SLOW TRAV

Durha

City, Dales & Coast

Local, characterful guides to Britain's special places

Gemma Hall

EDITION 1

Bradt Guides Ltd, UK
The Globe Pequot Press Inc, USA

First edition published February 2023
Bradt Guides Ltd
31a High Street, Chesham, Buckinghamshire, HP5 1BW, England
www.bradtguides.com
Print edition published in the USA by The Globe Pequot Press Inc,
PO Box 480, Guilford, Connecticut 06437-0480

ISBN: 9781784779498

British Library Cataloguing in Publication Data
A catalogue record for this book is available from the British Library

Photographs © individual photographers credited beside images & also those from picture
libraries credited as follows: Alamy.com (A); Dreamstime.com (DT); Shutterstock.com (S);
Superstock.com (SS)

Front cover A view of Durham Cathedral and the River Wear (Loop Images Ltd/A)
Back cover High Force (Graeme J Baty/S)
Title page Chemical Beach (Dave Head/S)

Maps David McCutcheon FBCart.S

Typeset by Ian Spick, Bradt Guides
Production managed by Zenith Media, printed in the UK
Digital conversion by www.dataworks.co.in

AUTHOR

Gemma Hall (⊘ gemmahall.co.uk) is a freelance travel writer from the North East who began her career in journalism writing for BBC magazines, then as deputy editor for the National Trust. She has written widely on the region and is the author of the Bradt Slow Travel Guide to Northumberland. Alongside writing, she spent ten years co-ordinating environmental projects abroad with The Conservation Volunteers (TCV) and, in the North East, for the RSPB. Her hobbies include birdwatching, camping, hiking, cycle touring and photography. She has walked and cycled many routes across Durham, and explored the North Pennines in search of special plant and bird life. Gemma is a fellow of the Royal Geographical Society.

AUTHOR'S STORY

I grew up in the North East and have rose-tinted memories of family weekends in the Deerness Valley: damming the river with stones; running through fields from an imaginary bull; messing about in hay barns; and sledging down hillsides on an old car bonnet. We'd visit Beamish museum and place coins on the trackway to be flattened by the Edwardian tram, and ride on steam trains at Tanfield Railway. And then there's a long gap in my recollection of times in Durham until I began visiting Upper Teesdale to go birdwatching as an adult. In 2012, I worked on the first guide to the North East for Bradt and extensively explored the county. But the Durham content had to be squeezed into two chapters and so I was delighted when Bradt commissioned this stand-alone guide.

For this new book, I spent six months revisiting every attraction and corner of Durham: cycling railway trails, poking around ruins, churches and nature reserves, camping out to go birdwatching at dawn; in and out of hundreds of cafés, restaurants, pubs and B&Bs; and searching for waterfalls (Jerry Force, I will find you one day), rare plants and elusive birds. Some moments are fixed in my mind: dusk at Baldersdale, all meadowland, wall and curlew under a pink sky; evensong at Durham Cathedral; Esh Winning's coal-fired chippy after a day hiking; walking the Durham Coastal Footpath with the continuous song of skylarks in my ears; and typing some pages of this book under Holwick Scars. Buildings figured heavily on research trips: a castle here, a Georgian manor there, but out of all the places I visited, it was Escomb Church I was drawn to more than anywhere else: its ancient churchyard and Saxon walls providing refuge after several long days on the road.

ACKNOWLEDGEMENTS

My thanks to Bradt for commissioning this new guide and especially to Anna Moores, the most efficient, astute and patient editor any guidebook writer could hope to work with, and Emma Gibbs for all her diligent work weeding out howlers from my manuscript, and polite requests to re-word chunks of texts. You were always right. Thanks to David McCutcheon for the maps and Rebecca Gurney, Susannah Lord and Ian Spick for your diligent behind-the-scenes work pulling the book together and finally to Daniel Austin for sourcing images.

I met many people on my travels in Durham who pointed me in the direction of places I would never have found without their local wisdom, or provided invaluable nuggets of information that found their way into the pages of this guide. They include staff at the Bowlees Visitor Centre, the North Pennines AONB, Teesdale Special Flora Research and Conservation Trust, the National Trust's North East office and Gibside estate, English Heritage, The Auckland Trust, and rangers at Natural England and the Durham Wildlife Trust. Thanks also to the wonderful employees and volunteers on the ground in many churches, museums, civic buildings and attractions who were generous with their time, particularly at Durham Cathedral, Durham Castle, East Durham Heritage & Lifeboat Centre, Spennymoor Town Hall, the Weardale Museum, Palace Green Library, the Oriental Museum, Killhope Lead Mining Museum, Locomotion, Bishop Auckland Town Hall, Saltholme, Gibside, Raby Castle, Beamish, Tanfield Railway and Escomb Church (sorry again about the keys, Joan).

Lastly, I could never have produced this guide without the support of friends and family who provided encouragement, insight and suggestions, especially Mary and Don; Ian, Lucy and Alexander; Owen and even, at times, my three young children!

DEDICATION

To Farne, Cheviot and Harthope

CONTENTS

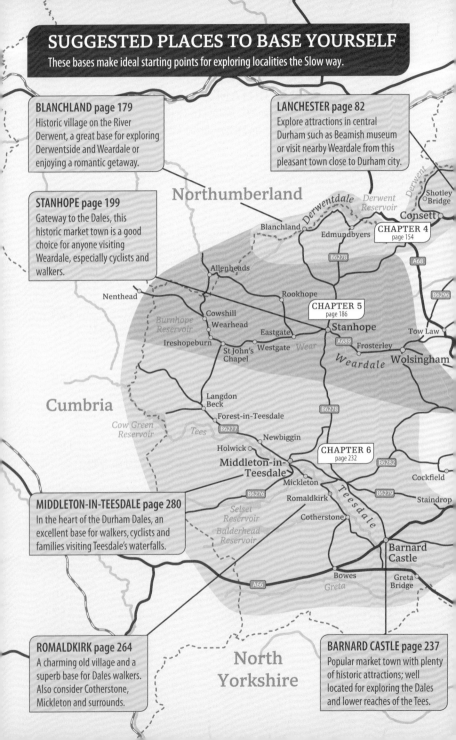

SUGGESTED PLACES TO BASE YOURSELF

These bases make ideal starting points for exploring localities the Slow way.

BLANCHLAND page 179
Historic village on the River Derwent, a great base for exploring Derwentside and Weardale or enjoying a romantic getaway.

LANCHESTER page 82
Explore attractions in central Durham such as Beamish museum or visit nearby Weardale from this pleasant town close to Durham city.

STANHOPE page 199
Gateway to the Dales, this historic market town is a good choice for anyone visiting Weardale, especially cyclists and walkers.

MIDDLETON-IN-TEESDALE page 280
In the heart of the Durham Dales, an excellent base for walkers, cyclists and families visiting Teesdale's waterfalls.

ROMALDKIRK page 264
A charming old village and a superb base for Dales walkers. Also consider Cotherstone, Mickleton and surrounds.

BARNARD CASTLE page 237
Popular market town with plenty of historic attractions; well located for exploring the Dales and lower reaches of the Tees.

Northumberland

Cumbria

North Yorkshire

Derwentdale

Derwent Reservoir

Shotley Bridge

Consett

Blanchland

Edmundbyers

CHAPTER 4 page 154

B6278

A68

B6296

Allenheads

Nenthead

Rookhope

Burnhope Reservoir

Cowshill

Wearhead

CHAPTER 5 page 186

Stanhope

Tow Law

Ireshopeburn

Eastgate

A689

Frosterley

Wolsingham

St John's Chapel

Westgate

Wear

Weardale

Langdon Beck

Cow Green Reservoir

Forest-in-Teesdale

Tees

B6277

Newbiggin

Holwick

B6278

CHAPTER 6 page 232

B6282

Cockfield

Middleton-in-Teesdale

Mickleton

Teesdale

B6279

Staindrop

B6276

Romaldkirk

Selset Reservoir

Balderhead Reservoir

Cotherstone

Barnard Castle

Bowes

Greta

A66

Greta Bridge

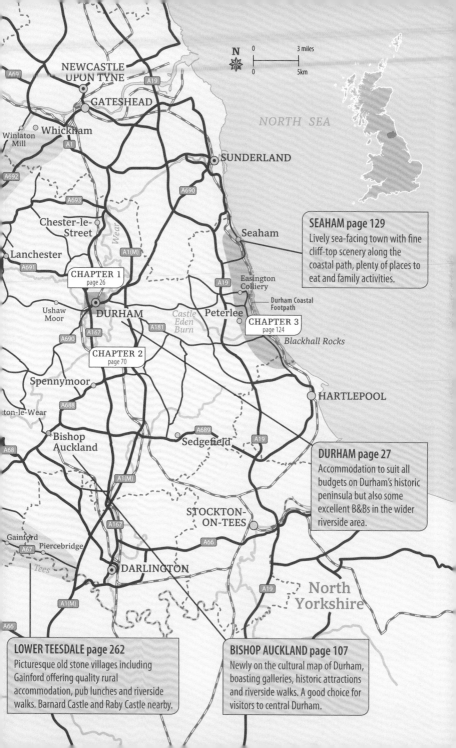

N

0 — 3 miles
0 — 5km

NORTH SEA

NEWCASTLE
UPON TYNE

GATESHEAD

A69

A19

Winlaton
Mill

Whickham

A1

A692

SUNDERLAND

A690

Chester-le-
Street

Lanchester

A693

Wear

A1(M)

Seaham

CHAPTER 1
page 26

SEAHAM page 129
Lively sea-facing town with fine
cliff-top scenery along the
coastal path, plenty of places to
eat and family activities.

A691

Ushaw
Moor

DURHAM

A167

A19

Easington
Colliery

Durham Coastal
Footpath

A690

*Castle
Eden
Burn*

A181

Peterlee

CHAPTER 3
page 124

Blackhall Rocks

CHAPTER 2
page 70

Spennymoor

A688

ton-le-Wear

Bishop
Auckland

A68

A1(M)

A689

Sedgefield

A19

HARTLEPOOL

DURHAM page 27
Accommodation to suit all
budgets on Durham's historic
peninsula but also some
excellent B&Bs in the wider
riverside area.

STOCKTON-
ON-TEES

A167

Gainford
Piercebridge

A67

A66

Tees

A1(M)

DARLINGTON

A66

A19

*North
Yorkshire*

A66

LOWER TEESDALE page 262
Picturesque old stone villages including
Gainford offering quality rural
accommodation, pub lunches and riverside
walks. Barnard Castle and Raby Castle nearby.

BISHOP AUCKLAND page 107
Newly on the cultural map of Durham,
boasting galleries, historic attractions
and riverside walks. A good choice for
visitors to central Durham.

DURHAM CITY, DALES & COAST

Always my boy of wish returns
To those peat-stained deserted burns
That feed the Wear and Tyne and Tees,
And, turning states to strata, sees
How basalt long oppressed broke out
In wild revolt at Cauldron Snout...

W H Auden, *New Year Letter*, 1940

Durham traded in coal and a cathedral for hundreds of years and these two features alone continue to define the region more than any others, despite the last coal mine closing 30 years ago. Increasingly, however, the county is doing a roaring trade in something less tangible, drawing adventure seekers to its remote landscapes in search of wilderness. Nowhere in England is truly wild and even Durham's most inaccessible expanses of upland terrain are managed in some way, but it's the sense of wildness experienced when striding alone across Stanhope Common, seeing High Force thunder over a dolerite cliff millions of years in the making, or finding Arctic alpine plants with a lineage to the Ice Age, that invigorates the soul and forges a connection with something primitive that is life-affirming. The poet W H Auden surely felt this when he peered through the glacial valley at the top of High Cup Nik in the North Pennines and found it 'one of the holiest places on earth'.

Durham is blessed with many holy places – real and imagined – that attracted famous writers and artists, coast-to-coast cyclists and

◀ **1** Hiking the Upper Derwent Valley moorland near Muggleswick. **2** The Durham Heritage Coast Path.

Pennine-Way walkers long before government officials finally decided in 1988 that the North Pennines was worthy of the accolade, **Area of Outstanding Natural Beauty**. Encompassing most of the **Durham Dales**, this vast AONB (the second largest of all the 46 AONBs in the UK, and bigger than most of the national parks in England and Wales) is recognised as one of the most unspoilt places in England, a 765 square mile expanse of meadowlands, wide valleys, heather moors and rivers. There's a raw beauty here unrivalled anywhere else in England with some of the country's darkest night skies and rarest upland habitats, geology and wildlife (red squirrels, ring ouzels, black grouse and scarce montane plants). It almost goes without saying that the rambler and cyclist who crave open scenery devoid of crowds will find the upper reaches of Weardale, Teesdale and the Derwent Valley fantastically rewarding.

In the **sub-Pennine hills** east of the Dales, the landscape steps down a gear and the villages and towns come every few miles, but there are still plentiful routes across open terrain, through semi-ancient woods, and for long stretches by the banks of Durham's famous rivers and on railway trails.

Those who set foot along the **Durham Heritage Coast** 11-mile clifftop path will cross unique limestone grasslands with much wildlife interest and enjoy bracing coastal views: towering cliff-faces and long rolling waves pounding rocky shores.

But what of the jewel in Durham's crown? Many pages in this guide are devoted to one of the most celebrated Romanesque cathedrals in Europe, an important place for Christian pilgrims from its founding in 1093, and the radiating medieval streets at the historic core of this **UNESCO World Heritage Site**. The River Wear ribbons around the wooded mount on which **Durham Cathedral** and **castle** preside, adding to the draw of the city – and offering lengthy riverside walks. Within a few miles of the city is 13th-century Finchale Priory and the National Trust's Crook Hall Gardens – both of which can be reached on foot by following the Wear.

Durham is proud of its distinguished cathedral and Anglo-Saxon churches, medieval castles, Georgian manors and Railway Age architecture, but the buildings that figure dominantly in the cultural imagination are the red-brick coal-mining terraces seen in almost every village and town in central and eastern Durham. The

THE SLOW MINDSET

Hilary Bradt, Founder, Bradt Travel Guides

We shall not cease from exploration
And the end of all our exploring
Will be to arrive where we started
And know the place for the first time.

T S Eliot, 'Little Gidding', *Four Quartets*

This series evolved, slowly, from a Bradt editorial meeting when we started to explore ideas for guides to our favourite part of the world – Great Britain. We wanted to get away from the usual 'top sights' formula and encourage our authors to bring out the nuances and local differences that make up a sense of place – such things as food, building styles, nature, geology, or local people and what makes them tick. Our aim was to create a series that celebrates the present, focusing on sustainable tourism, rather than taking a nostalgic wallow in the past.

So without our realising it at the time, we had defined 'Slow Travel', or at least our concept of it. For the beauty of the Slow movement is that there is no fixed definition; we adapt the philosophy to fit our individual needs and aspirations. Thus Carl Honoré, author of *In Praise of Slow*, writes: 'The Slow Movement is a cultural revolution against the notion that faster is always better. It's not about doing everything at a snail's pace, it's about seeking to do everything at the right speed. Savouring the hours and minutes rather than just counting them. Doing everything as well as possible, instead of as fast as possible. It's about quality over quantity in everything from work to food to parenting.' And travel.

So take time to explore. Don't rush it, get to know an area – and the people who live there – and you'll be as delighted as the authors by what you find.

association of coal with Durham endures here (and in many place names, monuments, memorials and annual mining celebrations) but for the rest of Durham, it was lead, not coal, that drove the economy of centuries past, and the discerning visitor may notice that settlements in the Durham Dales are distinctly different to the coalfield villages of the centre and coast, with more in the way of stone-built houses, and villages bound by meadowland and stone walls and fewer pony paddocks and hedgerows.

To make sense of this varied county, it helps to divide the area into four broad areas: Durham city; the coal-mining valleys of central Durham (here referred to as the 'Vale of Durham'); the coast; and the

Durham Dales to the west, including the valleys of the Derwent, Wear and Tees – and this is roughly how I've arranged this guide.

GEOLOGY & PLANT LIFE

In a large part it is geology and industry that underpin the four distinct areas of Durham that in turn have given rise to their own cultural narratives: lead defines the Dales; coal the centre and coast; and an industry of learning focused in Durham city. Geologically, Durham is a fascinating county and it pays to understand a few processes to assist with interpreting landscape forms and scenery, particularly at the coast and in the North Pennines, a **UNESCO Global Geopark** (one of seven such areas in Britain).

Many of the scenic features of the North Pennines owe their appearance to the **carboniferous period** 350 million years ago with repeated layers of limestone, shale and sandstone creating terraced hillsides and mighty waterfalls where the softer shale and sandstones have weathered rapidly, undercutting the harder limestone and whinstone (page 292) to create lips in the riverbed. The best examples are along the Tees, particularly where whinstone (or **whin sill**) – formed by volcanic intrusions some 295 million years ago – outcrop in the river, creating the magnificent High Force and Cauldron Snout falls, and elsewhere in the valley where they appear as impressive curtain-like cliffs. This volcanic activity was landscape-shaping in other dramatic ways too, the tremendous heat of the magma 'baking' the limestone, which crumbled into a sugary white rock visible today on the highest fells of Upper Teesdale. Known as '**sugar limestone**' (page 300) it is one of the special features of the valley, hosting a unique group of montane plants collectively described as the '**Teesdale Assemblage**' (page 300) for they are found here and almost nowhere else in England and include the endemic Teesdale violet and local populations of the stunning blue spring gentian.

Cutting through these rocks are 'veins' of minerals, notably **lead**, that profoundly transformed the North Pennines for a few hundred years as

---

1 The Great Whin Sill. **2** & **3** The Teesdale violet and spring gentian are two species in the 'Teesdale Assemblage' – a unique group of montane plants found in the region.
4 The high-altitude mining village of Rookhope in Weardale offers spectacular views as well as industrial archaeology. ▶

DURHAM HIGHLIGHTS

In this diverse county it can be hard to know where to start when planning a trip. Below, in the order they appear in this guide, I've listed some of the most popular attractions in Durham to get you started. For some lesser-known gems, see the box on page 18.

Durham city & cathedral (page 27) Hugely romantic and atmospheric, there is no other city like it in England.

Beamish, the Living Museum of the North (page 78) Period streets brought to life in a nationally-renowned outdoor museum featuring tram rides, a Victorian fairground, steam train, Georgian farm, Edwardian high street and a 1950s town.

Bishop Auckland's castle, chapel and galleries (page 107) A programme of investment has brought new life to this handsome market town centre on the outskirts of Durham.

Durham Heritage Coast (page 125) Flower-filled meadows cap the cliffs of Durham's striking coastline recognised for its wildlife and semi-ancient wooded denes.

Gibside, Derwent Valley (page 161) Georgian pleasure ground above the River Derwent with a Palladian chapel, walled garden and a lively programme of National Trust events.

Derwentdale The upper reaches of the Derwent Valley open to the wider Pennine landscape, enticing walkers and cyclists to the moors and historic villages of Blanchland (page 179) and Edmundbyers (page 177).

Dales' market towns Barnard Castle (page 237), Middleton-in-Teesdale (page 280) and Stanhope (page 199) are some of the most appealing places to stay in the Durham Dales.

mining activities honeycombed the hillsides and workers flooded into the valleys. Besides lead ore, mineral crystals are still found around old mines and in rivers.

The other special stone associated with the Dales is **Frosterley marble** (page 198), a fossiliferous black limestone polished to beautiful effect and showcased in churches throughout Durham.

Limestone appears dramatically along Durham's coast too as **magnesian limestone** (page 126), forming soft cliff walls supporting rare grasslands and invertebrates peculiar to the North East coast. Glacial meltwater carved channels to the sea that became wooded over time and these gorges – or denes – clothed in ancient trees are a distinctive feature of the Durham coast, celebrated for their plant life and scenic beauty.

Weardale Railway (page 200) An 18-mile heritage railway line between Bishop Auckland West and Stanhope.

Killhope Lead Mining Museum, Weardale (page 218) Superbly engaging museum, still with its original mine amid rugged hills.

Bowes Museum, Barnard Castle (page 242) Housed within the lavish surroundings of a purpose-built 19th-century mansion modelled on a French château is this vast collection of European art, porcelain and furniture.

Raby Castle, Barnard Castle (page 248) An impressive medieval fortress set in a deer park. Inside, the castle is a treasure-trove of antiques and artefacts; outside, there's an adventure play area and walled garden.

Teesdale villages Featuring great pubs and walks, the old stone villages of Romaldkirk (page 264), Cotherstone (page 262), Mickleton (page 268) are three of the most unchanged places along the Tees.

Gibson's Cave & Summerhill Force, Teesdale (page 293) A well-trodden footpath through woods leads to this elegant spout of a waterfall in a limestone and shale cave.

High Force, Teesdale (page 296) England's biggest waterfall crashes 70ft into a boiling pool at one of the most scenic spots along the Tees.

Cauldron Snout & Cow Green Reservoir, Teesdale (page 304) Well known to hikers and botanists is the spectacularly bleak expanse of water and fells at Cow Green and its dramatic waterfall that gushes down a staircase of dolerite boulders.

MINING HERITAGE

The boom in mining and expansion of **colliery villages** during the 19th and early 20th centuries transformed the communities and physical landscape of central and eastern Durham. The industry peaked in 1921 when there were 160,000 miners (up from 15,000 a hundred years earlier) excavating and exporting volumes of minerals only possible with the aid of an extensive railway network, which by then was reaching every colliery village and valley in the region. But the industry was on the wane by the middle of the 20th century and the last Durham coal pit closed in 1994. Unemployment rocketed and many places fell into decline; others were redeveloped and reinvented. The winding wheels and chimneys that once towered over the uniform terraces are now gone, though many settlements retain elements of their colliery-town character (plain brick terraces with back lanes, working men's clubs, welfare centres, Aged Miners' homes and colliery brass bands) and a strong mining identity as seen at the annual Durham Miners' Gala, known affectionately as 'The Big Meeting' (page 61). Central Durham remains criss-crossed by the old mining **railway lines,** many of them now converted into leisure trails (page 157) permitting off-road travel county wide and connecting north and central Durham with Tyneside, Sunderland and the Pennines.

At the **coast,** an area blighted for many decades by colliery waste, the natural landscape was transformed following an intensive restoration project launched at the turn of this century. Since the removal of 1.3 million tonnes of debris, Durham's 'black beaches' are now some of the greatest natural attractions the county has to offer, matching stretches of the North Yorkshire and Northumberland coasts in their rugged beauty. The National Trust and Durham Wildlife Trust care for much of the land as nature reserves.

As for the **lead-mining** communities of the Dales, which were once at the centre of biggest lead industry in the world, they are markedly different architecturally, scenically and culturally from the colliery villages of central Durham with their stone 18th and 19th-century miners' homes, reading rooms, Methodist chapels and enclosing wall and meadow landscape. Museums exploring this heritage include the wonderful **Killhope Lead Mining Museum** and the **Weardale Museum** in Ireshopeburn, but visitors will find ruined mines in a number of remote valleys, memorably at **Rookhope, Nenthead** and **Hudeshope Valley.**

WALKING

Durham has a rich and varied landscape, from the remote Pennine fells and waterfalls of the Dales to the forested denes and high cliffs of the coast, and beautiful river, meadow and woodland scenery in the central Durham valleys. While there are plenty of fine walks in the Pennine foothills, walkers heading west of Derwent Reservoir, Stanhope and

1 The Pennine Way. **2** Knitsley Farm Shop. **3** Cycling near Blanchland.
4 Teesdale Cheesemakers, Butterknowle. ▶

LESSER-KNOWN PLACES TO VISIT

Durham Miners' Hall, Durham (page 63) Red-brick mansion housing Durham's famous 'Pitman's Parliament' and described as one of the finest trade union buildings in Europe.

Tanfield Railway, near Beamish (page 81) Keeping alive the legacy of one of the oldest railways in the world with steam-train rides.

Field's fish & chip shop, Esh Winning (page 91) The faint smell of burning coal wafts through the door of this old coal-powered chippy. Could there be a more authentically Durham experience?

St Cuthbert's Chapel, Ushaw Historic House (page 92) Originally the work of Augustus Pugin, the chapel is richly decorated and one of many fascinating buildings in this former Catholic seminary.

Escomb Anglo-Saxon church, near Bishop Auckland (page 96) Simply one of the most moving places to visit in Durham, containing Roman masonry and Frosterley marble within its boxy 7th-century walls.

Cockfield Fell, Cockfield (page 104) England's largest scheduled ancient monument, this exposed area of open grassland reveals the farming and mining activities of centuries past.

Locomotion railway museum, Shildon (page 120) Historic engines and carriages, and nearby Victorian railway buildings on the line of the famous Stockton & Darlington Railway, draws local families to this superb museum.

Glass Beach, Seaham (page 133) Beachcombers pick through the rounded coloured pebbles at the north end of this popular seaside town in search of tiny pearls of coloured sea glass.

Barnard Castle will find the landscape becomes increasingly remote with some impressive fells and moorland scenery readily accessible from the main access roads shadowing the upper reaches of the Derwent, Wear, Tees and Greta. Upper Teesdale is especially unparalleled in its scenic beauty and variety of features and wildlife, with marked trails onto the likes of Widdybank and Cronkley fells and along the Tees. The Pennine Way takes in much of this landscape. The **Teesdale Way** (page 234) and **Weardale Way** (page 74) follow their respective rivers from the hills to the coast, linking superb Dales countryside with stone river-facing villages.

North–south routes crossing the hills between valleys are supremely desolate in parts and offer tremendous views from the Waskerley area, Stanhope Common, above Rookhope, Burnhope Moor, Chapel Fell and

Apollo Pavilion, Peterlee (page 137) Awesome 1960s sculptural walkway and a unique example of modernist design.

Castle Eden Dene NNR, Peterlee (page 137) Well-known to locals, this deep, thickly wooded gorge is an important wildlife reserve on the Durham coast which connects walkers to the shore near Blackhall Colliery.

Easington Colliery pit shaft cage (page 141) A moving tribute to the coal-mining industry that once defined Durham's coastline.

Rookhope, Weardale (page 203) A favourite spot of the poet W H Auden, this high-altitude old village offers superb hill walks and riverside trails, plunging valley views and historic lead-mining architecture.

Greta Valley (page 255) Once the haunt of Turner, Cotman and Sir Walter Scott, the wooded banks of the River Greta are exceptionally scenic and peaceful, particularly at Brignall Banks.

Baldersdale (page 270) A stunning North Pennine valley with quintessential Dales scenery and superb bird and plant life.

Hudeshope Valley, Middleton-in-Teesdale (page 284) Desolate, eerily quiet valley beneath some hefty moors where time has stood still since the lead mines closed.

Holwick, Teesdale (page 286) A dead-end lane leads to this old hamlet flanked by a dolerite cliff wall known as Holwick Scars. The meadows leading from Holwick to the Tees' famous waterfalls are a botanist's delight.

Langdon Common – all areas with extensive areas of Open Access Land where you'll need to form your own route across much of the terrain.

LIST OF WALKS

The pages of this guide are peppered with suggestions of short walks outlined in the text but I've included more detailed walk descriptions and maps for the following routes:

Blanchland & the River Derwent Derwentdale, page 184
Ireshopeburn hay meadows walk Weardale, page 212
Barnard Castle to Egglestone Abbey Teesdale, page 244
Hannah's Meadow Baldersdale, page 274
The Kings Walk & Hudeshope Valley Middleton-in-Teesdale, page 280

GETTING THERE

Getting to Durham from elsewhere in the country and abroad is straightforward by all the usual forms of public transport including by **train** to Durham city (direct from London in little over 2½ hours on the fastest services; and around two hours from Edinburgh). See below for more information. I've also provided an overview of local public transport options at the beginning of each chapter.

In a region famous as the birthplace of the railways and once extensively connected by train lines, a skeleton service now exists operated by Northern (⊘ northernrailway.co.uk), connecting the likes of Seaham, Newton Aycliffe, Shildon and Bishop Auckland with the main London–Edinburgh East Coast Main Line at either Darlington, Durham or Newcastle.

For **bus** routes, two major bus companies operate in Durham: Go North East (⊘ gonortheast.co.uk) and Arriva (⊘ arrivabus.co.uk/north-east/bus-travel-in-durham), as well as smaller companies in some of the valleys (see the *Getting Around* section at the beginning of individual

BY TRAIN TO DURHAM

Pulling into Durham station is one of the most memorable arrivals into any English city by train, with the cathedral and castle raised above the Wear in direct view of the East Coast Main Line from Edinburgh to London. Operated by London North Eastern Railway (LNER; ⊘ lner.co.uk), the service is direct to Durham from Edinburgh in little over two hours and around 2½–3 hours direct from London.

For the cheapest fares, book in advance and choose off-peak tickets (avoiding departures from London Monday to Thursday before 08.00 and between 16.00 and 18.00. There are no restriction at the weekend). Trains take four bikes but you must reserve a space in advance (you can do this online).

First-class ticket holders are in for a treat with complimentary meals and drinks served to your seat. One of three menus will be served on your train with 'Dine' (weekdays only) the most special, offering a full English breakfast on morning trains and hot plates for lunch and dinner (such as roasted Scottish salmon). Go online to find out which menu will be served on your train.

–3chapters). Durham County Council's travel webpages provide links to all relevant travel operators at ⊘ durham.gov.uk/publictransport. Generally, bus travel in Durham is fairly comprehensive with central Durham, the coast, Durham city and the Derwent Valley particularly well connected. Travel in the lower reaches of Teesdale and Weardale is feasible by bus but the upper, more remote stretches of both valleys have very infrequent services.

Newcastle International Airport is the closest for **flights** from mainland Europe and London (Teesside International really only serves a local holiday crowd heading to European resorts). To reach Durham from Newcastle Airport, it's a fairly swift journey by Metro to Newcastle Central Station (25 minutes) where you can transfer to train for the onward journey of 12 minutes.

SAVOURING THE TASTES OF DURHAM

Durham offers some of the best trout and salmon fishing in England in its reservoirs and rivers, while hill farms and shooting estates in the Dales stock restaurants, farm shops and farmers' markets with quality lamb, beef, venison, game and dairy products.

A few reliable places to find regional produce include the **food markets** at Barnard Castle, Durham, Sedgefield and Bishop Auckland; **butchers** such as William Peat and MacFarlane's in Barnard Castle and Castle Bank Butchers in Stanhope; and some of the excellent **farm shops** in the region including Cross Lanes Organic Farm Shop (page 258), Knitsley Farm Shop (page 172), and Broom House Farm (page 84) and Piercebridge Organic Farm Shop & Butchery (page 254), as well as at summer **agricultural shows**, notably at Wolsingham (page 191).

Local speciality **cheeses** you may see on café and restaurant menus include Cotherstone Cheese, Weardale Cheese and Teesdale Cheese, which can also be sampled at the farm's on-site café (page 104). Also look out for Durham Brewery **beers** and **gins** from the Durham Distillery (30–31 High St, Durham DH1 3UL; book distillery tours at ⊘ durhamdistillery.co.uk).

Every April sees the return of the lively Bishop Auckland **Food Festival** (⊘ bishopaucklandfoodfestival.co.uk) showcasing some of the very best foods produced in the North East.

HOW THIS BOOK IS ARRANGED

Durham's major valleys, city and coastal strip are generally well understood as distinct geographical places and so you'll find a chapter devoted to each of these areas. Boundaries become more fluid in the central area of Durham where I have brought together the lowlands between the coast and the Pennines into a chapter of its own (the Vale of Durham). Darlington and Hartlepool are boroughs in their own right and are not included in this guide, with the exception of a few places of significance to the wildlife watcher and railway enthusiast. I've strayed over the county border elsewhere too, at Allenheads, Nenthead, Blanchland and a few other places just outside the county boundary.

MAPS

The numbered points on the maps at the beginning of each chapter correspond with the numbered headings in the text. They are mostly larger settlements (not necessarily the most interesting places to visit) with attractions and smaller places nearby listed within them.

Suggestions of **walks** are highlighted throughout this guide, with maps included for some – but it should be noted that they are not a substitute for Ordnance Survey maps (see individual walk boxes for which OS maps to take with you).

ACCOMMODATION

While researching this guide I visited a range of independent hotels, B&Bs, youth hostels, campsites, bunkhouses and holiday cottages and picked a small selection of some that caught my eye to recommend to readers. Green credentials, local food for breakfast, unique features, historic buildings and any place with a friendly welcome and a high

1 High Force Waterfall, Teesdale. **2** Durham Illuminations. ▶

standard of cleanliness and décor (not necessarily the most plush) tended to be what I was looking for. They are all listed at the back of this book (page 308) and referenced in chapters under the heading in which they are located, with hotels and B&Bs indicated by 🏠, self-catering with 🏡 and campsites and hostels with 🔺. Go to ∂ bradtguides.com/durhamsleeps for full reviews.

ACCESSIBILITY

A ♿ symbol appears next to visitor attractions, accommodation and places to eat where there is step-free access and a disabled toilet. Some restaurants and museums have worked really hard to welcome those less mobile, but really good access remains patchy or so complicated that the effort of getting around can overshadow a visit. Old villages and towns tend to be difficult to navigate owing to a dominance of uneven and narrow pavements and lack of dropped kerbs, but some villages and hamlets are so quiet that you may be able to use the tarmacked roads. Note that Durham city centre is largely car-free during the daytime and pedestrians and wheelchair users spill into the medieval lanes around the Cathedral.

FEEDBACK REQUEST AND UPDATES WEBSITE

At Bradt Guides we're aware that guidebooks start to go out of date on the day they're published – and that you, our readers, are out there in the field doing research of your own. You'll find out before us when a fine new family-run hotel opens or a favourite restaurant changes hands and goes downhill. So why not tell us about your experiences? Contact us on ∂ 01753 893444 or ✉ info@bradtguides.com. We will forward emails to the author who may post updates on the Bradt website at ∂ bradtguides.com/updates. Alternatively, you can add a review of the book to Amazon, or share your adventures with us on social:

📘 BradtGuides 🐦 BradtGuides 📷 BradtGuides

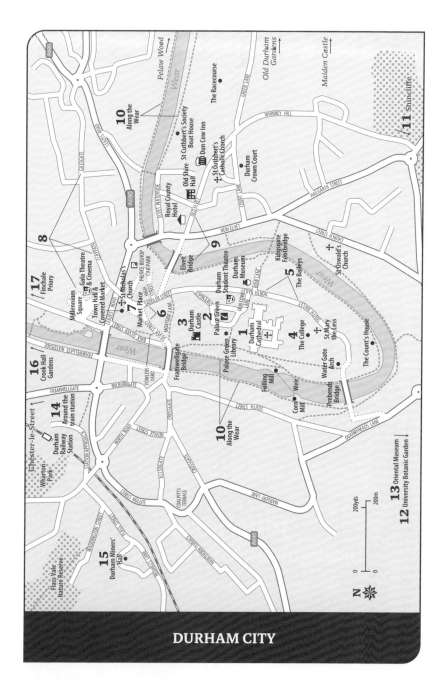

DURHAM CITY

1
DURHAM CITY

As the London to Edinburgh train approaches Durham station, all heads in the carriage turn to the east to savour the view of **Durham Cathedral** standing halfway to heaven on a rocky promontory above the River Wear. In the late afternoon sun, the Norman masterpiece is golden and magnificent. The cathedral faces **Durham Castle** – once the seat of the ruling Prince Bishops but now owned by Durham University – its keep raised on a Norman motte, its walls embattled, doorways framed by Romanesque arches. Combined, the cathedral, castle and outlying streets fronted by Georgian townhouses form the core of the compact peninsula and **UNESCO World Heritage Site**.

Durham grew around the cathedral in the 12th century, but growth was limited in a place perched on a natural cul-de-sac and bound by water on three sides. For that reason, the city is not somewhere one chances upon or passes through; it must be sought out. Millions of pilgrims over the centuries have done just that, ever since monks from Lindisfarne in Northumberland came to rest here with the body of St Cuthbert in AD995. A monastic community of Benedictine monks flourished in Durham, centred on the saint's shrine, which was moved to the cathedral on its completion in 1093.

"As the train approaches Durham station, all heads in the carriage turn to savour the view of Durham Cathedral."

Over time, the city did expand beyond the Wear to embrace a wider area, and visitors today will find much outside the historic peninsula to enrich a stay: the ruins of 12th-century **Finchale Priory**, the **University Botanic Garden** and **Oriental Museum**, the National Trust's medieval **Crook Hall Gardens**, and several miles of riverside trails. Half-day excursions a little further afield could also take you to **Beamish museum** (page 78) or historic **Bishop Auckland** (page 107), while **Durham's Heritage Coast** (page 125) can be reached by train for fabulous clifftop walks.

GETTING AROUND

By London North Eastern Railway (LNER) **train** (⏃ lner.co.uk) from London it is around three hours direct to Durham, 1 hour 40 minutes from Edinburgh and 12 minutes from Newcastle. The **Cathedral Bus** (⏃ gonortheast.co.uk; tickets £1/£1.50 return; every 20 minutes daily, except Sun, public holidays and during the Miners' Gala ⏁) connects the train station with the city centre and cathedral. Buses from Durham to outlying towns and villages in the Vale of Durham and along the coast are frequent. A couple of useful routes include Go Northeast services to Bishop Auckland (#X21) and the Angel 21 bus to Newcastle via Chester-le-Street. Arriva run regular services to Sunderland via the coast (#22 & #24) as well as through the Deerness Valley for Ushaw Historic House (#43). For Beamish museum, you need to change at Chester-le-Street for the #8 or #28.

There's a two-word response to how best to get around Durham city: on foot. I've noted a few practical details on page 29 and suggested a couple of pleasant walks in the city.

Cyclists will find the city centre pretty inaccessible in comparison to pedestrians and not an enjoyable place to visit on wheels. This is especially so if coming from the train station as you must descend towards the river and navigate across some very busy roads before climbing up the banks of the peninsula, where you'll find the streets so crowded that your bike is a hindrance. That said, the riverside paths are great for getting about by bicycle and you can reach a number of attractions very easily (the National Trust's Crook Hall Gardens for example, page 64).

If you are arriving from other parts of the county by bike along the network of old railway paths, cycling to the outskirts of Durham is a joy, following the Lanchester Valley Railway Path (page 85) or other routes that converge on the city's fringes at Baxter Wood (before Broompark). The official Route 14 to Durham centre takes a fiddly course via Pennyferry Bridge.

Durham's peninsula is not easily reached by **car**; the streets are cramped, and a £2 congestion charge (⏲ 10.00–16.00 Mon–Sat, excl bank hols; ⏃ 0191 3846633 to pay ⏃ durham.gov.uk) operates on the

---

ℹ TOURIST INFORMATION

Gone are the days of bells-and-whistles tourist information centres in Durham (now reduced to a **phone line-only service** operated by helpful staff ✆ 03000 262626), but there are still a few places offering face-to-face advice, even if more informally. They include the **World Heritage Site Visitor Centre** within Palace Green Library (page 41) on Palace Green, a few paces from the cathedral, where you can pick up city maps. Staff at the **cathedral** (page 30), **Town Hall** (page 50) and **Durham Museum** (page 48) are also useful sources of info.

---

roads around the cathedral to deter motorists. The hassle of paying it (it's not straightforward and you can't pay online) is another deterrent. A much better option is the **Prince Bishop car park** (DH1 3UJ), a five-minute walk from Palace Green and the cathedral. Alternatively, leave your car outside the city and use the **Park & Ride** service (three locations around Durham; car park ☉ 07.00–19.00 Mon–Sat; buses every 15 minutes ⊘ durham.gov.uk/parkandride).

♿ **Disabled Blue Badge holders** are exempt from the toll (but you still have to phone ✆ 0191 3846633 to register your car). Park in front of the cathedral by calling the office to book a slot or speak to the porter on arrival.

WALKING

From the train station it is a short 15-minute up-and-down **walk** to the cathedral via Framwellgate Bridge, or 25 minutes via some of the city's most intact historic streets on South Street, across Prebends Bridge and then up South Bailey. Once you reach the peninsula, everywhere is pretty accessible and in walking distance (most places are reached in five to ten minutes or so).

Durham is a city for the flâneur. Its winding pedestrianised streets on the peninsula and connecting medieval alleys (called 'vennels') make exploration **on foot** not just the most practical way of getting around but rather exciting too. Away from the likes of Saddler Street, Silver Street and Market Place, the main shopping areas in Durham, the crowds fizzle out and you can find quiet corners in many places (walk from North Bailey to South Bailey and then to the river if you want to be convinced of this, or visit the cathedral close called The College, page 46).

Paved and dirt footpaths on both sides of the River Wear make accessing the centre and wider city often quicker than calling a cab. Many of the places described in this chapter can be visited quite easily on foot this way and if you keep following the river for long enough (15 to 20 minutes or so) you will soon be in countryside – or open green space at least.

TAXIS
Belmont Taxis ☏ 07884 307489 ♿
Durham Taxis ☏ 0191 3942468
Lenny's Taxis ☏ 0191 3779299 ♿
Will's Taxi Services ☏ 07927 401652

DURHAM'S CATHEDRAL PENINSULA

🏠 **Durham Castle** (page 308), **Castle View Guest House** (page 308), **Hatfield College** (page 308)

The historic core of Durham city, a UNESCO World Heritage Site, is the steep-sided wooded peninsula with the **cathedral** and **castle** at its centre, in an area known as Palace Green. Set behind Palace Green is the Market Place with connecting narrow streets and alleys and plenty of independent shops and places to eat. The peninsula is compact, crowded at times, and the streets narrow and fiddly, but this makes it a wonderful place to explore on foot, with beckoning passageways leading to unexpected corners. Mostly these 'vennels' descend to the Wear where a walk along its riverbanks is rewarded with some of the most beautiful river scenery in the whole of the county, framed by medieval bridges and shrouded by trees. You can also hire rowing boats from under Elvet Bridge (page 52) and take in the view of those famous cathedral towers peeping through the treetops above the gorge.

1 DURHAM CATHEDRAL

Palace Green, DH1 3EH ☏ 0191 3387178 ♂ durhamcathedral.co.uk ⏰ 10.00–16.00 Mon–Sat, noon–16.00 Sun; evensong 17.30 Tue–Sat, 15.30 Sun (also a sung Eucharist at 11.15); tours 10.30, 11.30 & 13.30 Mon–Sat; tower climbs on the hour 10.00–15.00 Mon–Sat; museum 10.00–16.00 Mon–Fri (times vary, check ahead online) ♿ Except St Cuthbert's Shrine, the Chapel of the Nine Altars and a few other places (see website for access information).

'Half church of God, half castle 'gainst the Scot' wrote Sir Walter Scott of Durham Cathedral. The much-quoted line is inscribed on the city's Prebends Bridge, from where you gain one of the most romantic views of the Norman church. Both a shrine to St Cuthbert and a display of power to the north, the cathedral held a complex political and ecclesiastical role for many centuries after its foundation stone was laid in 1093 on the site of an earlier wooden Saxon church established by the monks of Lindisfarne in the late 10th century.

Adjacent to this new stone church built soon after the Norman Conquest were the monastic cloisters and associated buildings. Incredibly, it took just 40 years to complete the wondrous stone cathedral that crowns the rocky eminence above the serpent Wear. Durham was already welcoming pilgrims at the time work began, but its fame as a place of pilgrimage was amplified in the years after completion and with it the wealth of the Bishop of Durham, whose affluence and influence was only second to the King of England.

Protected on three sides by the river, the location for St Cuthbert's resting place and home for the Benedictine community of monks must have been strategic though nothing could stand in the way of King Henry VIII's commissioners who entered Durham around 1539 to dissolve the priory (and strip Cuthbert's shrine of its treasures). The last service as a Benedictine monastery was in 1539 but, unlike at Lindisfarne and Fountains Abbey, Durham survived by making a swift transition to becoming an Anglican cathedral two years later: the monks became cannons; the priors deans.

DURHAM ILLUMINATIONS

Originally staged as a one-off show, *Lumiere*, the UK's largest light festival has returned biannually since 2009, transforming Durham's famous buildings and public spaces into an open-air theatre of light over four nights in November. Specially commissioned local and international artists use the landscape and built heritage of the city to project spectacular and mesmerising beams and moving images on to the sides of buildings, walls and across the city's bridges and streets.

The popularity of the event has grown over the years with the city centre closed to traffic to allow pedestrians to take over the roads which swell with visitors from dusk. In previous years the show has included a miniature 'city' made with illuminated paper lanterns, a giant snow globe, the projection of a whale onto the Wear, and many buildings and bridges playing host to moving scenes and abstract light beams, but the star attraction is the lighting of Durham Cathedral in some years. A spectacular installation in recent years saw the building set on 'fire' with projected flames flickering from gallery windows. See ⊘ lumiere-festival.com.

Over the following century, the cathedral suffered at various times and especially during the Civil War when 3,000 Scottish fighters imprisoned in the cathedral by Cromwell used the choir stalls as firewood. It's why almost all the woodwork you see today, except the clock and a few other pieces, date from the post-Civil War refurbishments of the late 17th century.

The Victorians too left their mark, replacing the stained glass and using caustic soda and wire brushes to clean the post-Reformation whitewash from walls. In doing so they also stripped away most of the Norman and medieval paintwork that lay beneath. They missed a few places though and you can see the original artwork that would have once decorated much of the interior: on a stone arcade in the north aisle and, most extensively, in the Galilee Chapel.

Today, Durham Cathedral is cared for with all the devotion you'd expect of a World Heritage Site monument and continues to be an important place of worship and pilgrimage for Christians from around the world. You can book **tours** of the building (see listing information, page 30) and, with a separate ticket, climb the central tower or visit the Durham Cathedral Museum (page 39) to marvel at the treasures of St Cuthbert's tomb as well as a mass of other historic finds. A varied programme of theatre, concert and craft events are held in the cloisters and elsewhere around the cathedral; details of all events are online.

A Norman cathedral

From Palace Green, the 500ft length of the cathedral is seen in its entirety. You may be thinking that the architecture feels somewhat Gothic, and you'd be right because the 13th-century eastern extension housing the Chapel of the Nine Altars, and the central tower, added in the late 15th century, are two of the most dominant features. But that's from the outside. It is not until you enter the cathedral through the north doorway with its bands of zigzags and then gaze down the **nave** to the rose window that the purity of the Norman architecture really hits you. At this moment it becomes clear why Durham is considered one of the finest Norman cathedrals in Europe. We're not just talking about a bit of chevron detailing here and there and some Romanesque

◄ **1** The nave. **2** Cosin's Hall. **3** The Chapter House. **4** The Rose Window.
5 The Sanctuary Ring. **6** The Cloisters.

THE ORIGINS OF DURHAM

How, when the rude Dane burn'd their pile,
The monks fled forth from Holy Isle;
O'er northern mountain, marsh, and moor,
From sea to sea, from shore to shore,
Seven years Saint Cuthbert's corpse they bore.

Sir Walter Scott, *Marmion: A Tale of Flodden Field*, 1808

The history of Durham cannot be told without reference to the secluded isle of Lindisfarne off the north Northumberland coast and its most famous bishop, Cuthbert. When he died in AD687 St Cuthbert was initially buried on the island, but 11 years later his body (reportedly undecayed) was moved to the mainland when the monastic community were driven out by Viking invaders. For seven years the monks wandered northern England with Cuthbert's coffin (and the Lindisfarne Gospels) until they came to Chester-le-Street at the end of the 9th century. Here they stayed for over a hundred years until Cuthbert was moved one last time.

The story goes that on nearing the wooded peninsula, today known as Durham, the cart carrying Cuthbert's coffin stopped and could not be budged. This was interpreted as a sign from the saint, and so a shrine was built on the facing rocky mound above the River Wear, referred to by a passing milk maid searching for her lost cow as 'Dun Holm'. The name explains the name Dun Cow Lane off Palace Green and the stone relief of two maids and a cow on the northwest tower of the cathedral.

arches; at Durham, the masonry is chiefly 11th- and 12th-century Norman. And there's a lot of stonework at Durham, almost all of it locally quarried sandstone.

Entrance

The cathedral is entered through the north door under three zigzag arches. Note the large replica **Sanctuary Ring** with its wild eyes and locks (the 12th-century original is on display in the cathedral museum). Until the early 17th century, those accused of criminal wrongdoing were offered temporary immunity from prosecution in the cathedral by knocking on the door. After 37 days of receiving shelter, they had to leave the country or turn themselves in and face trial.

Housed at the western end of the nave, the most eye-catching feature of the marble **font** is its 40ft-high wooden canopy, both of which date to the refurbishment of the cathedral in the late 17th century, in the decades after the Civil War. It's one of the largest and most ornate you will find anywhere in England.

The nave, crossing & transepts

The immense body of the cathedral – the **nave** – is quite jaw-dropping with its thumping 7ft-wide drum piers carved with geometric patterns, and alternating columns soaring past the arcades and galleries to form a series of elegant arches spanning the vaulted ceiling, 75 dizzying feet above. It is the combination of rounded ribs and pointed arches that gives the ceiling such formidable strength. Before Durham, no stonemason had attempted to create a vaulted ceiling like this on such a scale. If you've arrived late in the afternoon, sit yourself at the back of the nave and take in this sight while the exquisite voices of the city's Chorister School come in waves through the church. **Choral evensong** at Durham is experienced every day during term time at 17.15 and on Sundays at 15.30.

At the crossing, look up into the 218ft **central tower** which can be climbed from the south transept (for a fee). A mere 325 steps later and you'll be taking in the view of Durham, its river scenery and distant countryside. Also in the south transept is the **Durham Light Infantry Chapel** (note the miners' banner) and a decorative medieval clock painted turquoise and gold.

The quire, sanctuary & Neville Screen

Beyond the crossing is the heart of the church (sometimes referred to as the chancel) from where the choir sing and Mass is performed. Beyond the choir stalls, the ornate **Bishop's Throne** (built under Bishop Hatfield in 1381, who is said to have ordered his throne to be two inches higher than the Pope's in Rome) and finely painted organ pipes, is the **sanctuary**, housing the high altar and one of the most celebrated and intricate stone structures in the cathedral. Completed in 1380 using a pale white stone from Caen in France, the Gothic **Neville Screen** rises all spears and spikes from behind the altar; it is still magnificent despite having lost its bright paintwork and the alabaster angels and saints that once stood in its 107 niches. The figures are said to have been buried by monks fearing their destruction during the Reformation, and have never been recovered.

The Neville family, incidentally, is a name you hear in many places around the city. Famous for his role in the victorious battle of 1346 against the Scots, known as the Battle of Neville's Cross, Ralph Neville (whose son gifted the stone reredos to the cathedral) was the first layperson to be honoured with burial in the nave. The **Neville Tomb** has been ravaged over the centuries but remains in situ in the south arcade of the nave.

St Cuthbert's Shrine

A plain stone slab engraved 'CVTHBERTVS' marks the saint's resting place that lies in a tranquil space beyond the high altar, reached by steps from the quire aisles. The simplicity of his shrine today is perhaps a more fitting tribute to the humble saint than the original lavish surroundings before the Dissolution commissioners paid a visit in 1539. On finding Cuthbert's body still 'fresh, safe and not consumed' they left it alone, but not before taking the gold and jewels that decorated his shrine. In the 19th century, his coffin was opened again and more treasures removed, some of which are now on display in the cathedral museum.

"The simplicity of his shrine today is perhaps a more fitting tribute to the humble saint than the original lavish surroundings."

A stone statue of Cuthbert holding the head of Oswald, King of Northumbria from AD634 to his death in AD642, keeps alive the record that the Northumbrian ruler's head was buried with the saint. Above Cuthbert's tomb is a modern brightly painted canopy depicting Christ.

The shrine area once marked the east end of the cathedral, but an extension (the Chapel of the Nine Altars) was added in the mid to late 13th century to accommodate the increasing number of pilgrims visiting Durham. You can still see this division in the floor, marked by lines.

Chapel of the Nine Altars & the Rose Window

The glorious **Rose Window** draws the eye through the nave to the sanctuary and the Chapel of the Nine Altars beyond which occupies the far eastern end of the cathedral. Originally medieval, the window was reconstructed in the 19th century with new glass depicting Christ in the centre surrounded by the 12 apostles. Externally it is best viewed from North Bailey.

When the cathedral was extended in the 13th century to accommodate swelling numbers of pilgrims, the land fell away to the east and so the flooring in this new area housing the **Chapel of the Nine Altars** was lowered, creating an even greater sense of height than already provided by the slender tiers of lancet windows.

The Chapel of the Nine Altars is as Gothic as the nave is Romanesque with its tall, narrow columns and pointed arches all classically Early English in design and contrasting with the heavy Norman piers and columns of the nave, the technology of the day having progressed to make use of glass over stone to create vertical lift. Interestingly, it took 40 years to build, the same length of time as it had taken to construct the rest of the cathedral some 200 years earlier.

One of the defining features of the columns is the extensive use of black Frosterley marble from Weardale. It's actually a limestone containing the fossilised remains of sea creatures that once swam in tropical waters 350 million years ago. You'll want to run your hand down the smooth, polished columns, but try doing the same round the back of the pillars and you'll find the stone in its raw form, which feels quite rough.

The Galilee Chapel

The walk along the nave to the western end of the cathedral allows you again to take in the tremendous power of the nave and the 14th-century west window. Crossing the thick black marble line by the font, you enter the only area of the cathedral that women were permitted in under the rules of the Benedictine community. For this reason it was also known as the 'Lady Chapel'. Another of the most celebrated parts of the cathedral, this area feels very different – quieter and more intimate because of the low height of the ceiling and because the open space with its many Romanesque arches rising from slender columns lends itself well as a gathering place. Indeed, ever since construction began in 1170, the Galilee Chapel has been used in this way before and after services, as seen in French churches of a similar period. The chapel's four arcades of Romanesque arches decorated with chevrons are remarkably well preserved and it has often been noted that the chapel's extensive columns and connected arches echo Andalusian architecture and specifically the Great Mosque in Cordoba, Spain, built centuries earlier. Structural similarities aside, the chapel is distinguished by its medieval stained glass and murals, particularly the Crucifixion that is narrated in scenes across one arcade, and the figures in the recesses by the altar, dating to

"The western end of the cathedral allows you to take in the tremendous power of the nave and the 14th-century west window."

the chapel's 12th-cenury construction, which are likely depictions of St Cuthbert and St Oswald.

Of course, mention must be made of the second shrine in the cathedral, dedicated to the Anglo-Saxon scholar, the **Venerable Bede**, who died in AD735 and whose great tomb chest with a black marble cover is housed in the Galilee Chapel. Bede documented St Cuthbert's life and was an important figure during the cultural flowering of Northumbria from the mid 7th to the early 9th centuries. Like Cuthbert, his body hasn't always lain in Durham: Bede was first buried in his home town of Jarrow on Tyneside before being moved to the cathedral in 1022.

The cloisters & monastery buildings

Originally the windows of the **cloisters** would have been glazed, some with coloured glass, and the cloisters would have felt much less airy than today though they still convey a strong sense of where most of the activities of the monastic community were centred in the years after the monks of Lindisfarne settled at Durham and work began on the cathedral. Originally built around the same time as the cathedral was underway, the cloister arcades were rebuilt in the early 15th century and later.

Chapter House is reached from the cloisters and was an important part of the daily proceedings in the monastery, where monks would gather along stone benches built into the perimeter wall and listen to a daily reading of a 'chapter' of the Rule of St Benedict. Today it functions as a kind of robing room before services and choir recitals, as you may see at the starting point of a museum tour. A peak under the rugs will reveal the burial sites of the earliest Norman bishops of Durham whose graves were uncovered in 1874; artefacts removed include episcopal rings (on display in the cathedral museum at the time of writing). Impressive to this day, the stone-vaulted room was remodelled in the late 18th century and then again a century later, returning it to something similar to its original appearance.

The **Priory Kitchen** (also known as the Great Kitchen) and **Monks' Dormitory** (see opposite) are hugely impressive, the former with a rib-vaulted ceiling said to be one of only two surviving medieval monastic kitchens in the country; the latter with a huge oak-beamed roof and medieval hall-like proportions (nearly 200ft long). Both rooms are used today as museum spaces and it is easy to overlook the impressive architecture when faced with the riches from St Cuthbert's coffin and the mass of artefacts in the dormitory. The same is true of the cathedral **café** and **shop** with more in the way of striking stone-vaulted ceilings.

Durham Cathedral Museum

Durham Cathedral ☉ 10.00–16.00 (last entry 15.30) Mon–Fri (times can vary so check online); access via the cathedral ⊘ durhamcathedral.co.uk ♿ limited access, see details online.

This awe-inspiring and important museum housed in the intimate surroundings of the monastery's medieval **kitchen** is chiefly focused on a small selection of exquisite items retrieved from St Cuthbert's coffin, but the collection embraces a wider selection of finds celebrating Northumbria's golden Anglo-Saxon era.

Treasures include St Cuthbert's gold pectoral cross with garnet inlay, an ivory comb, a silk stole made with the finest gold thread (one of the earliest pieces of Anglo-Saxon embroidery in the country) and the saint's 7th-century wood coffin (now in fragments) carved with depictions of the apostles and Christ. It is remarkable that it has survived at all. These precious items are beautifully displayed in glass cases under the rib-vaulted ceiling of the old monastic kitchen (note the old bread oven) alongside

"Over 300 manuscripts and 60 printed books survive, making this the most complete in situ medieval monastic library in the UK."

a digital copy of the Lindisfarne Gospels (the original travelled with St Cuthbert on his century-long journey to Durham and is now housed in the British Museum in London) and the cathedral's original 12th-century Sanctuary Ring – or Knocker – that formerly hung from the main entrance, its fiery eyes once filled with red glass. Dating to the same period is the Conyers Falchion, a type of sword so rare that only four are known to still exist in Europe.

The museum continues at a different pace upstairs in the former **Monks' Dormitory** – a tremendously long medieval hall – showcasing Anglo Saxon and medieval finds alongside a hoard of Roman stones, and interactive displays documenting the antiquities and their uses: Viking grave covers, 7th-century log coffins and Roman altar stones. A recreated cubicle with a bed recalls the room's former use. You'll also notice many cabinets containing books that belong to the **library**, first established in various parts of the cloisters under Bishop William of St Calais in 1083, with manuscripts dating to the 7th and 8th centuries,

HARRY POTTER AT DURHAM CATHEDRAL

There's a scene in the film of *Harry Potter and the Philosopher's Stone* when Harry releases his owl, Hedwig, into the skies above the snowy grounds of Hogwarts. If you've visited the cathedral cloisters in Durham you may well recognise it as the setting for this famous shot: the cloister garth covered in fake snow, the stone basin once used by monks at its centre, and, surrounding the quad, the stone walkways of the cloisters. As Hedwig climbs, fleeting glimpses of the cathedral's galleries and towers appear which are transformed by digital technology to appear like Hogwarts.

The cloisters appear many times in the first two *Harry Potter* films, memorably as the setting for the 'Eat Slugs!' scene when Ron's spell backfires and he vomits slugs on the grass; but mainly the walkways serve as the corridors between classrooms. The cathedral's Chapter House stood in as the teaching room of Professor McGonagall and her transfiguration lessons.

some from Lindisfarne. Over the centuries, the cathedral's collection expanded (though many items were lost during the Reformation and Civil War) and today over 300 manuscripts and 60 printed books survive from the early collection, making this the most complete in situ medieval monastic library in the UK. The rarest manuscripts are stored in the university library in Palace Green (see opposite), along with the Durham Gospels (a precursor to the more famous Lindisfarne Gospels) created on Lindisfarne in the 7th century.

2 PALACE GREEN

'Le Place' as it was known after the Norman Conquest was eventually Anglicised to 'Palace', but the green, bound along its south side by the length of the cathedral and on its other sides by a higgledy mix of historic buildings and the castle, retains its open character. Little effort is needed to imagine this area as a bustling market square in the years during and after the construction of the cathedral; it was moved a short way north to its current location in the 12th century, however, and for a long time served as the executive centre for the Prince Bishops whose residence was in the castle.

Close to the corner of Owengate by the red telephone box is **Moneyer's Garth**, now a 19th-century university building, but for 400 years until 1536 this was the site of the bishops' mint (those extraordinary powers bestowed upon the bishops of Durham by the king including the right to mint their own coins). Next door is the fine 21-window façade of

Cosin's Hall (now the university's Institute of Advanced Study), which is thoroughly Georgian in very obvious ways: the use of brick, the flat, uniform façade and all those rectangular windows. Note the decorative doorway with its ornamental columns and leaf-carved frieze. Contrasting with the splendour of the Georgian mansion next door is a modest row of stone **almshouses** built in 1666. Tucked away out of sight at the end of the row is a plain Georgian building, **Abbey House**, once also known as 'The Dovecote' by male students when in 1899 it became a hostel for the first female undergraduates. It is now the Department of Theology and Religion. On the side of Dun Cow Lane,

"Little effort is needed to imagine this area as a bustling market square during and after the construction of the cathedral."

you'll see an exposed section of a medieval wall that was integrated into the current building. On the west side of Palace Green is the Tudor-styled **Pemberton Building**, which looks much older than its early 1930s construction. It is home to one of the earliest university debating societies in the world, founded in 1842. The medieval-looking **Palace Green Library** buildings adjoining it are as old as they appear, dating to the mid 15th century onwards (see below). At the end of the row is the **Exchequer Building**, built under the rule of the Prince Bishops for administrative purposes.

Palace Green Library & Cosin's Library

☉ Palace Green: 10.00–17.00 daily (19.00 Thu); Cosin's: 11.00–15.00 Wed–Sun

In the aftermath of the English Civil War, Bishop Cosin ordered a large amount of restoration and repair work to the cathedral and castle and the construction of the almshouses and library facing each other across the green (the library is the last building before the castle). Opened in 1669, **Cosin's Library**, as it is known today, downstairs from Palace Green Library, has been restored in recent years and its dark-wood bookcases and painted portraits of authors, historians and philosophers (indicating the subject matters on shelves below) are looking their best. The library contains around 5,000 books, many of them from John Cosin's private collection, the bishop being an ardent collector of theology, history, law and philosophy works. It's an exquisite historic room and well worth visiting but note that only ten visitors are allowed in at any one time so you may have to wait a short while.

Palace Green Library also cares for a number of other collections including the Durham Cathedral Collections and 100 rare medieval manuscripts. In all there are an astonishing 70,000 books here printed before 1850.

Besides a Special Collections library, the building houses the **Durham Light Infantry collection** and serves as a useful **tourist information point** (this being the World Heritage Site Visitor Centre) where you can pick up maps and book tours of the castle. The **Museum of Archaeology** on the ground floor provides an interesting introduction to thousands of years of history in Durham from the Bronze Age to the Romans: axe heads to altar stones; pottery to coins.

3 DURHAM CASTLE

Palace Green, DH1 3RW ✆ 0191 3342932 ⌨ dur.ac.uk/durham.castle ☺ guided tours only; book online or in the Palace Library.

> **Though nature had made the city a fortress, he made it stronger and more imposing with a wall.**
> A monk writing about the 11th century Bishop Flambard who ordered the construction of a bailey wall surrounding the castle and cathedral on the already naturally defensive peninsula.

On the orders of William the Conqueror, a fortress was built at Durham in 1072 as a show of strength, to supress local uprisings in the wake of Norman rule – and to keep Scottish invaders at bay. To this aim, the king gave secular powers to the Bishop of Durham to control large areas of northern England in return for loyalty to the Crown, hence the title 'Prince Bishop' afforded to successive heads of the Diocese of Durham. The castle has changed over the centuries: the bailey walls removed, bits added here and there, rooms reconfigured, galleries added and so on, but some of the earliest parts from the time around the Conquest, conspicuously the early Norman chapel, remain intact making it the oldest built structure in the city – older than the cathedral by several decades.

In future centuries, the castle would be developed into a luxurious palace fit for a prince (bishop) and later – much later – into accommodation for university students when it came into the ownership of University College in 1836. It remains in use by the university, maintaining the continual occupation of the fortress since the 11th century.

Architectural writer Nikolaus Pevsner described Durham Castle as 'one of the most completely preserved and most easily appreciated

DURHAM UNIVERSITY

Durham University is formed of 17 colleges mirroring the structure of Oxford and Cambridge universities, though it is much younger, established in 1832. Those first students were all men and were required to live in the castle, attend mandatory chapel services and study a few restricted subjects, mainly theology. Drinking in the city's taverns was forbidden. A very different learning environment exists today, of course.

Students at Durham belong to a college with their own sports clubs, arts institutions and traditions.

For a hundred years, the students were largely confined to the peninsula until the university expanded south of the city in the 1920s, where most of the science departments are based to this day. Durham Castle came into the ownership of the university a few years after its founding, becoming known as University College; today it is home to nearly 1,500 students. The Keep on the mound was refurbished into student accommodation and is still used by first and fourth year students – as well as visitors (looking for inexpensive accommodation) in the city out of term time (page 308).

Norman strongholds in the county.' Let's overlook the fact that the octagonal **Keep**, raised on the original Norman mound – or 'motte' – and looking tremendously imposing and old, actually only dates to the mid-19th century when it was reconstructed from the original 11th-century building (probably made of timber). But Norman masonry survives in the chapel and gallery – both of which you can admire on guided tours.

The fort is entered through the **gatehouse** from Palace Green, with clear signs of Norman stonemasonry in its bands of zigzags and rib vaulting (but that's nothing compared to the doorway into Tunstall's Gallery, page 45). The hefty doors at the gateway are early 16th century; they open into a central courtyard surrounded by medieval buildings that once formed the **inner bailey** walls of the castle.

Little remains of the **outer bailey** castle walls that once girdled both castle and cathedral (though they are recalled in the street names: North Bailey and South Bailey). The castle's defences were further strengthened by a **dry moat** located behind the keep and still existent today, albeit restructured into a walkway connecting Silver and Saddler streets.

Part of the castle walls formed the external wall of the intimate **Norman Chapel** which explains why it is so tremendously thick – at least 6ft. At its core stand half a dozen central supporting pillars made

of local sandstone, beautifully patterned with natural swirls formed by iron deposits, their capitals carved with rudimentary beasts and faces – all with meanings that can only be speculated on but include two leopards, a serpent (symbolic of eternal life) and a mermaid, thought to be the first depiction of its kind in England.

A newer place of worship, the **Tunstall Chapel**, was built shortly after the Reformation in 1540 under Bishop Tunstall, marking the break away from the Catholic church. Tunstall's portrait in the chapel is telling because the rosary once held in his hands was painted out to appease the newly Protestant monarch.

Other features worthy of mention are the misericords (seats), taken from Auckland Castle, which predate the chapel itself. Some are carved with humorous fables on their undersides including a man in a skirt (some wonder if this is a medieval joke at the expense of the Scots) pushing a woman in a wheelbarrow; and a bear with a muzzle, bearbaiting being a popular sport at the time.

Tunstall added a gallery to the south side of the castle to allow access to his new chapel without having to cross the courtyard. The castle side of the **Tunstall Gallery** was clearly once an external wall and it is also the reason why the doorway into the gallery, known as **Le Puiset's Door**, once an exterior opening, is so well preserved. The detail across the thick trio of arches is wonderfully detailed with octagons, zigzags and other geometric shapes. It is, according to Pevsner, 'the most sumptuous piece of Norman work in the county'. Today the gallery contains artefacts acquired over the centuries including a huge heavily time-worn chest that would have probably once stored important documents.

Other buildings fronting the courtyard include the early 14th-century **Great Hall**, similar to those dining rooms found in Oxbridge colleges. Meals are still prepared in the medieval kitchen for students in the hall who dine below a display of Napoleonic armour and one of the largest collection of rifles in England. St Cuthbert is easily identified in the stained glass, holding the head of St Oswald.

Also memorable is the leaning **Black Staircase**, built in 1662 from wood, with carved pineapples as a sign of the bishop's wealth and prestige. The fruit was so expensive in the 17th century that judging by

◀ **1** Durham Castle. **2** Stalls at the Victorian covered market. **3** Silver Street.
4 Durham Cathedral crowns a wooded peninsula above the Wear.

their interpretation the carpenters had clearly never actually seen one before. Take note of the wide 'floating' staircase with its open well where the wife of a bishop allegedly fell to her death. Her ghost is said to appear from time to time, her presence signalled by the scent of lavender. A ghost hunt for the Grey Lady is staged by students annually, which I am told becomes more elaborate every year.

4 THE COLLEGE

Nothing to do with the university, this beautiful village-like green – really a cathedral close – with an eye-catching water tower and surrounded by Georgian-looking houses was built for the college or 'community' of the Priory and today is home to the Dean of Durham Cathedral and members of the clergy as well as the Chorister School (past alumni include former Prime Minister Tony Blair, and Rowan Atkinson, better known in some parts of the world as Mr Bean). At one time an infirmary, guest hall, prison and brewery serviced the community. All these buildings remain – or at least parts of them, though some were remodelled in the 17th and 18th centuries, giving the medieval buildings the outward appearance of houses. Access for visitors is through the medieval gateway where North Bailey meets South Bailey.

5 THE BAILEYS

Durham's old centre and cathedral is reached in a few ways but none is more peaceful or saturated in historic buildings than the approach from Prebends Bridge, following an uphill path and under the **Water Gate Arch** (also known as Bailey Gate) of 1778 where it meets with South Bailey. The arch was built into the old city walls and frames the sinuous lane of cobbles ahead. Lined with Georgian townhouses and lit by old lamps, **South Bailey** brings to mind streets in Oxford, and indeed, most of the buildings now belong to Durham University, mainly to the colleges of St John's (blue paintwork) and St Cuthbert's (green paintwork), but the history of the passage goes back almost 1,000 years to when it formed part of the outer bailey wall of the castle, and you can still see evidence of the defensive structure in a few places.

Of the three churches dedicated to St Mary in Durham, the smallest (evoked by its name) is **St Mary the Less**, which began life in 1140 but was substantially rebuilt in 1847 and is now the chapel of St John's College with services at 08.30 and 17.15 on weekdays during term time. Some memorials to look out for: inside, to a famous Polish-born entertainer known as the 'Little Count' (page 55); on the outer wall, memorial slabs including one of Frosterley marble encrusted with many fossilised sea creatures millions of years old, and another with some curious spellings but, from what I can decipher, it remembers a woman called 'Joan Lever' who was the 'wife' of someone called 'Nicholls' who died in the month of 'Maie', 1599. God bless you Joan and everything you were besides a wife.

South Bailey becomes **North Bailey** at The College gatehouse (see opposite) and hereon the lane is dominated by Hatfield and St Chad's colleges, and various university department buildings. Glimpses of the cathedral come into view from behind the street wall and soon the dazzling Rose Window on the east face of the cathedral appears right in front of you. Opposite is St Mary-le-Bow Church, housing the **Durham Museum** (page 48).

Two cobbled lanes branch in opposite directions away from North Bailey at this point: **Dun Cow Lane** recalls how the city became known as Durham (page 34) and connects to Palace Green for visits to the cathedral; **Bow Lane** trails down the side of the heritage centre – all cobbles, old stone and Georgian brick – to meet with the modern age and a fine span of reinforced concrete known as **Kingsgate footbridge**. 'Dramatic, beautifully detailed and ingenious' is how Historic England

"Glimpses of the cathedral come into view and soon the dazzling Rose Window on the east face of the cathedral appears."

describe the slender crossing over the Wear which is Grade I listed and a wonder of 1960s design. It is the work of esteemed modernist architect Ove Arup who considered it his finest structure. It was also his last. Erected in 1963 without the use of scaffolding, the crossing was raised in two parts on each side of the riverbank, which were then swivelled on bearings to meet in the middle to be joined with bronze expansion joints.

Back on North Bailey, the **Durham Student Theatre** (⊘ durhamstudenttheatre.org) puts on a large number of productions every year and is housed in the former 18th-century Assembly Rooms, identified by its reworked Art-Deco entrance. Facing the theatre is another church, now Hatfield College Chapel. Saddler Street continues the lane's run to Market Place.

Durham Museum

North Bailey, DH1 3ET ✆ 0191 3845589 ⏁ durhammuseum.co.uk ⊙ Apr, May & Oct 11.00–16.30 Sat, Sun & bank hols; Jun–Sep 11.00–16.30 Wed–Sun

This informative little museum explores the city's heritage from the Normans through to the 20th century and includes displays about local industries in medieval and Victorian Durham and daily life under the control of the governing bishops. Highlights include a set of four Victorian backlit stained-glass panels depicting members of the illustrious Neville family; a sedan chair known to students at Durham School as the 'death chair' as it was used to carry sick pupils to the local infirmary; and the 17th-century Chancellor's Bench – a relic from the days of prince bishop rule in Durham.

"The museum explores the city's heritage from the Normans to the 20th century and includes displays about local industries."

The church itself – no longer in use – is historically interesting, having been partially reconstructed in the late 17th century after an arch (the 'bow' in the church's name) connecting the tower to the city walls collapsed, taking the tower down with it. Woodwork dating to around the time of the rebuild are worth a moment's pause, including the rood screen and panelling.

A sculpture garden to the rear of the museum displays a couple of works by Durham sculptor Fenwick Lawson, best known for his bronze of monks carrying St Cuthbert's coffin in Millennium Square (page 51) and whose works appear across the North East.

6 SADDLER STREET & SILVER STREET

Two of the best-known streets, Saddler Street and Silver Street, form a wishing bone in the old city centre converging at Market Place. **Silver Street** is a lively pedestrianised shopping lane with plenty of places to enjoy a coffee while taking in the scene. It is many visitors' first impressions of the cathedral peninsula on crossing the Wear over **Framwellgate Bridge**. And what an entrance: the castle crowning the leafy prominence ahead; the wide river gliding below. First built around the time of the cathedral, the two hefty arches spanning the Wear today are medieval but were widened under the Victorians.

Fowlers Yard art and craft workshops (⏁ fowlersyarddurham. co.uk) on Back Silver Street is a hidden hub of creative talent in the

DURHAM MUSTARD

Saddler Street was once known for the production of mustard. In 1720, a local woman called Mrs Clements developed the process of grinding mustard seeds in a mill to produce a distinctly hot powder. Her mustard became legendary and was said to be enjoyed by King George I. Durham Mustard was later produced by a number of local firms until the last was absorbed into Colman's of Norwich.

city and is reached in a few fiddly ways but the easiest route on foot is by descending a stepped passageway from Silver Street, a short way up from Framwellgate Bridge and just before Moatside Lane. Textile artists, jewellery makers, painters and printmakers, among other artists, occupy a tranquil lane of old red-brick buildings where there is a quiet café with outdoor seating away from the bustle of nearby Silver Street. The road is also home to **City Theatre** (⊘ durhamdramatic.co.uk) where five annual shows are performed by the Durham Dramatic Society, a long-running and much-loved amateur dramatic group.

Continuing along Silver Street, you'll reach Market Place but you can also wander through the gorge-like passageway, **Moatside Lane** (a dry moat), that winds under the castle walls connecting with Saddler Street on the other side of the peninsula. It's one of a number of narrow alleyways in the city.

Saddler Street has always been a bustling route to the cathedral, the independent cafés, shops, bars and restaurants standing where once there were shoemakers, fishmongers, butchers and other traders in medieval times. Closed to traffic, except the Cathedral Bus, for much of the day, visitors wander freely in and out of shops including a vintage clothing shop and some quirky bistros serving lunch (page 67). **The Shakespeare** tavern claims to be the most haunted pub in England. To the side of the pub is the east entrance to Moatside Lane. Saddler Street connects with **Owengate** – a short venerable street with almshouses dating to 1830 that provides a fittingly historic walk up to the cathedral, which appears straight ahead across Palace Green.

7 MARKET PLACE

Pedestrians spill into spacious Market Place from Silver Street, Saddler Street and Claypath. A mix of Victorian and Georgian frontages and the length of St Nicholas's Church flank the busy, largely pedestrianised square enclosing a few monuments. **Neptune** stands baring his muscles, buttocks and tumbling locks above a doomed sea creature; he may be ten miles from the sea but he keeps alive the memory of an unrealised plan in the 1720s to connect Durham city with the coast by canal and river.

Also with coastal connections is the double life-size copper figure of the **Third Marquess of Londonderry** on horseback. Unveiled in 1861, the statue was commissioned by his wife in recognition of his influence in the county as an important colliery owner and the creator of a port for Durham at Seaham that dramatically increased the coal output along the coast.

Altogether more humbling is the bronze statue of a **soldier** from the Durham Light Infantry marking the end of the Korean war in 1953. The historic regiment, whose origins go back to 1758, is remembered elsewhere in the city as well as in the Town Hall behind the sculpture, in a striking glass window depicting marching soldiers beneath Durham Cathedral.

The **Town Hall** is a complex of administrative buildings and rooms occupying the northwest corner of Market Place, next to the covered market entrance. It's open for tours on Saturdays only (⊙ 10.00–15.00 Sat; free entry) – but you'll find staff on the front desk (⊙ daily) are a useful source of informal information if visiting Durham during the week. The highlight inside is the **Guildhall** of 1665 with its hammerbeam roof and much-admired west window – an intensely coloured work of glass art commemorating the Feast of Corpus Christi festival, a popular tradition during medieval times with a procession from Market Place to the cathedral. Portraits and plaques line the walls identifying notable residents of the city made Freemen, including former footballing legend

DURHAM MARKETS

Reached through an archway next to the Town Hall is the restored **Victorian covered market** (⌂ durhammarkets. co.uk ⊙ 09.00–16.30 Mon–Sat ♿ but corridors are tight) – a warren of stalls selling secondhand books, fresh local produce, vintage finds, old records, hardware, jewellery and take-away food. There's a café upstairs from where you can view the market's wonderful roof.

A regular **Saturday outdoor market** is held in Market Place, run by independent stallholders showcasing a range of art, local delicacies, clothes and crafts. A **food and craft market** occupies the same space on the third Thursday of the month.

Sir Bobby Robson, Desmond Tutu and Bill Bryson (chancellor of the university until 2011). On your tour, look out for the ornate Jacobean fireplace and overmantel, an old jail cell and a suitably diminutive exhibit of clothes and belongings of local 19th-century celebrity, the Little Count (page 55) as well as his portrait.

St Nicholas's Church dominates the north side of Market Square and dates to the mid 19th century, built on the site of a 12th-century church that once stood at a gateway into the city and whose north wall formed part of the old city wall. When rebuilt in Victorian times, it was the only church with a spire in the city, and that remains the case to this day.

8 MILLENNIUM SQUARE, CLAYPATH & GILESGATE

Heading north away from the historic centre, beyond St Nicholas's Church and over the flyover, is **Claypath**, a long, busy road that, though not hugely attractive at first, is flanked by old, pastel-coloured houses where it becomes **Gilesgate** (particularly by the green and not far from the university's School of Education).

By the flyover is the modern **Millennium Square**, an open space dominated by the **Gala Theatre** and cinema (⌀ galadurham.co.uk) hosting screenings of major releases as well as comedy nights, music concerts, children's theatre, Shakespeare plays and dance shows. *The Journey* by acclaimed Durham sculptor, Fenwick Lawson, is a moving life-sized bronze in the spacious square depicting six monks carrying St Cuthbert's coffin. It matches a sculpture in elmwood by the same artist on the Isle of Lindisfarne, marking the beginning and end points of the monks' 100-year-long journey to Durham.

THE WIDER CITY & RIVERSIDE

🏠 **Forty Winks Guest House** (page 308), **The Victoria** (page 309) 🏠 **Durham Riverside Apartment** (page 309), **Woodland Barn Holiday Cottage** (page 309)

Away from the peninsula, the rows of Victorian brick terraces around the **railway station** contrast with the medieval streets and Georgian houses lining the lanes near the cathedral and this whole area feels very different – more work-a-day in parts, but it has its own history, some very attractive old streets, parks and places of heritage interest.

Other areas in the wider city of interest are the **University Botanic Garden** and celebrated **Oriental Museum**, both in the dense university complex south of the peninsula. Heading east off Elvet Bridge into **Old Elvet** are streets famous for staging the annual **Durham Miners' Gala** (page 61), and a good few miles of riverside paths linking the peninsula with areas of open countryside, remnant woods and 18th-century **walled gardens and orchards** (page 57). If you keep on this path tracing the Wear upstream (that is, south), you'll reach the old village of **Shincliffe** (page 58) where a good pub lunch awaits. In the opposite direction, north out of Durham from Framwellgate, the riverside connects to **Crook Hall Gardens** (page 64) in ten or 15 minutes by foot.

9 ELVET BRIDGE & OLD ELVET

🏨 **Hotel Indigo** (page 308) 🏠 **52 Old Elvet** (page 309)

Durham's medieval streets were once crammed with traders and the shops on Saddler Street would not have come to the abrupt halt on meeting Elvet Bridge as they do today, but made good use of the multi-arched crossing as well, where there were also two chapels. Only one building survives today on the peninsula side.

Elvet Bridge dates in part to the 12th and 13th centuries and often features on postcards of the city, usually with rowing boats below its

---

BOATING ON THE RIVER

On sunny days there can be few activities more pleasurable in Durham than messing about in a wooden rowing boat. Whichever direction you travel in from the boat-hire station at Elvet Bridge, you'll pass under three of Durham's historic crossings and enjoy views of the River Wear tugging gently on overhanging branches as it curls lazily around the peninsula.

Motor cruises on the open-topped *Prince Bishop* depart three times a day all year round from the same spot next to The Boathouse restaurant and bar, and travel as far as the weir, taking in views of the cathedral, castle, bridges and mills. The commentary by the knowledgeable skipper provides a good introduction to the city.

Browns Rowing Boats Elvet Bridge, DH1 3AF (between the bridge & The Boathouse restaurant & bar) ✆ 0191 3863779 ⊙ mid-Mar–Sep 10.00–18.00 daily (last hire 17.00). Boats £8/£5 per adult/child per hour.

Prince Bishop River Cruiser ✆ 0191 3869525 (information line) ⊙ 12.30, 14.00 & 15.00. Sightseeing motor tours of the river. £10/£5 per adult/child for one hour. No booking required.

stone arches gathering like ducks to bread. Connecting Saddler Street with Old Elvet, the pedestrian bridge is unusual in that only four of its arches actually span the water; below one of the dry arches is an old **prison** with two cells dating to the early 17th century. Now a drinking hole, the Bridewell Gaol Bar at Jimmy Allens recalls the building's former use and the legend of its most famous inmate, a renowned piper from a famous gypsy clan in Northumberland who died in the cell and whose tunes are said to haunt the riverside.

The bridge connects the medieval streets of the peninsula with **Old Elvet**, a grander and more spacious area with its wide avenue and Georgian frontages (nearly every building is listed), including the famous **Royal County Hotel** where left-wing dignitaries and Labour Party representatives traditionally watch the Miners' Gala (page 61) parade from the balcony.

Muscling its way into the run of 18th-century buildings is the Victorian **Old Shire Hall**, an imposing red-brick mansion with a bright turquoise copper dome. Originally built for Durham County Council in the 1890s, it is now a large boutique hotel and restaurant (Hotel Indigo) – but its sumptuous interior is really worth seeing on account of its extensive decorative tiles and stained glass. The former Council Chamber, a spacious, circular room with rich glazed wall tiles, has been remodelled into an upmarket steakhouse restaurant and cocktail bar (page 66).

"The bridge connects the medieval streets of the peninsula with Old Elvet, a grander and more spacious area."

A little further uphill is the **Dun Cow Inn**, an old, squat pub dating to the late 17th or early 18th century whose name remembers the city's beginnings.

Cross the small triangle green opposite the Dun Cow Inn and veer right, passing **Durham Crown Court,** admired architecturally for its early 19th-century façade by Ignatius Bonomi, the same architect who designed two churches nearby: **St Cuthbert's Catholic Church** and St Oswald's (page 54). After the Reformation and the refounding of the cathedral as an Anglican church, Catholicism persisted secretly in the city but not without reprisals for Catholic priests and their followers, some of whom were executed. Persecution continued into the 17th and 18th centuries, and it wasn't until 1778 that punishments for priests were abolished. The present church of St Cuthbert dates to 1827.

In a city with one of the finest Norman churches in Europe, it is hard to rouse interest in any other building from the same period, and if it weren't for Durham Cathedral perhaps more would be made of **St Oswald's** (Church St ☉ Mon–Fri & for Sun services) whose rear churchyard (a wildlife haven) faces the cathedral on the far side of the Wear. Easy access from the riverside path via steps makes for a straightforward – and worthy – diversion.

It is the interior that's special, with its 12th-century round columns and arches at the east end of the nave, and 14th-century octagonal piers to the west. The choir stalls, roof carvings and tower are all medieval; the rest came later under a rebuild by architect of the day around here, Ignatius Bonomi, in 1834, including stained-glass narrating the life of St Oswald in the west window under the tower (the work of William Morris & Co).

10 ALONG THE WEAR

It's hard to think of a more glorious stretch of urban river scenery than where the Wear curls around Durham's wooded peninsula on its way to the coast at Sunderland. Paved and earth paths stay close to the water's edge on both riverbanks, offering several miles of contrasting views and points of interest – of meadows and woodland, university college boat houses, orchards, old mills, a Victorian folly, and, most memorably, of the cathedral towers rising above the gorge. The city's historic stone bridges (and one splendid modern crossing) provide the foreground for many a photo and facilitate circular walks along the waterside and through the city. While you may think you don't need a map, it can be confusing to work out where you are because the river coils serpent-like around the city, so my advice is to take a free paper one (available at the Palace Green Library visitor centre).

On the peninsula side of Framwellgate Bridge (page 48), steps lead to the banks of the Wear where you can follow a paved path with the river on your right to **Prebends Bridge**, under half a mile away. At this glorious 18th-century crossing, you have a few options, but whichever you choose, a long pause on the bridge to savour the view of the cathedral with the weir and mill below is the quintessential Durham experience. Turner famously captured this scene, bathing the landscape in a lemon light in 1835, though he tilted the cathedral to include more of the towers. It's worth pointing out here that this romantic vista was part of a landscape-scale plan by cathedral clergy embracing the Picturesque movement of the 18th century, and many of the beech and sycamore trees crowding the rocky slopes below the cathedral were planted during this period at the same time as a network of walkways was developed.

An old **fulling mill** stands below the cathedral at the weir and has held many uses over the years, but it was originally built in medieval times (though the current building is 17th and 18th century) to clean and process woollen cloth. Facing it at the other end of the weir is a former **corn mill** (also known as the water mill), again, originally medieval but rebuilt after a huge flood in 1771. It's a timeless scene worthy of more photos, both of the mill and the view of the cathedral.

From the peninsula end of Prebends Bridge you can either stroll uphill and enter the city under Water Gate Arch, walking along the Baileys to reach the cathedral; or continue on the wooded riverside path a little further to the miniature Palladian-style hall, Count's House (see below) and, beyond, Kingsgate Bridge (page 47). Ahead is Old Elvet Bridge, from where a rowing-boat hire company and boat-tour company operate (page 52).

An alternative route back to Prebends Bridge is to cross to the west side of the Wear (away from the peninsula), turn left and follow the river downstream under the churchyard of St Oswald's (see opposite) where you can access the streets around Old Elvet. A popular **walk** is to pick through the streets to the Iron Age hillfort, **Maiden Castle**, which stands on a steep-sided wooded hill east of the city, and then on

THE LITTLE COUNT

Durham has many distinguished former residents but one of the most colourful city legends was Jozef Boruwlaski, a Polish-born musician, entertainer and local curiosity. Born in 1739, he was better known as the 'Little Count' for he stood just 3ft 3in tall. Boruwlaski toured Europe, performing in theatres and to royalty but spent most of the latter half of his life in Durham, where he died aged 97. He is buried outside the cathedral by a gravestone bearing his initials.

Boruwlaski's clothes and belongings (including his violin) form an exhibit in the Town Hall (page 50), which also includes a life-sized model of the man. A mock miniature country 'mansion' known as 'Count's House' on the banks of the Wear near Prebends Bridge (by the side of the riverside footpath) was never inhabited by Boruwlaski but the name of the Victorian folly is suggestive of his enduring fame during the 19th century.

to Shincliffe. Or return from Maiden Castle to the city centre via the Racecourse (see below).

Alternatively, head upstream from the west side of Prebends Bridge, walking back in the direction of Framwellgate Bridge via the corn mill (page 55) and **South Street** with its almost unbroken run of early 18th-century houses and intermittent cathedral views – a scene best admired in the late afternoon light.

The Racecourse & around

Tracing the Wear east out of Durham, not far from Old Elvet, is a wide grassy area known locally as the **Racecourse**, which recalls its former use as a horse-racing venue at least as far back as the 1730s. Today it is used as a sports and cricket ground by the university and for the annual Miners' Gala, first held on the site in 1872 (page 61). If following the riverside path you'll pass a bandstand, large cow sculpture (a nod to the legend of the Dun Cow from where Durham gets its name) and **St Cuthbert's Society Boat House**, a lovely old red-brick building dating to the late 19th century. Several other university boat clubs occupy this stretch of the Wear and this is the location for the **Durham Regatta** – a huge annual event since 1834 enjoyed by thousands on the second weekend in June, making it the second oldest regatta in the UK predating the more famous Henley Regatta by five years.

Old Durham Gardens & Pelaw Wood

DH1 2RY; reached via the riverside path or through the university sports ground; access by road from Bent House Lane olddurhamgardens.co.uk Lower walled garden & orchards always open; upper walled garden Apr–Sep 14.00–16.00 Thu & Sun. Pelaw Wood is always open.

Just a mile from the city and easily reached from the riverside footpath, the orchards, terraces and walled grounds in **Old Durham Gardens** deserve to be better known, though its tiered grassy areas are well-used by university students who visit with their picnic blankets in the spring and summer continuing a tradition of public enjoyment for several hundred years. Once attached to a manor house (now demolished), the gardens were first laid out in the mid 1600s. Over the years they have

◀ **1** Elvet Bridge on the Wear. **2** Durham Miners' Gala. **3** Boating on the Wear. **4** The old fulling mill.

served many purposes but almost always as a place of recreation and entertainment: a one-time bowling green, tennis court, public park, 18th-century open-air music concert venue and al fresco dance floor between the wars.

Flowering damson, apple and pear trees – all varieties from the 17th century – put on a stunning show of flowers in early spring. They are maintained by a committed group of volunteers involved in a long-term restoration project of the grounds and gazebo (built into the wall of the garden).

Adjacent to the gardens, and also reached from the riverside footpath east of Durham (or from St Giles Close), is **Pelaw Wood** (⌀ pelaw-wood.org.uk), a 30-acre area of predominately beech and oak woodland with open areas (offering views of the cathedral) covering a steep-sided bank above the Wear.

11 SHINCLIFFE

An evening stroll through old Shincliffe, a village a few miles outside Durham, is quite the Georgian experience. Period cottages with porch lanterns light the way for diners coming out of the Seven Stars inn (page 67) and walking down the otherwise dimly lit High Street. It's all very atmospheric and pleasingly timeless. Curiously, the village name comes from the old English 'scinna' meaning 'spectre'. Whether the village was ever associated with a ghostly tale, I cannot find out, but keep this in mind as you take that night-time wander, particularly when a mist is rising from the Wear.

The Weardale Way footpath travels south from Shincliffe village through its namesake **woods** above the river; in the other direction, along the riverside path north, you'll eventually reach Durham city centre in a few miles, a journey on foot of under an hour. Bus 58 from Darlington stops outside the pub if you're in need of a lift back to Durham.

12 UNIVERSITY BOTANIC GARDEN

Hollingside Ln, South Rd, DH1 3TN ⌀ 0191 3342887 ⊙ Mar–Oct 10.00–17.00 daily; Nov–Feb 10.00–16.00 daily ♿ much of the gardens and glass houses are accessible but some paths are steep and stepped in places.

Set in 25 acres of woodlands and wildflower meadows to the south of the city is this peaceful site. A series of paved and earth paths link glasshouses at the top of the gardens by the visitor centre, shop and café (there's a well-placed outdoor seating area overlooking the gardens) with distinct botanical zones showcasing habitats and plants from across the world: Japanese cherry trees, thickets of bamboo, a Himalayan dell with birch trees, and magnesian limestone grasslands native to Durham (a large wildflower meadow with picnic benches here makes for a lovely lunch spot). Woodland dominates much of the lower areas where in spring snowdrops then bluebells carpet steep banks sloping to a stream.

Glasshouses, while hardly on the scale of Kew Gardens, have some interesting corners and include an orchid collection with tropical species seized by border agencies and donated to the university. The cactus collection is one of the highlights, with a fine specimen of *Echinopsis pachanoi*, better known as the hallucinogenic 'San Pedro', which I noticed is missing a few stems.

Children will enjoy the goldfish pond, garden sculptures, and tropical bug cases home to tarantulas, scorpions and huge exotic moths. No child should leave without hitting an inviting button in the rainforest glasshouse with the instruction 'push the button for rain!', where upon a fine mist showers plants – and visitors – from overhead sprinklers. Fancier museums and attractions pour money into making their exhibits 'interactive' and engaging for children when sometimes the simplest ideas are the best, and this is a fine example.

> *"Woodland dominates much of the lower areas where in spring snowdrops then bluebells carpet steep banks sloping to a stream."*

13 ORIENTAL MUSEUM

Elvet Hill, DH1 3TH ✐ 0191 3345691 ⬦ dur.ac.uk/oriental.museum ◷ 10.00–17.00 Tue– Fri (19.00 Thu), noon–17.00 Sat & Sun ♿

This is a fantastically rich museum with a huge number and variety of objects spanning thousands of years of history from Egypt, the Himalayas and Southeast Asia, Japan and North and South Korea across four floors.

Housing one of the largest Ancient Egyptian collections in the UK is the engaging **Thacker Gallery**, with much besides mummys and painted funeral masks to interest, including a display of cosmetic pots, utensils and jewellery; scribe's tools; and an intriguing cabinet containing ceramic Bes jars once storing milk for children. Created around 500BC (give or take a few hundred years) the large vessels carved with child-like line drawings of animals are uncannily modern.

A large section of the famous Deir el Bahri relief from a wall in the mortuary temple of Queen Hatshepsut at Luxor is one of the gallery's most treasured possessions.

Elsewhere in the museum, there's a fascinating Silk Road exhibition exploring the complexities of the East–West exchange of goods and beliefs beyond the prevailing notion of a single trade route focused on spices and silk, with the gallery looking at the exchange of ideas, faiths, literature and science, as well as foods and textiles.

Modern-day exhibits include an elaborately decorated Buddhist shrine from the 1980s, objects highlighting the influence of Korean pop culture in the 21st century, and some fascinating Communist Party artefacts: a Red Army cap and Little Red Book from Maoist China, and a prayer rug depicting Lenin from the time of the Soviet–Afghan war in the 1970s and 80s.

The museum **shop** is superior to your average gift store and stocks a small range of ceramics and artworks and authentic small items, all very reasonably priced. While there's no café at the museum apart from a hot drinks machine and a few snacks and cold drinks, visitors often combine their trip with the Botanic Garden (page 58), a ten-minute walk away, where there is a café and plenty of picnic spots.

14 AROUND THE TRAIN STATION

The Victorian terraces southwest of the railway station and 1857 stone viaduct – a stomping crossing of many arches and great height – are some of the most intact traditional terraces in the whole of the region. The likes of Hawthorn Terrace, Mistletoe Street and Lawson Terrace evoke memories of what many residential areas in the northeast used to look like at the height of coal mining in the 19th and early 20th centuries. Typically red brick or stone, they feature back lanes – some of them still cobbled and with their old coal chutes. Six stone houses on **Coalpitts Terrace** (numbers 1–6, raised above Alexandra Crescent) date to the mid-1800s and are listed for their collective heritage value, as are the ones at **58-61 Hawthorn Terrace**, which face red-brick houses on the other side of the street. Looking up the elegant curve of Alexandra Crescent with Hawthorn Terrace splintering to the right and divided by the rounded masonry of the **Colpitts Hotel** (an old pub with much character; page 66) is one of the most unchanged 19th-century views in the city.

DURHAM MINERS' GALA

On the second Saturday in July, the streets of Durham are filled with the sound of brass instruments, drums and rousing speeches during the annual miners' parade, a tradition in the city since 1871, which remembers the country's coal-mining heritage. But it is much more than that: a county-wide celebration and coming together in a show of solidarity and shared history. The Gala is also an opportunity for trade unions and Labour Party representatives to raise pressing political issues. There's an exuberant, carnival-like atmosphere with folk dancers and musicians in costume, but most of the parade is formed of brass bands marching with their historic colliery banners held above a crowd of 150,000.

Historically, colliery bands from every pit village would march through their streets early in the morning to converge in Durham.

Today the procession principally gathers in the city in Market Place around 08.30 and at the **Durham Miners' Association** headquarters (page 63), 'Redhills', near the Railway Station before marching to Old Elvet and on to the **Racecourse** on the riverside for the 'Big Meeting' around 13.00. Stalls, food stands and rides for children make this a fun family day out for many. A special service is later held in the cathedral and is a stirring experience if you get the opportunity to attend.

A focal point of the proceedings is the **Royal County Hotel on Old Elvet** (page 53) where left-wing royalty gather on its famous balcony. Traditionally the leader of the Labour Party joins trade union leaders and local dignitaries, but the invitation has been declined by a number of modern-day politicians, notably Tony Blair for every one of his 13 years as leader.

Wharton Park & Flass Vale Local Reserve

Wharton Park, Framwellgate Peth, DH1 4FJ; ☉ café & toilets 10.00–16.30 Wed–Sun; car park gates dawn–19.00 (summer from 07.30) ◌ durham.gov.uk/whartonpark

Conveniently located behind Durham railway station, **Wharton Park** is a popular green space in the city, and its playgrounds, open spaces, modern amphitheatre and café are well used by local families. It's worth checking online for upcoming events staged in the amphitheatre – a feature of the park since its opening in 1857, though modernised since. Brass-band concerts are often held during the summer.

William Lloyd Wharton was an industrious landowner, businessman and one of the directors of the North Eastern Railway company, with interests in science, astronomy (he built the nearby obelisk for the university) and sports (founder of the Durham Regatta). He created the park from wasteland as a public space, adding features including a mock castle, known as 'the Battery' (so named because of a large field

gun used in the Crimean War which stood here for some years) Then, as now, the raised platform offers a wonderful view of the cathedral. He also planted an oak in memory of Queen Victoria's husband, Prince Albert, who had died two years previously. It grows to this day near the North Road (A1) entrance to the park and is marked by an inscription that was read by Wharton on its planting in 1863: 'While we have time, let us do good to all men'.

Flass Vale Nature Reserve is within a short walk of Wharton Park and has a number of access points from surrounding roads including Ainsley and Waddington streets, both close to the train station and Wharton Park. A remnant of semi-natural woodland, the reserve is forested across much of its 12 acres with glades of grasslands and wetlands in places. It is much quieter than the nearby park with no infrastructure apart from a network of rights of way.

15 DURHAM MINERS' HALL
15 Flass St, DH1 4BE ✆ 0191 3868413 ⌂ redhillsdurham.org

Known affectionately as 'Redhills', the historic home of the Durham Miners' Association headquarters strikes an emotional chord with communities of the Durham Coalfield and is pictured on a number of miners' banners. Out of 100 buildings identified by Historic England for their significance in shaping England, the 1915 Miners' Hall is up there alongside the likes of St Paul's Cathedral and the Palace of Westminster. It is, they say, 'one of the finest trade union buildings in Europe'. The 150ft-long façade with its domed roof and porch is a commanding frontage – a proletarian retort in red brick to the stone country manors of mine owners, and a muscular display of the collective might of the 200,000 coal miners the union once represented.

A key institution of the Labour movement, Redhills was central to the Durham coalfield communities. Through subscriptions, the Durham Miners' Association built welfare halls, libraries, health centres and homes for retired miners; it continues to provide support and legal advice to ex-miners. Though the last Durham coal pit closed in 1993, the colliery villages and towns in the county are still culturally connected to the industry in many unshakeable ways, and Redhills remains a

---

◀ **1** Crook Hall. **2** University Botanic Garden. **3** An exhibit in the Oriental Museum.
4 Finchale Priory. **5** Shincliffe Woods.

community hub (undergoing renovations at the time of writing; check online for updates) with music, arts and local groups utilising the building, and from where the annual Gala is organised. In coming years it will become a centre of learning for schools, the local community and wider public.

The Council Chamber, more memorably known as **'The Pitman's Parliament'** is an elegant oak-panelled debating chamber with 298 numbered seats, each corresponding to a Durham colliery.

16 CROOK HALL GARDENS

Frankland Ln, Sidegate, DH1 5SZ ⊙ Feb–Oct 10.00–17.00 daily, Nov–Dec 10.00–16.00 Fri– Sun, winter opening & café may differ – check website; ♿ level access to the gardens which are winding, narrow & bumpy in places; National Trust

Crook Hall is really three historic buildings – a Georgian mansion, a Jacobean house and an 800-year-old banqueting hall – that have recently come into the care of the National Trust who have reopened the medieval hall and gardens to the public (the other properties are holiday cottages run by the Trust). They huddle together on a low hill gazing at Durham Cathedral a mile south and are enclosed by ten acres of flower-filled gardens, an orchard and moat pond, all connected by winding paths.

Originally owned by Peter del Croke in the early 14th century, from whom the hall gets its name, the building passed hands to the Billingham family in 1372 where it remained for 300 years. The hall has housed some colourful families and visitors over the centuries including medieval knight John de Copeland, who stayed here the night before the nearby 1346 Battle of Neville's Cross, during which he captured King David – and later retired a wealthy man. From 1834 to 1858, a well-known historian and cathedral librarian, James Raine, lived at Crook Hall where he entertained many distinguished guests including William and Dorothy Wordsworth, Walter Scott and John Ruskin. Perhaps they were keen to hear what he saw when he opened St Cuthbert's coffin on 17 May 1827 and removed the Saint's Saxon treasures.

The main interest for visitors are the Elizabethan and Georgian walled gardens which overflow with rambling roses, bossy lupins, oriental poppies and oxeye daisies in summer, and shelter plenty of peaceful spots to lay a picnic blanket or take in the distant cathedral views from benches.

A box-hedge maze by the purpose-built café (no ticket required) will occupy children for the duration of a coffee and slice of cake.

Crook Hall Gardens is reached by a ten-minute walk on a paved footpath from Durham's Framwellgate Bridge, following the west bank of the Wear north for half a mile (keep the river on your right and follow it upstream).

17 FINCHALE PRIORY

Finchale Av, Framwellgate Moor DH1 5SH ☺ 10.00–17.00 daily (Oct–Mar until 16.00); free entry (though there is a parking charge in force); English Heritage

Enclosed in a wooded bend of the River Wear, 13th-century Finchale Priory (pronounced 'Finkle') occupies a secluded spot a few miles northeast of Durham. A caravan park presents something of an initial intrusion into the otherwise timeless surroundings, but once you are within the priory, it's just you, a handful of visitors and the sound of the rushing Wear. It is a peaceful place to while away an hour or two, enjoy a picnic or walk along the river. A crossing allows visitors to stroll along the opposite bank which is wonderfully lush.

"Finchale is remarkably well preserved with enough arcades, huge piers and lancet windows to create quite an impression."

As far as medieval monastic buildings go, Finchale is remarkably well preserved with enough arcades, huge piers and lancet windows still standing to create quite an impression. Nonetheless, it takes some time to make sense of the layout and individual buildings (now roofless), and to locate the church and all other structures you would expect to find in a monastic complex; but they are all here: a cloister, refectory, dormitory, church and chapter house. A vaulted undercroft below the refectory remains particularly intact.

The priory's origins date to the early 12th century when St Godric, a retired pedlar and later a sea captain and pilgrim, founded a hermitage in the sheltered location by the riverside where he lived in seclusion for over half a century. On his death at over 100 years old, St Godric was laid to rest in a chapel, of which little remains. The priors of the monastery at Durham Cathedral took over the site and, in 1196, founded the Benedictine priory you see today, described by Pevsner as 'by far the most important monastic remains in County Durham'. By the mid 14th century, Finchale had become a holiday retreat for monks from Durham, until the disbanding of the monasteries resulted in its decline from 1538.

The **Weardale Way** connects Durham with Finchale Priory in three miles across farmland and along the river making for a rewarding excursion from Durham on foot, despite the route skirting round Franklin Prison. The final descent from farmland into the wooded banks of the Wear is rather special with the priory ruins before you.

¶ FOOD & DRINK

Cafés and inexpensive restaurants are plentiful on Durham's peninsula with somewhere to eat or drink housed in every other building on the likes of Silver and Saddler streets. Along the riverfront, tables are sought after for the views, and again there's a fair amount of choice, but the city is not particularly known for its fine dining. Below are some of my favourites but this is not an exhaustive list – just a selection of some of the places I enjoy while in the city.

For a special occasion, there are a couple of reasonable choices including **Finbarr's Restaurant** one mile northwest of Durham (Aykley Heads DH1 5TS ♪ 0191 3077033 ☉ Tues–Sun), which serves small plates of modern French and British dishes; expect to pay around £150 for a three-course meal for two. Closer to the centre is a **Marco Pierre White Steakhouse Bar & Grill** (Old Shire Hall, 9 Old Elvet DH1 3HL ♪ 0191 3293535 ☉ daily). Part of Hotel Indigo, the restaurant occupies a Victorian former Council Chamber and is noted for its sumptuous period tiling and modern furnishings. Steaks and crowd-pleasing plates: fish and chips, macaroni cheese, calamari, and burgers, plus a kids' menu and Sunday roast.

Bells Fish Restaurant Market Sq (corner restaurant curving into Saddler St), DH1 3NE ♪ 0191 3848974 ☉ 11.00–20.30 Mon–Sat; noon–15.30 Sun. Reliably good fish suppers to eat in or take-away; around £10 for cod (more for haddock and other fish). Children's portions ('strictly for under 12s') available.

The Boat Club Elvet Riverside (peninsula side, under old Elvet Bridge), DH1 3AF ♪ 0191 3866210 ☉ 10.00–late daily. I list the Boat Club for the river views from its first-floor outside terrace, where a cocktail on a balmy summer's evening makes a fine way to start – or indeed end – your evening. This steakhouse and bar caters for a youthful crowd and visitors on boat trips (which operate from just outside the restaurant), trading in hangover cures (a Bloody Mary cocktail with a steak and fried egg, for example) – or inducing them (this also being a club venue on weekend nights with live music). Later in the day and for evening meals, it's steak all round (with five sauces to choose from) but there's a separate vegan/vegetarian menu.

Colpitts Hotel meeting of Colpitts Tce & Hawthorn Tce, DH1 4EL ♪ 0191 3869913 ☉ daily. No longer a hotel, just an understated pub in a beautiful stone building near the railway viaduct with simple furnishings and full of local chatter. Victorian fireplaces, Sam Smiths beers and much traditional appeal.

Flat White Kitchen 40 Saddler St, DH1 3NU ✆ 0191 3840725 ⊙ 09.00–16.00 daily (from 10.00 Sun). It seems too obvious that this would be a favourite place for coffee and breakfast but it really is a reliable spot to ease yourself into the day; the problem is that a lot of people know that and so the queues trail along the street. All day. Inside, it's full of greenery and young, eager things and the noise level is high. Morning pancakes are weighted down with toppings and include a vegan option. Alternatively, you could opt for sourdough loaded with eggs, avocado, bacon, mushrooms or halloumi, while from 11.30 fish-finger sandwiches, a salt-beef bagel, beetroot and black been burger, and a Korean chicken burger are added to the menu (as well as a few other dishes). Afternoon tea drinkers are catered for with the ultimate North East cuppa, Ringtons. To accompany your hot drink, there's a calorific display on the counter: sticky date and caramel cake, lemon and pistachio or a peanut butter, chocolate and pistachio bar.

La Spaghettata 66 Saddler St, DH1 3NP ✆ 0191 3839290 ⊙ daily. Italian restaurants are predictably plentiful on the peninsula's touristy streets but this is a firm favourite that's been around for years, serving low-cost pizza and pasta dishes to a lively crowd of students (to whom the restaurant is affectionately known as 'Spags'). Big portions, fast service and no, you can't book.

Leonard's Coffee House Fowlers Yard, Back Silver St, DH1 3RA ✆ 0191 3840647 ⊙ daily. Finding this laid-back café is your first challenge but once you do, you're away from the crowds with your morning paper and stacked pancakes or avocado on sourdough with a great coffee. Later on it's paninis or falafel for lunch followed by a sweet offering dribbling with gooey sauce. Open for breakfast, brunch and lunch with seating on two floors in an old brick workshop and highly appealing outdoor tables in a sunny, peaceful spot. Access is via a few fiddly routes, including taking a stepped alley from Silver Street or from the rear of the indoor market on Market Place (see Fowlers Yard, page 48 for directions) but it's worth the effort.

Riverview Kitchen 20–21 Silver St, DH1 3RB ✆ 0191 3845777 ⊙ 09.30–16.30 Mon, Wed, Thu & Fri, 09.00–17.00 Sat & Sun. Under the Silver Street side of Framwellgate Bridge and reached by the riverside path or from a steep vennel (alley) descending from Palace Green, is this modern café with conservatory tables leaning over the riverbank. This must be one of the finest river views in the city, with Framwellgate Bridge leaping across the Wear. Tuck into towers of toppling American-style pancakes for brunch or posh burgers, open sandwiches or, the regional speciality, a stottie bap (with sausage and red onion perhaps?) for lunch.

Seven Stars High St North, Shincliffe DH1 2NU ✆ 0191 3848454 ⊙ 11.30–21.00 daily (to 19.00 Sun). This old inn has always served great dishes, but the quality of the food is even better now. Local venison (served blue), pork belly (with the crispiest of crackling) and scallops, a few chicken and fish dishes and several other British/European plates were on the menu when I last visited. The food is superb, right down to the perfect twice-cooked chips and the moreish puddings: apple and rhubarb cobbler, bread and butter pudding, sticky toffee pudding served with butterscotch and vanilla ice cream.

Shaheen's Indian 48 North Bailey, DH1 3ET ✆ 0191 3860960. Within paces of Palace Green and Durham Cathedral, Shaheen's has been serving locals and visitors for decades. Their popularity is clear when you try and book a table for Saturday evening. Nothing complicated or fancy on the menu – just great baltis, biryanis and curries.

Teelicious Tearoom 88 Elvet Bridge (opposite end from the peninsula), DH1 3AG ✆ 0191 3401393 ☉ 10.00–16.00 Wed–Sat. A frilly place for afternoon tea or light lunch on Elvet's historic bridge: all pastels, bunting and vintage tiered cake stands – the kind of place that must get booked up weeks in advance for Mothers' Day. And look at those cakes: great big curling stones of sponge smothered in dollops of buttercream icing and piled high with strawberries and all manner of other sweet toppings. Some favourites: chocolate mint, Vicky sponge, treacle ginger and lime. And let's not ignore the tea – loose in jars on shelves (all 24 varieties) including Durham Miner's Brew (you may roll your eyes but this is a great tea with a lot of depth thanks to its base of Assam). Soup and sandwiches on offer too, including an option filled with Durham's favourite cheese from Cotherstone.

The Undercroft Durham Cathedral, Palace Green, DH1 3EH ✆ 0191 3863721 ☉ 10.00–16.00 Mon–Sat & noon–16.00 Sun ♿. For a coffee and slice of cake in historic surroundings, nowhere in Durham can match this unassuming café in the old monastic cloisters of the cathedral. While modern seating and tables and a busy crowd of visitors distracts somewhat from the setting, there's no missing that stonking vaulted ceiling. A small, no-frills menu of inexpensive soup, sandwiches, quiches, scones and cakes and all the usual hot drinks is just enough to set you up for a cathedral tour.

Vennel's Café Saddlers Yard (reached via an alley off 71 Saddler St), DH1 3NP ☉ 09.30–16.30 daily (from 10.30 Sun). The words 'Everything baked on premises' will catch your eye, but so will the price for your quiche and salad, pie or sandwich (don't expect much change from £10). But this is the centre of Durham, just off one of its busiest streets, where you will probably have to queue (and then wait for your food). All that aside, it's nice to be away from the bustle, taking in all the nooks and character of the building or sitting back in the 16th-century courtyard where there is outdoor seating.

The Victoria 86 Hallgarth St, DH1 3AS ✆ 0191 3865269. A wonderful find east of the river on a long road of Victorian and Georgian houses and one of a small number of traditional pubs in the city with beers from the North East. The Victoria has much old-world charm and has remained true to its 19th-century heritage with a wood-panelled interior, period coal fire and bare floorboards. No TV, no music, no fruit machines, no food – just good beers and cheerful banter. Guest room accommodation upstairs.

Durham's Victorian terraces and stone viaduct dating to 1857. ▶

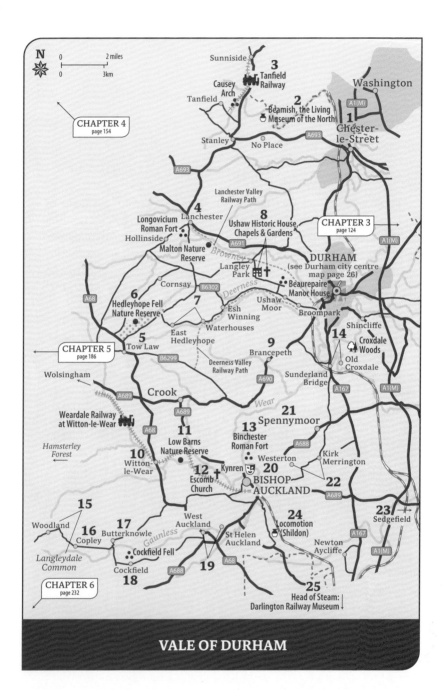

N

0 — 2 miles
0 — 3km

Sunniside

3 Tanfield
Railway

Causey
Arch

Tanfield

page 154

2 Beamish, the Living
Museum of the North

Washington

A1(M)

1
Chester-
le-Street

A693

Stanley

No Place

A693

Lanchester Valley
Railway Path

4 Lanchester

Longovicium
Roman Fort

Hollinside

Malton Nature
Reserve

8 Ushaw Historic House
Chapels & Gardens

A691

Browney

Langley
Park

page 124

A1(M)

DURHAM
(see Durham city centre
map page 26)

Béaurepaire
Manor House

Cornsay

B6302

Deerness

Ushaw
Moor

Broompark

Shincliffe

6
Hedleyhope Fell
Nature Reserve

A68

7

Esh
Winning

Waterhouses

East
Hedleyhope

5 Tow Law

B6299

Deerness Valley
Railway Path

9
Brancepeth

Sunderland
Bridge

14
Croxdale
Woods

Old
Croxdale

A167

A1(M)

Wolsingham

A689

Crook

A689

Wear

A690

21
Spennymoor

Weardale Railway
at Witton-le-Wear

A68

11
Low Barns
Nature Reserve

13
Binchester
Roman Fort

A688

A688

Kirk
Merrington

22

*Hamsterley
Forest*

10
Witton-
le-Wear

12 Kynren
Escomb
Church

Westerton

20

BISHOP
AUCKLAND

A689

23
Sedgefield

A167

A1(M)

15

Woodland

16
Copley

17
Butterknowle

Gaunless

West
Auckland

St Helen
Auckland

24
Locomotion
(Shildon)

Newton
Aycliffe

*Langleydale
Common*

Cockfield Fell

A688

A68

19

18 Cockfield

page 232

25
Head of Steam:
Darlington Railway Museum

VALE OF DURHAM

2
VALE OF DURHAM

Old colliery villages trail through the valleys and lowlands between Durham city and the North Pennine hills, an area characterised by old stone and red-brick mining terraces, outlying allotments and pony paddocks, wooded denes and old railway trackbacks. Architecturally and culturally these villages lend much character and distinctiveness to Durham with their long terraces and stepped roofs and features that make them conspicuously coal-mining settlements. While this may be a heavily populated area, there is much to entice those who enjoy the outdoors, particularly the further west you venture where the low-lying hills begin their gallop into the Dales.

Durham's industrial legacy comes to life in a number of outstanding attractions. **Beamish**, the famous landscape-scale outdoor museum with recreated period streets, is one of the most visited places in the North and is not to be missed. Shildon's awesome railway museum, **Locomotion**, and Darlington's **Head of Steam** on the line of the famous 1825 Stockton & Darlington Railway are also terrifically engaging, as is the wonderfully unchanged **Tanfield Railway**, the world's oldest railway still in use, now operating steam train rides. Elsewhere, the social history of the coalfields is movingly narrated through the works of painters such as the renowned **Norman Cornish** whose canvases appears in a few galleries, notably in his hometown of Spennymoor, and the Mining Art Gallery in Bishop Auckland.

Sedgefield, **Chester-le-Street** and **Bishop Auckland** are three of the largest towns in the area; between them they boast a number of historic attractions that will enrich a visit to Durham's hinterlands, including Sedgefield's **Hardwick Park** and Bishop Auckland's absorbing **castle**, **parkland** and **art galleries**. The story of early Christianity is quietly told at Chester-le-Street, one of the last resting points for monks carrying St Cuthbert's body before they reached what is now Durham city (page 34). Anyone interested in ecclesiastical architecture or the history of Catholicism in the region should visit **Ushaw Historic House, Chapels & Gardens**, a one-time seminary and now an important attraction in the Deerness Valley with its many historic buildings and Pugin-designed chapel.

I've divided this chapter into five sections whose boundaries are somewhat fluid: **North Durham** including Chester-le-Street and outlying places of interest; the **Browney**, **Deerness** and **Gaunless** valleys whose respective rivers flow eastwards from the edge of the Pennines towards Durham city; places of interest along the **River Wear** from just outside Wolsingham as far as Durham; and **South Durham**.

GETTING AROUND

A vast railway network once connected nearly every town and village in the county; today only a handful of **train stations** in the Vale of Durham are operational including at Shildon, Newton Aycliffe, Bishop Auckland and Chester-le-Street, with connecting services to Durham and Darlington.

Dismantled lines converted into leisure paths for cyclists and walkers are a familiar feature and you'll find **cycling** a great way to get around (page 157).

Besides the railway paths, all outlying areas around Durham city, including remote parts and many hillside colliery villages, are well serviced by roads and established **bus** routes linking most settlements with Durham. Arriva (arrivabus.co.uk/north-east) run many lines in and around Durham city, connecting to places covered by this chapter including Bishop Auckland, Chester-le-Street and the Deerness Valley. Go North East (gonortheast.co.uk/services) similarly provide comprehensive links between larger urban centres.

WALKING & CYCLING

Where there was coal, there were railways. Central Durham was once dotted with collieries and though they are all closed, the **old train lines** that serviced them remain and are now mixed-use leisure paths forming useful off-road corridors for **cyclists** (and walkers) connecting the Tyne with the Wear via many back of beyond places. Piecing together a cross-county route without hardly needing to put wheels on a road is highly

---

ℹ TOURIST INFORMATION

Bishop Auckland is the most reliable place for tourist information with **Auckland Tower** (page 107) a good first port of call. Auckland Castle (page 111) and the Spanish Gallery (page 109) are similarly staffed by locals who are a helpful source of knowledge. Likewise, the friendly staff at **Bishop Auckland Town Hall** (page 108) and **Spennymoor Town Hall** (page 117) will point you in the right direction and offer informal advice on where to go and how to reach places.

---

rewarding. How you get back is another matter, unless you form a circuit with another railway trail or take your bike on a train using the modern rail network. Durham County Council lists all the routes on their website alongside downloadable maps and information sheets. Search for 'railway paths' on ⌀ durham.gov.uk. They are also clearly marked on maps of the region. Equipped with Ordnance Survey maps ✳ 305, 307, 308 and OL31, you can plot your off-road route right across Durham.

Three of the longest and best-used railway trails, all of which converge at Broompark on the outskirts of Durham, are: the **Lanchester Valley Railway Path** (page 85) from Consett via Lanchester and the Browney Valley, which connects with the **Consett & Sunderland Railway Path** and the **Waskerley Way** (for access to the Pennine moors) at its northern end; the **Deerness Valley Railway Path** (page 89) from Crook via the Deerness Valley; and the **Brandon–Bishop Auckland Railway Path** linking Durham with Bishop Auckland. There are other railway routes besides these ones, such as the **Auckland Way Railway Path** between Spennymoor and Bishop Auckland via Binchester Roman Fort. I could go on, but the best thing is to check out the council webpage for their useful overview map. Many of the lines trace their respective river valleys and so you'll often be accompanied by river scenery and woodland much of the way.

For the most part, **walkers** can make good use of railway paths too for local routes but their linear nature means the return leg can feel repetitive unless you take a bus or cobble together a fiddly return via public rights of way.

The other stand-out feature of the Vale of Durham is the **river** network which, like the railway paths, forms several arterial routes across the county. This is particularly so of the River Wear that takes a meandering route through many of the places mentioned in this chapter and is walkable along almost its entire west–east course thanks to the **Weardale Way** footpath. Connecting Weardale with Wolsingham, Bishop Auckland, Durham and Sunderland, the 45-mile route offers many options for long, linear routes as well as circuits linking with other public rights of way.

Away from the riverside and railway paths, the countryside is hilly with numerous steep inclines and plenty of high passes with views for many miles. For long stretches over open moors and grasslands, you'll need to head west of Wolsingham into Weardale; whereas here, in the Pennine foothills, the landscape is more varied with villages, pony paddocks, fields, waterways and historic architecture including Saxon churches, castles, Roman forts and, of course, railway buildings: station houses and disused platforms.

CYCLE HIRE & REPAIRS

A few sole **bicycle mechanics** operate in the region, offering low-cost repairs, including **Durham Bike Repairs** (☏ 07741 490565) who will travel to your location within ten miles of Durham city centre; and **Mark's Bicycle Workshop** (☏ 077287 43485) based in New Brancepeth.

THE PITMAN POET

Me aad sangs hev kept me in beer an' the floor o' the public bar hes bin me stage for forty years. Aw'd sing, we'd drink, aw'd sing, we'd drink agen, sangs wi'oot end, amen.
Tommy Armstrong

Songwriter Tommy Armstrong (1848–1920) was born in Shotley Bridge but lived for most his life in the Tanfield area, working in the mines from the age of nine, and writing songs about the lives of miners. His ballads recall mining disasters, strikes and daily life in colliery towns. He achieved fame in his lifetime but died penniless. One of his famous songs, *The Sooth Medomsley Strike*, tells the story of how miners were evicted from their homes by colliery owners and managers. The opening verse includes these lines:

*The miners of South Medomsley they never will forget
Fisick and his tyranny and how they have been tret;
For in the midst of danger, these hardy sons did toil,
For te earn their daily bread se far beneath the soil.
Te make an honest livelihood each miner did contrive,
But ye shall hear how they were served in eighteen eighty-five.*

Infinity Cycles Langley Moor DH7 8ET ✆ 0191 3784209 ☉ Mon–Sat. Run by knowledgeable cyclists.

Halfords Pity Me DH1 5GF ✆ 0191 3754620 ☉ 08.00–20.00 daily (shorter opening times at the weekend). For general parts, accessories & repairs.

Mountain High Cycles Ferryhill DL17 8AT ✆ 01740 657500 ☉ Mon, Tue & Thu–Sat. Independent bicycle shop and workshop.

TAXIS

Also see page 30 for the area around Durham city

Deneside Taxis Lanchester ✆ 01207 528882
GMC Taxis Bishop Auckland ✆ 07935 684022
Henderson's Taxis Beamish area ✆ 01207 258337
Nightingale Taxis Stanley ✆ 01207 529729 ♿
Riverside Taxis Chester-le-Street ✆ 0191 3888688

NORTH DURHAM

⌂ **Lumley Castle Hotel** (page 309)

The Wear departs Durham city on a laboursome journey to the sea at Sunderland. Here we follow its winding course as far as **Chester-le-Street**, a busy town with a commanding medieval castle (now a hotel) and an important church. A few miles away is **Beamish, the Living Museum of the North**, one of the most popular places to visit in the whole of the North of England, and the engaging heritage attraction, **Tanfield Railway**, keeping alive the legacy of the oldest railway line in the world in continuous use.

1 CHESTER-LE-STREET

An 11-arched railway viaduct strides across this workaday town halfway between Durham and Newcastle, best known for its church, castle and cricket ground. Chester-le-Street has Roman origins (it was once known as Concangis), but very little remains from that period except for some stones marking the outline of barracks to the rear of the Parish Centre on Low Chare (round the corner from the church of St Mary and St Cuthbert).

In the years following Danish raids on the Northumberland isle of Lindisfarne in the 9th century, the monks from the priory travelled the North East for seven years with the body of St Cuthbert (and the Lindisfarne Gospels) before settling at Chester-le-Street in AD883 for over a century. The story of St Cuthbert's journey to Durham is told in a painted panel in the chancel of the **church of St Mary and St Cuthbert** (Church Chare, DH3 3QB ☉ 10.00–12.30 Mon, Tue, Wed & Fri & for services: 10.45 Thu service; 08.00, 10.00 (family service) & 18.00 Sun worship ☏ 0191 3883295 ♿), an important place in the history of early Christianity. In modern times, the church welcomed a rather different crowd one October evening in 1936 when the 'Jarrow Crusade' marchers protesting against unemployment and poverty on Tyneside made their first stop here on their month-long walk to London.

Originally, a wooden shrine was built within an old Roman fort which was then rebuilt in stone in the mid 11th century. Saxon masonry reveals itself in the sanctuary and chancel, but the rest of the building is mostly medieval and Victorian. The tall spire, visible for miles around, dates to the 1400s. Even if you are only travelling through Chester-le-Street, it is worth making the short uphill walk or drive out of the centre to see some of the curious relics housed inside, including 14 stone effigies known as

"Fourteen stone effigies known as the Lumley Warriors are laid head to toe in two rows along the nave wall."

the **Lumley Warriors** laid head to toe in two rows along the nave wall. In order to squeeze them in, some of their feet have been hacked off. Most are not as old as you'd think. Architectural historian, Pevsner, wrote: 'The majority of the monuments are Elizabethan, but in imitation of the medieval style, an extremely interesting case of early, self-conscious medievalism'. Also on display is a wonderful facsimile of the celebrated **Lindisfarne Gospels**. Note also the stained-glass windows depicting the book's creation.

Adjoining the church is an anchorage that was built in the latter half of the 14th century and once housed a religious recluse. The Anker's House is now a small **museum** over two floors (☉ same times as the church) displaying Saxon and Roman finds.

The one-time seat of the Lumley family, **Lumley Castle** (DH3 4NX ☏ 0191 389111 🖱 lumleycastle.com) stands on a prominent hill bearing down on the town, its cricket club and golf course. A complete castle, dating largely to the 1300s, with four battlemented turrets marking the corners of a quadrangle, Lumley has changed little over the last

600 years (except for some internal restructuring by Vanbrugh in the early 18th century) and is now an upmarket hotel and wedding venue, though non-guests can enjoy cream teas or dine in the intimate Knights Restaurant (advance booking for both essential). Elizabethan banquets are held throughout the year.

The castle provides a wonderful backdrop to the International Cricket Ground, home of the **Durham County Cricket Club** (𝒟 durhamccc. co.uk). If you're just passing and want to see the pitch, you can access the outside areas of the stadium from The Sticky Wicket bar and restaurant (𝒥 0191 3882290 ☉ Wed–Sun). A well-used riverside path runs past the cricket club and through the popular **Riverside Park** with its café and play areas, including a children's splash park (☉ summer).

For countryside views, head to **Waldridge Fell Country Park** to the west of the town, an area of lowland heath spanning 250 acres with a network of trails through the heather and woodlands that are accessible from several parking areas.

A longer **walk** from Chester-le-Street with wonderful riverside scenery is the 7½-mile route to Durham Cathedral, much of which follows the Weardale Way along the River Wear; it loops around wonderful Finchale Priory (page 65) before entering Durham city across Framwellgate Bridge and offering one of the finest historic vistas in the North of England. While the route is marked with 'Cuddy's Course' red crosses, you will need ❈ Ordnance Survey 308 to help keep you on the right

THE VILLAGE OF NO PLACE

No Place was too intriguing to overlook while researching this book. I hoped the village west of Stanley wouldn't disappoint like Pity Me – just outside Durham – which is terribly ordinary and, I discovered, doing just fine. But, what about No Place? The row of bungalows with immaculate lawns and hedges on the edge of the settlement could be in fact Any Place, but the centre of No Place is a very neat block of miners' houses built in the late 1800s for workers at nearby Beamish Mary Colliery. They are arranged along three long terraces with back lanes between each row, a plain Victorian school and a decent pub, the Beamish Mary Inn. The village once had a jazz band that formed during the general miners' strike of 1926. In the 1980s residents hotly objected to council plans to change the name of the village to the rather more humdrum 'Co-operative Villas', which explains why road signs now use both names to this day.

path. Trains from Durham to Chester-le-Street make the return journey in a few minutes or you can take the Angel 21 bus in half an hour or so (⊘ gonortheast.co.uk/services).

¶¶ FOOD & DRINK

In a town scattered with take-aways, cafés and pubs, there's somewhere to refuel within paces of anywhere in the centre of Chester-le-Street, particularly so on Front Street where there are low-cost Italian restaurants, bistros and drinking holes every few doors. One stand-out café is REfUSE (see below) and, for its 1950s-era décor and ice creams, **Citrone's Café** (130 Front St ☉ Mon–Sat 08.30–17.00 (sometimes earlier) ⊘ 0191 3883908). For a decent lunch or evening meal (also known for its cocktails), you could try **Hollathan's** (6–9 Ashfield Tce, DH3 3PD ☉ Tue–Sat noon–20.00 (bar open later) ⊘ 0191 3880090 ♿ bar area only) at the bustling south end of Front Street. It's a modern restaurant and bar serving plates of pasta, pizzas, meat and seafood dishes. They have a vegan menu and good-value early bird two-course meals with a glass of wine.

REfUSE 143 Front St, DH3 3AU ☉ Tue–Sat 10.00–16.00 & Thu evenings ⊘ 07561 765264 ♿. Wonderful community café run by a friendly team of volunteers transforming edible food waste from local retailers into creative lunches: soups, sandwiches, salads and some hot plates too. Blackboards list the day's offerings, which usually include around six options (shepherd's pie, a curry, toasties and baked potatoes were on offer when I visited). Inside, it's vibrant and modern with mismatched chairs and tables and exposed brick walls; a bit of colourful bunting here, a cheese plant there; and on some days there's live music. While there are set prices for drinks, a 'pay as you feel' system operates for the food menu.

2 BEAMISH, THE LIVING MUSEUM OF THE NORTH

Beamish DH9 0RG ⊘ 0191 3704000 ⊘ beamish.org.uk ☉ Apr–Oct 10.00–17.00 daily; Nov–mid Dec 10.00–16.00 Wed–Sun; mid-Dec–early Jan 10.00–16.00 daily (some dates in winter closed; check online before visiting) ♿ not accessible throughout

Beamish museum blurs reality and theatre so convincingly that you feel the years have rolled back when you step into the museum's recreated period streets. The 300-acre open-air museum, famous nationally, tells the story of the local area in the Georgian and Edwardian periods, 1940s wartime and the 1950s. It is superlative on so many levels, particularly for its authenticity (the houses, shops, farm, pit, stables,

---

1 Tanfield Railway. **2** Beamish, the Living Museum of the North. **3** Aerial view over Chester-le-Street. ▶

railway line, bars, signage and whole streets are largely genuine), and variety of buildings and experiences (tram and train rides, brass-band concerts, fairground rides, hairdresser appointments and a walk down a real mine). Entire buildings and cobbled streets were taken from elsewhere in Durham, brought to the rural landscape at Beamish and reconstructed brick by brick alongside some existing buildings including the drift mine, farm and Georgian house. You won't find many interpretation boards or 'do not touch' signs; instead you'll see staff in costume working in the fields, making hay, ploughing farmland with heavy horses, making boiled sweets to sell in the confectionary shop, chatting in the street, tending to the Georgian garden, changing barrels in the Edwardian pub, feeding pigs and making bread. It is hard to get round Beamish in one day, so make sure you come early (tickets are valid for a year, however).

"Many people's favourite is the Co-operative store with genuine dry goods in boxes on shelves."

The Edwardian town is where most people alight first on taking the tram (which offers a 'hop on, hop off' service round the site) from the entrance hall. Here you'll find a period dentist, bank, solicitor's office, printer's shop, pub, sweet shop, garage and, many people's favourite, the Co-operative store with its genuine dry goods in boxes on shelves, alongside hardware and drapery. Those of a certain age will be recalling their 'divi' number as soon as you set foot inside – something I vividly remember my grandmother doing on one visit.

¶¶ FOOD & DRINK

Period fish and chip shops, a restaurant and pub keep most visitors to Beamish museum well fed during their trip but if you're looking for an evening meal once the museum doors close, there are a number of options very close by.

Shepherd & Shepherdess Inn Beamish DH9 0RS ℰ 0191 3700349 ☉ daily ♿. The child-sized figures above the old doorway of this family-friendly 18th-century pub right next to the entrance to Beamish museum are the wrong way round (either that or the pub should be renamed the 'Shepherdess and Shepherd'). The landlady will tell you that one day the young couple ran off into the woods and when they returned, they stood in the other's position by mistake. Apparently, the figures date to the Napoleonic wars when lead was covertly imported from the continent as ornaments to be melted and used in weaponry, but these two figures escaped the furnace. On the food front, expect all the usual pub classics:

steak, fish and chips, lasagne (meat and veggie), scampi and so on, plus Sunday roasts and a children's menu – all reasonably priced. There's also a beer garden and children's playground. **The Stables** Beamish Hall, Stanley DH9 0YB 🕿 01207 288750 ⊙ noon–20.30 daily (until 20.00 on Sun) 🚻. Beamish Hall is a grand, early 19th-century villa set in glorious parkland close to Beamish museum and now an upmarket hotel hosting back-to-back weddings during the summer, and with a restaurant. It's a good choice for lunch (paninis and hot food) or evening dinner (standard gastro-pub fare: fish and chips, roasts, fish and veg dishes, posh burgers). On bright days, you'll probably want to eat outside in the sun-filled courtyard (this being the old stable block for Beamish Hall). A path to the rear of the contemporary restaurant leads to a large adventure playground where there's also a café.

3 TANFIELD RAILWAY

Marley Hill, Gateshead NE16 5ET 🕿 07508 092365 🖉 tanfield-railway.co.uk ⊙ times vary throughout the year so check website 🚻; Newcastle–Stanley buses X30 & X3 stop close to all stations except East Tanfield; additionally, Newcastle–Consett buses X70 & X71 stop close to Sunniside station.

Horses were pulling wagons on wooden tracks at Tanfield from 1725, transporting coal from Stanley and Marley Hill to the River Tyne, a hundred years before the Stockton & Darlington Railway. In the 19th century they were replaced by locomotives and metal rails but this is where rail transport began and Tanfield is credited as being the world's first operating line still in use. It closed in 1962 but was brought back to life by a group of friends and is still staffed by devoted volunteers.

Of all the heritage railway lines in the North East (and there are a fair few in this part of the country), Tanfield Railway is my very favourite. It's wonderfully low-key and authentic without intrusive barriers and modern signage or feeling commercialised. Steam engines and their Victorian carriages run along the standard gauge, six-mile track from Andrews House station to East Tanfield year-round, stopping at Causey Arch and Sunniside. Some operate a special afternoon tea service on board.

The rural setting, period station architecture and steeply wooded Causey Valley with its much-photographed stone bridge are hugely atmospheric, enhanced by the sound of hissing steam, screeching carriages and engine whistles. But Tanfield is much more than just a trip on a steam train. My lasting impression when I visited as a young child was the **Marley Hill Engine Shed** (access from the parking area at Andrews House Station), the oldest working engine house in Europe, built in 1854. I remember the thrill of touching the wheels of a steam engine; the oil, soot and smell of coal; and men in overalls working on the bellies of locomotives. It's still the same today (except there was a woman in overalls driving one of the engines on my last visit).

There are four stations along the line with car parks and facilities at **Andrews House station** (NE16 5ET), **Causey Arch station** (NE16 5EG) and **East Tanfield station** (DH9 9UY). Andrews House is the main station on the line and has a café. Note there are no facilities at the end of the line at **Sunniside station** (NE16 5EF).

A popular **footpath** tracing Causey Burn and crossing the famous **Causey Arch** viaduct runs through the same wooded gorge as the railway line, making a return trip on foot possible using ❀ OS Explorer 307 & 316. Built in 1727 to carry coal wagons across the steep Causey gorge, this 105ft-wide stone arch is the oldest railway bridge in the world and was once the largest single span arch in Britain. Today it stands as a monument to the region's great railway past – and makes an eye-catching focus for a walk. There's a picnic spot near Causey Arch Station.

FOOD & DRINK

Bayberry Hollow Tanfield village DH9 9PX ✆ 01207 230580 ◷ 10.00–16.00 daily. Old pub dating to the 1600s now converted into a modern country-style café serving good food (breakfast, lunch and afternoon teas): chunky quiches, pies, rolls and soup. Great scones and cakes, all freshly baked.

Shield Row Chippy 1 Duncombe Cres, Stanley DH9 8RG ◷ 17.00–20.00 Mon–Wed, 11.30–13.00 & 17.00–20.00 Thu & Fri, 11.30–13.00 Sat. Well off the tourist trail, this great little fish and chip shop is on the main A-road through Shield Row, a couple of miles west of Beamish. I waited 45 minutes in a queue that snaked round the corner but that alone should tell you this is a very good place to pick up a fish supper.

LANCHESTER & THE BROWNEY VALLEY

🏠 **Burnhopeside Hall** (page 309), **The Old Post Office** (page 309)

The River Browney rises in the Pennine foothills among swelling heather moors but for the most part the waterway takes us on a journey through arable land with remnant oak woodlands here and there, past historic Lanchester, a pit village or three and a nature reserve before merging with the River Deerness on the outskirts of Durham. If you walk or cycle along the **Lanchester Valley Railway Path**, the river will accompany you much of the way.

While the Browney is not rich in attractions as such, the valley as a whole holds some appeal and those with a fondness for moseying through old places may like to pause at the likes of **Hollinside** with its picturesque old farm and stone miners' cottages (one of the best preserved rows of its type, according to Historic England), and the old hilltop village of **Cornsay** (not to be confused with Cornsay Colliery), for its wide views across the Browney and Deerness valleys, stone houses and curious post box (housed in an old well). Closer to the river is **Malton Nature Reserve** (page 86) and, gazing across the valley from the north, the medieval ruins of **Beaurepaire Manor House** at Bearpark.

4 LANCHESTER & SURROUNDS

Smart Georgian cottages face a broad green bound by a knot of roads in the centre of Lanchester, a convivial village (though you may assume a town on account of its size) eight miles west of Durham city. Look closely at some of the houses, some of which were likely built with dressed stone from the nearby Roman fort of Longovicium, the outline of which stands on a hillside above the village (page 84).

There's a lively scene in the **village centre** around the hub of cafés and shops at the north end of the green on Front Street; from here you'll find access to the **Lanchester Valley Railway Path** (page 85) for walks and cycle rides into the surrounding countryside.

Before you head out of Lanchester, do pay a visit to the celebrated 12th-century **All Saints Church** (Durham Rd, DH7 0LJ ✆ 01207 529166 ◷ mornings Wed & Sun), on the main road through the village, which is full of treasures. It is perhaps not surprising to find Roman masonry here and there: some columns from Longovicium and a Roman altar to the goddess Garmangabis, its inscription and motifs still astonishingly clear. Other things of note include medieval cross slabs; a chest in the chancel dating to the 16th century that once contained parish documents and records; and the stone figures of Christ and two angels carved above the vestry doorway that have survived almost 800 years, albeit with the loss of Jesus's head. Note too, the 13th-century stained glass in the southwest

"There's a lively scene in the village centre around the hub of cafés and shops at the north end of the green on Front Street."

chancel window and the wonderful chancel arch, clearly Norman, showing three bands of chevrons.

Once commanding the top of a hill half a mile west of Lanchester are the now grassed-over ramparts of **Longovicium Roman Fort** (DH7 0HJ; viewable from Cadger Bank (B6296), ½ mile southwest of Lanchester ♀ NZ159469), built in AD122. It faces Dere Street, an important Roman road from York to Hadrian's Wall, and would have been a staging post between the forts at Ebchester and Binchester. Its design is typical of Roman forts: rectangular with one gateway in each side and housing barrack blocks, a commander's house, granaries and a bath house (none of which are visible). Though there's currently no public access, you can see the ramparts from the road.

¶¶ FOOD & DRINK

On Lanchester's Front Street you can pick up take-away sandwiches and quiches at a very good butcher and deli (**Hanley & Sons**), stop for cake and a hot drink outside a little coffee shop, or dine at one of the good restaurants listed here.

Broom House Farm Witton Gilbert, DH7 6TR ✆ 0191 3718839 ☉ 09.00–17.00, closed Mon ♿. Hill-top organic farm with Browney Valley views; well-stocked farm shop and café serving mainly breakfast food all day. Adventure playground open spring and summer.
Crinnions 21 Front St, DH7 0LA ✆ 01207 520376 ☉ 09.00–23.30 Mon–Sat, 09.00–21.00 Sun ♿. Café, restaurant, pub – popular Crinnions covers all bases serving breakfast (until 11.00), lunch and dinner. Pub favourites (fish and chips, lasagne, scampi, roasts, as well as a seafood menu and steak nights) and a lively atmosphere.
Lanchester Garden Centre Bargate Bank, DH7 0SS ✆ 01207 521669 ☉ 09.00–17.00 daily ♿. Hilltop views from this local restaurant 1½ miles south of Lanchester, set in farmland with much to see – besides the usual plants, gifts and garden furniture – once you've had lunch, including Potter's World (a mini zoo with exotic animals, a bird of prey centre and children's play areas). The conservatory-style **Greenhouse Restaurant** offers all-day breakfasts, scones and cakes, sandwiches, quiches and pricey hot lunches (baked potatoes, burgers (including a vegan option), fish and chips, pies, sausage and mash and so on), Sunday roasts and afternoon teas. Good-value **deli** counter in the main shop which also stocks quiches, pies, cakes and pantry items.
The Pavilion Iveston Ln, DH8 7TE ✆ 01207 509144 ☉ noon–14.00 & 18.00–23.00 daily. People drive for many miles to this great Chinese restaurant on the Lanchester to Consett road. While the menu is fairly standard with all the usual chicken, beef, king prawn and noodle dishes on offer, the plates of food are really excellent.

Ravello 9 Church View, DH7 0ES ✆ 01207 528825 ⊙ noon–22.30 daily. Well-regarded, authentic Italian, hence the queues outside (make sure you book ahead), with a full offering of Mediterranean favourites (pizza, pasta, risotto, steaks, chicken and seafood) as well as Sunday roasts but best known for its seafood (their seafood linguine comes highly recommended). Expect to pay upwards of £13 for most non-pizza dishes and substantially more for some of the best fillet steaks you will find anywhere in Durham (the filleto Rossini is wrapped in parma ham, topped with pâté and served with a Madeira sauce; filleto steak dolce latte is with blue cheese).

Yannis 21 Front St, DH7 0LA ✆ 01207 438161 ⊙ 17.00–21.00 Mon–Thu, 17.00–22.00 Fri & Sat. This modern Greek restaurant has been around for years serving authentic dishes including chicken and pork souvlaki, gyros and moussaka (evenings only).

Lanchester Valley Railway Path

Locals make good use of Lanchester's disused 1862 railway line for countryside strolls, dog walks and to commute by bicycle to Durham city, and you'll find the path is in constant use. A cycle ride along the 12-mile line to Broompark is highly recommended. To reach the path, head north on Lanchester's Front Street, past all the shops. Turn left onto Newbiggen Lane and follow the signs to a car park a short way along the road on your left that fronts the railway path. Once on the trackbed, turn left in the direction of Durham; turning right will take you to

"Locals make good use of Lanchester's disused 1862 railway line for countryside strolls, dog walks and to commute by bicycle."

the foothills of the Pennines where the line joins with another railway path, the Waskerley Way (page 173) leading to Weardale. On autumn days, the oak, hazel, birch and sycamore trees flanking either side of the line are particularly scenic. At points on the trail, the canopy thins permitting views of farmland and the River Browney twinkling in the valley floor.

Heading towards Durham from Lanchester, **Malton Nature Reserve** (page 86) and picnic area is the first place of interest along the riverbank. Not long after, the old pit village of **Langley Park** (page 86) butts up against the line, though it is easily missed. Also easy to overlook are the ruins of medieval **Beaurepaire Manor House**, which looks rather picturesque through the trees on the far side of the valley. Its 13th-century walls are all crumbling and in fragments now. Ahead, near Broompark, is a **farm café** by the side of the path offering light lunches (soup, sandwiches, cakes), ices, bags of sweets and teas.

When you get to **Broompark**, on the outskirts of Durham, the path merges with two other railway trails: the Brandon–Bishop Auckland Railway Path and the Deerness Valley Railway Path (page 89). To access Durham, you'll need to follow NCN Route 14 from Baxter Wood (a short way before you reach Broompark) which is signed off the railway path. There's a popular picnic ground at Broompark where you may wish to rest your legs.

Malton Nature Reserve

DH7 0TH; signed off the A691, one mile southeast of Lanchester. Buses from Durham to Consett stop on the A691 at the entrance to the reserve.

A colliery once stood where now you see meadows, woodland and wetlands by the banks of the River Browney; it closed in the 1960s and the once complete pit village with terraces housing workers, a school, the colliery and so on, are all demolished now, with the exception of one terrace, known as Officials Row, and the Miners' Welfare Hall. Durham Wildlife Trust manage the site, which is today a very pleasant place to picnic by the river and where children can throw pebbles in the shallow waters.

You can access the reserve from the Lanchester Valley Railway Path in little over a mile from Lanchester on foot or bicycle or by following signs from the A691 to Malton Picnic Area where there is parking.

Langley Park

Cyclists and walkers following the Lanchester Valley Railway Path (page 85) will pass this old pit village close to the trackbed, 3½ miles east of Lanchester. As is common in these parts, the terraces were built by the colliery to house miners, and the railway line constructed in part to transport coal away from the mine (as well as iron ore to Consett steelworks). Note the remarkably unchanged Railway Street running parallel to the line. Each house faces its coal shed on the other side of the road.

There's not much to see in the village but if you were to pause here for refreshments, pay a visit to the **Langley Park Hotel** which is just off the railway path, where Railway Street meets Front Street. A 19ft-high stone wall to the rear of the beer garden is a most intriguing relic from when Langley Park was a working colliery village. Miners used the wall to play hand ball – or 'fives' as it was known – between shifts in the mine and it is now Grade II listed. They were once found in many pit villages but this is one of very few still existent.

THE DEERNESS VALLEY

The River Deerness flows through woods, pastures, and below a string of colliery villages on the edge of Weardale before merging some ten miles later with the River Browney on the outskirts of Durham. Following the Deerness is a line of an old railway, now the **Deerness Valley Railway Path** (page 89), which makes for a peaceful countryside walk or cycle ride. For the most part, villages like Esh Winning (its very name evoking colliery machinery) and Ushaw Moor, remain out of sight and you will need to seek out places of interest including a coal-powered fish and chip shop (page 91) and the hilltop **Ushaw Historic House, Chapels & Gardens** (page 92), once a Catholic seminary and now a fascinating heritage attraction famous for its chapels.

THE WIZARD OF ESH

When I met Robert Liddle, an elderly man from the former colliery village of Esh Winning in the Deerness Valley, he told me about his knowledge of medicinal herbs learned from his grandmother who lived in nearby Waterhouses. She used to treat locals for common ailments in the days before the National Health Service and modern healthcare. On her death, Robert, aged nine, took over the 'practice' which he ran from his living room. He would return from school to find a queue of people outside his front door. 'I'd use herbs collected from hedgerows, fields, woodland edges and the beck. Most were ordinary plants like foxgloves, dandelions, clovers, nettles and watercress,'

he explained. Robert treated miners' boils, colds, rashes, infections and so on. During the course of our conversation it became clear that he also learned about what some once called witchcraft.

'My gran told me water could hold a wish. If you can magnetise water for a short period, which should be impossible, why can't it hold a wish?' He mentioned that she was the local witch doctor or 'wise woman'. Once common in many rural areas for several centuries, the 'profession' had almost completely died out by the early 20th century. Robert must have been one of the last community herbalists of his era when he died in 2013.

The sub-Pennine villages hunkered below **Hedleyhope Fell** in the upper reaches of the valley are not infrequently cut off in winter when a snow storm blows in, but what makes the exposed head of the valley vulnerable to snow drifts makes it a special place to explore on foot during spring and summer and there are fine countryside views from many spots. If you set off on foot from **Tow Law**, **Waterhouses** or **East Hedleyhope** in March and make the climb out of the valley, you'll be greeted with the sound of curlews announcing the onset of spring.

5 TOW LAW

A thousand feet above sea level, winds whip through Tow Law's streets on the edge of Weardale and the village as a whole feels rather bleak and down on its luck. A hundred years ago it was quite different, with coal mining and a booming ironworks providing employment to a few thousand workers. The jobs fizzled out over the course of the 20th century until the coal mines closed completely in the 1960s. Little remains of these industries except for some restored beehive coke ovens on Hedleyhope Fell, reached off Inkerman Road (a mile or so northwest of Tow Law) where there are also far-reaching views into Weardale and some rewarding bird-filled grasslands (see below).

"A hundred years ago coal mining and a booming ironworks provided employment to a few thousand workers."

6 HEDLEYHOPE FELL NATURE RESERVE

Tow Law DH7 9ET; main car park 2½ miles north of Tow Law on the B6301 between Tow Law and Cornsay Colliery ♿

Open scenery is enjoyed in every direction from this high vantage point at the top of the Deerness Valley, particularly in August when the bell heather comes into flower turning large areas of this important mid-altitude heathland bright pink. Three footpaths (one of which is wheelchair accessible) traverse the 200-hectare reserve through a mosaic landscape of bilberry, cotton grass, crowberry, bracken, heather and acid grasslands. From early spring, lapwings, curlews, oystercatchers and skylarks fill the sky with their courtship flight displays and repetitive notes and you may even see a black grouse or snipe in the rushy grasslands. In summer, butterflies (some twenty species) are the draw for wildlife enthusiasts, and this is also a good time to spot a slow worm, common lizard or even an adder.

7 EAST HEDLEYHOPE & WATERHOUSES

The village of Waterhouses is in many respects a model one. It is entirely new, and the houses of the men, well built of fine brick, are two stories high, containing front and back rooms. A good-sized plot of ground suitable for a vegetable garden is attached to each, and for the benefit of such miners as are disposed for the fattening of livestock, a pigsty is placed at the end of the garden.

The sinking of the pit, a most difficult and really troublesome work, was completed only some three or four years ago, and now there exists in this almost utopian village a good and commodious schoolhouse, and, what is of more importance, a competent school master.

Victorian view of the typical colliery village, Waterhouses, in around the 1860s

THE DEERNESS VALLEY RAILWAY PATH

Coal wagons used to trundle along the 8½-mile line from Crook to Broompark (on the edge of Durham city) via Waterhouses, Esh Winning and Ushaw Moor for almost a hundred years from when the Deerness Valley Railway opened in 1858. Though the line was built to serve the collieries in the valley, passenger trains became a familiar sight from 1877 with the opening of Waterhouses station. According to newspaper reports, such was the demand for the service that it operated for 20 hours a day during weekdays. A relative told me that, according to local legend, when Queen Victoria visited Durham, the royal train was parked at Waterhouses station at the end of the line. It must have been quite a sight for residents who were used to seeing coal wagons passing their houses.

Today, the old trackbed is well-used by dog walkers, cyclists, horseriders and wheelchair users (the wide path is fully ♿ accessible but it is a bumpy and at times muddy ride in places).

Travelling upstream from Broompark (a spacious picnicking area where you can also leave your car) on the outskirts of Durham city to Crook, the track stays close to the River Deerness much of the way, skirting the edges of fields and pony paddocks, and the sites of old open-cast mines (though you'd never know it); but for the most part the scenery is heavily wooded and the path cuts through broadleaved woodlands with some old oaks and plenty of hazel, birch and holly among a scattering of conifers. The bluebell woods around Waterhouses are particularly scenic come mid spring.

If you didn't want to walk the return, this being a linear route, you could take the Stanhope–Durham X46 bus from Crook which stops at Langley Moor (not far from Broompark) and Durham.

Coal lorries make regular rounds to the old miners' cottages standing side by side above the River Deerness, where for much of the year the smell of burning fuel wafts through the hillside terraces that make up these two villages at the head of the valley. To the rear of the cottages on Hedley Hill Terrace in **Waterhouses** are back lanes with vegetable plots, coal bunkers converted from outside loos and a pigeon cree. If this sounds like a caricature of an old Durham pit village, it's not intentional, it's just that's what it is really like around here. Streets in the village of **East Hedleyhope** once had the names of Chapel Row, Reading Room Row, School Row, Post Office Row and Office Row, reflecting the typical colliery village layout so prevalent in these parts.

The enclosing hillsides are dotted with farmsteads and wildflower meadows inhabited by breeding wading birds. Nearby Hedleyhope Fell (page 88) is one of the best places to see the birds and other wildlife and offers a taste of the Dales' scenery that becomes increasingly dominant the further west you venture.

I have fond childhood memories of playing in the Deerness around Waterhouses, and of exploring Stanley and Waterhouses woods which conceal the river for several miles on its run between Tow Law and Esh Winning. The best way to access the river and enjoy the woodland scenery is to follow the Deerness Valley Railway Path (page 89) but you can also reach the waterway from the main road through the villages via several informal as well as official footpaths. The stretch of railway footpath below Waterhouses cuts a clear course through a mixed woodland with all the usual bird species present, and is treasured locally by walkers, cyclists (and the occasional horserider). Look out for deer if taking a quiet stroll late in the afternoon.

¶¶ FOOD & DRINK

Field's Fish & Chips 4 Durham Rd, Esh Winning DH7 9NW ✆ 0191 3734385 ⊙ 16.30–20.00 Mon–Thu, 11.30–13.30 & 16.00–20.00 (sometimes later) Fri & Sat. Buckets of coal sit by the coal-powered range in this wonderful step-back-in-time fish shop in the former pit village of Esh Winning (one mile northeast of Waterhouses). Still with its 1930s green, cream and black glass tiles, Field's has been in the same family for over a century, and staff seemed to know the names and orders of half of those queuing ('Hiya Betty, three open chips and scraps on top?'). While my fish supper was fine, the experience of Field's

◀ **1** Brancepeth Castle. **2** Ushaw Historic House.

was truly memorable and I enjoyed watching the range being refuelled as I waited for my food to fry: the yellow flames and scent of burning coal more gratifying than I let on, stood as I was among locals. I left with my fish supper wrapped in newspaper – a rare thing these days.

8 USHAW HISTORIC HOUSE, CHAPELS & GARDENS

Woodland Rd, Ushaw Moor DH7 7DW ℘ 0191 3738500 ⬙ ushaw.org ◷ 11.00–16.00 daily ♿

'It looks like a town' remarked the Pope in a letter to the President of St Cuthbert's College, Ushaw in 1859. At the time, the hilltop Catholic seminary training men for the priesthood was indeed like a small settlement, with a farm, walled gardens, bakery and dairy servicing the hundreds of staff and pupils at the college (some 500 men lived here at its peak), comprising a main quadrangle and a number of connecting chapels. There was once even a tailor's, cobbler's, an infirmary, ice rink and extensive sports grounds.

Around the time of the French Revolution, an English religious community from Douai in northern France settled at Ushaw, purchasing enough land to live almost self-sufficiently (Protestant England was still an unwelcoming place for priests so the relative isolation of the site between the Deerness and Browney valleys would have provided a level of security). Centred upon the main quadrangle buildings and chapels, Ushaw received its first pupils in 1808 and closed in 2011.

Now a registered independent charity, Ushaw puts on a varied programme of events and exhibitions throughout the year (there was a vintage railway poster exhibition on when I last visited; and classic car shows and music concerts feature during the summer).

"The Catholic seminary training men for the priesthood was like a small settlement, with a farm, walled gardens, bakery and dairy."

Ushaw's buildings, chapels and terraced gardens are open to the public; highlights include the gardens (see opposite), **refectory** (now a simple café offering light lunches, scones and coffees), the **old library** containing rare books including illuminated manuscripts (open for special tours; check dates online) and **St Cuthbert's Chapel**. Originally built in 1847 by the famous Gothic architect, Augustus Pugin, of Houses of Parliament fame, much of St Cuthbert's Chapel dates to a reconstruction at the end of the 19th century when the college was expanding and more space was needed in the chapel, but it remains elaborately decorated and hugely impressive with its decorative Victorian tiles, lofty pointed ceiling painted gold, pale blue and burgundy, and ornate altar. Pugin's original **High Altar,** one of the crowning jewels at Ushaw, was moved to the Sacred Heart Chapel where it is admired for its elaborate stone carvings across a richly decorated screen. His workmanship is seen elsewhere at Ushaw with stained glass, fittings, metalwork, furniture and several other buildings in the complex attributed to the architect and designer – and his descendants. Ushaw holds work of other members of the illustrious family and is said to be the only place in the world where you can see designs by all six Pugins.

Laid out below the striking Georgian-looking frontage of the main quadrangle are the formal **gardens** planted with rhododendrons and azaleas that put on a colourful display in late spring. Below them is the old pond, now a kind of wild bog garden, but once it functioned as an ice-skating rink in winter. Close by are the sports grounds, still showing evidence of popular games once played by the young residents of the college in the 19th century including 'Fives', a form of handball played in many pit villages in these parts, and 'Cat', a team game with similarities to rounders, played around a ring, that originated in Douai.

On a slope southwest of the main buildings is the **home farm,** an imposing solidly mid-19th-century sandstone block of factory proportions housing haylofts, cowsheds and stables. You may see it on one of the side roads leading to Ushaw; unfortunately there's no access and the buildings are sadly much dilapidated.

9 BRANCEPETH

The leafy surroundings and long, wide avenue of stone-built houses leading away from Brancepeth Castle make this village on the western outskirts of Durham one of the most distinctive and attractive places in the valley. An old photograph of this street, The Village, from the turn of the 19th century shows the Georgian cottages covered in ivy and looking a little run down. It's easy to identify the location because all the houses have remained the same, except they are smarter today. The Village is capped at its southern end by the pillared driveway to impressive Brancepeth Castle; to the north, beyond the crossroads, the houses are more imposing and have Tudor styling. There's not a huge amount to *do* here and there is no bustling village hub, but if you time your visit around open days at the castle you could join a tour.

Some say the name 'Brancepeth' is a corruption of 'Braunspath' which recalls a fearsome boar (a 'braun') that was said to roam the area many hundreds of years ago. If you pass the Brancepeth Castle Golf Club (set in the castle's old deer park), you'll see the boar motif.

Hidden along a quiet lane just off The Village is **St Brandon's Church**, which dates back 1,000 years though very little remains of the oldest parts. In 1998, a fire gutted the interior and destroyed precious woodwork, but once the flames were extinguished over a hundred medieval stone coffin covers were revealed in the damaged walls. The collection is thought to be the largest in the North East, some of which are displayed in the restored church interior. Of interest are the engravings of cross heads with multiple points and shafts carved as a Tree of Life with sprouting foliage.

The two round gate towers and high curtain wall of **Brancepeth Castle** (brancepethcastle.org.uk) are brutes and give the appearance of a mighty Norman fortress. If you have the chance to get up close, perhaps on one of the weekly tours run throughout the year or at a craft fair, you'll see the stonework is a little too neat and pristine to be so old. Indeed, though a Norman castle did once stand here, most of what stands dates to the early and mid-19th century.

The castle played a role in the 1569 Rising of the North involving the then owner, Charles Neville, the Earl of Westmorland, and Thomas Percy, the Earl of Northumberland. The unsuccessful attempt to depose Queen Elizabeth I and place Mary, Queen of Scots on the throne resulted in the execution of Percy and the ousting of Neville from his castle. He fled to Holland and the crown took over Brancepeth. Over the following 400 years, the castle changed hands several times and is now in private ownership.

ALONG THE RIVER WEAR: WITTON-LE-WEAR TO DURHAM

 Dowfold House (page 309), **The Saxon Inn** (page 309)

On leaving the Pennines, the Wear flows into the lowlands and is shrouded in woodland for long stretches on its run to Durham where it loops scenically around the cathedral city before changing course and heading north. Here we follow the Wear from outside Wolsingham (page 192) to the old stone village of **Witton-le-Wear**, past **Escomb** and its important Saxon church, before skirting Bishop Auckland (page 107) under an impressively tall viaduct. A mile or so downriver is **Binchester Roman Fort**. The countryside around **Sunderland Bridge** and Shincliffe (pages 100 and 58) on the outskirts of Durham offers yet more fine glimpses of river scenery. Tracing the river along its entire course is the **Weardale Way** long-distance footpath (page 74), which opens up many options for walks and circular routes making use of connecting rights of way.

10 WITTON-LE-WEAR

A red telephone box stands prominently in the centre of Witton-le-Wear, catching the eye of anyone passing through this picturesque village on edge of Weardale. Facing it across the sloping green is an old pub, the Victoria Inn, and some handsome stone cottages. It's all rather lovely round here with plenty of old buildings of interest including a pele tower at the far west of the village, dating in part to the 16th century, and the **church of St Philip and St James**, housing a font made of Frosterley marble and 13th-century stonework (look up to admire the arches in the nave). While there is little to amuse in the village itself, the nearby castle, **heritage railway** (for services to Stanhope; page 200), river and connecting footpaths make for an enjoyable half-day visit.

Witton Castle stands in open countryside a short ride from the village (or a mile-long amble following the Weardale Way from the western edge of High Street) and is reached by crossing the River Wear over the glorious two-arched **Witton Bridge** of 1788. A **footpath** on the far side of the Wear from the village offers a few miles of riverside trails. Otherwise, continue ahead on the Weardale Way to reach the castle. Around the time work was completed on the aforementioned bridge,

"Witton Castle stands in open countryside and is reached by crossing the River Wear over the glorious two-arched Witton Bridge."

much of the interior of Witton Castle was destroyed by fire. You won't get to see the inside, however, as it is closed to the public but the grounds are accessible via footpaths. A caravan park dilutes the romance of the setting somewhat, but the castle is impressive with its embattled turrets.

Unlike many other fortresses in the North, little is known about Witton but it is essentially early 14th century with a fair amount of 18th- and 19th-century alterations.

11 LOW BARNS NATURE RESERVE

DL14 0AG ✆ 0191 5843112 ☺ reserve always open; visitor centre & café open 10.00–16.00 daily ♿

At dusk, mammals and birds emerge from the reedbeds and woodlands within this secluded 47-hectare wetland reserve three miles west of Bishop Auckland. When I walked the 1¼-mile circuit of Low Barns one late afternoon in winter, I had the reserve to myself and I came within yards of roe deer grazing on the edge of birch woodland, and watched wildfowl dabbling in the shallows of lakes created many years ago from flooded gravel pits, but what I was really hoping to set eyes on was an otter, kingfisher, bittern or perhaps even a starling murmuration over the reedbeds. All these species are not infrequently spotted at Low Barns. As the light dropped, I climbed away from the lakes and up the lane to the exit but I turned back one last time to see a rippling V-shaped trail of something cruising across the water below. In the dim light, it was hard to see if it was a duck or something else, though I like to think it was an otter.

To the rear of the nature reserve, the River Wear rushes wildly along the southern boundary, lapping at the woodland edge and adding to the appeal of the site – and the diversity of species encountered. In spring and summer, warblers, reed bunting and many tits and finches breed in and around the lagoons.

At the visitor centre there is a sheltered **café** with outside tables, a butterfly garden and wetland areas accessible via boardwalks (look out for damselflies and dragonflies hereabouts). Elsewhere, four large hides are spaced around the reserve and are all accessible for those in wheelchairs.

12 ESCOMB CHURCH & SURROUNDS

'One of the most important and most moving survivals of the architecture of the times of Bede', says the Pevsner architectural guide of the 7th-

1 Sunderland Bridge. 2 Bridge near Witton-le-Wear. 3 Escomb Saxon church.
4 Binchester Roman Fort. ▶

century church which stands in the centre of Escomb ('Escum'), ringed by 1960s houses where kids play on bicycles and neighbours chat from one side of the village to the other. Unless you're walking the Weardale Way, you'll probably have to go out of your way to see one of Britain's most complete Saxon churches. But, it is a detour well worth making.

Of all the many historic sites in Durham, Escomb Church is somewhere I'm drawn to more than any other building. To stand in its circular churchyard, unchanged for 1,300 years, and gaze at the lines on its venerable sundials and the uneven, pitted, scored and worn stones in its walls, wondering which were pillaged from the nearby Roman fort of Binchester, instils a sense of permanence and continuity; a connection to a time so long ago it is hard to imagine how a building could have remained intact for so many years. But here it stands: still a place of Christian worship; still telling the time.

A visit starts at number 28 Saxon Green, where the **keys** to the church hang outside the front door, the home of a friendly lady called Joan (who will not be cross when you accidentally leave the keys in the church and close the door behind you, as I did once). On entering the **churchyard** (which contains some good examples of medieval gravestones), even those without an interest in church architecture will immediately appreciate that Escomb is special with its strikingly high walls, box shape and small windows. Experts say it is distinctively northern (Saxon churches in the south of England are wider and shorter).

The church booklet for sale inside explains how the building has survived through love and the conservation efforts of villagers and because the prince bishops of Durham 'had other things to do than build anew in a little outlying village'. Those who care for the building have done a superb job explaining all its wonderful curiosities and narrating its significance and place in history. The **porch** alone is a mini exhibition space containing stone crosses and various Saxon artefacts.

Inside the simple limewashed building, the eye is immediately drawn to the tall, hairpin **chancel arch** (and the medieval fresco painted on its underside) which probably came from Binchester (page 99). Roman stones have been widely recycled in the walls and there are many examples of diamond broaching (cross hatches carved into stones). One piece of masonry near the sanctuary on the north wall (to the left of the small window) has the sideways inscription 'BONO REI PUBLICAE NATO' ('To the man born for the good of the state'). The barely visible letters may have been carved on a Roman plinth. On hot days, listen carefully and you may hear the resident whiskered bats shuffling around in the timber-framed roof.

A black grave cover made from Frosterley marble (page 198), encrusted with hundreds of fossilised sea creatures, lies in front of the **altar**. The stone cross on the wall behind the altar may have been a 'preaching cross' used by missionaries in the early days of Anglo-Saxon Christianity and before this church was built. Outside, many irregular stones are found in the church walls. Look for a horse mount, Roman altar stones and a grooved slab possibly carved by chariot wheels. Their origins are not altogether clear but it is certainly enjoyable looking for these stones and pondering their former life. As for the Saxon **sundial** (not the one above the porch but to the right on the south wall), its three lines mark the time of services.

A short circular **walk** takes you to the banks of the Wear and around little **Escomb lake** before returning to the church. It only takes 30 minutes or so and is very pleasant at any time of the year.

With your back to the church and pub, turn right along Saxon Green turning off left down Dunhelm Chare which soon bears left becoming a dirt track leading to the river. At the Wear, turn left and follow the footpath along the bottom edge of a field until you reach the lake, where you might see swans, ducks and great crested grebes. Follow an obvious track through trees which skirts around the edge of the lake in an anti-clockwise direction until you're roughly halfway round the water. Where the path forks, turn left and continue across some muddy fields with allotments (you may be able to hear the calls of cockerels on your right). Exit the field over a stile next to a metal farm gate and continue ahead to an opening between a fence and a metal post where you re-enter the village. Escomb Church appears quite scenically between houses.

13 BINCHESTER ROMAN FORT

DL14 8DJ ⏀ 01388 663089 ⏀ durham.gov.uk/binchester ⏀ 1 Apr–31 Oct daily ♿

The largest Roman fort in the county, founded in AD80, Binchester stands above the River Wear in farmland 1½ miles north of Bishop Auckland. Like the forts at Lanchester and Ebchester, Binchester lies on the Roman road, Dere Street, which ran from York to Corbridge, across Hadrian's Wall and into Scotland; the difference at Binchester is that you can actually see a visible a stretch of this ancient route, complete with its stone guttering and river cobbles. Excavations are ongoing and archaeologists unearth new structures every year including a Roman barrack block and civilian settlements in pasture lands outside the fort.

As well as a short section of Dere Street, you'll see the foundations of some buildings including the commandant's house and the fort ramparts (like earth mounds). What most visitors come for is the commandant's private **bath house**, said to be the best example in Britain. Close up viewing of the hypocaust is provided inside a museum that stands over the bath house to protect it. Hot air circulated through the brick stack pillars, heating the floor tiles of the changing and bathing rooms above.

Roman re-enactment events are staged in the surrounding farmland – check online for details. It's possible to **walk** to Binchester from Bishop Auckland by following the River Wear for a mile or so and then heading uphill through farmland.

14 SUNDERLAND BRIDGE & OLD CROXDALE

Whiling away the years on a shelf above the Wear three or four miles south of Durham is this quiet village with two facing rows of cottages and a Victorian church. You're in for a treat if you arrive on foot from the Weardale Way as the path crosses the river by way of the village's namesake **bridge**, a handsome four-arched crossing that is quite obviously of some age. The middle section is actually 14th century; the rest was rebuilt and then widened at various times in the centuries that followed.

A tranquil **walk** through woods, accessed from the eastern end of the village or by following the Weardale Way along the river's edge, rewards with views of the Wear taking a difficult route to Durham and of **Old Croxdale** with its largely 18th-century Hall and eye-catching medieval chapel, the oldest parts of which are Norman.

THE GAUNLESS VALLEY & BISHOP AUCKLAND

🏠 **Dowfold House** (page 309), **Park Head** (page 309), **Thomas Wright House** (page 309) 🧀 **Teesdale Cheesemakers** (page 309)

Three becks merge below the village of **Copley** in the foothills of the Pennines to form the Gaunless, a secluded river which travels largely unnoticed through one of the least-known Durham valleys, passing a scattering of villages and pastures grazed by sheep, cattle and horses, until it emerges alluringly below Bishop Auckland's castle at the confluence of the River Wear.

At the western edge of the valley and the closer you travel to Langleydale, the landscape becomes increasingly Pennine like with drystone walls and sloping green valley sides; heather and snow posts appear by the sides of the highest passes.

Bishop Auckland has undergone a transformation in recent years and is now a highlight on the cultural map of Durham, both for its visual arts and historic buildings.

15 WOODLAND & LANGLEYDALE COMMON

The old colliery village of **Woodland** keeps watch from the highest point in the Gaunless Valley on its single road, known fittingly as The Edge – and it really feels like it up here at over 1,000ft above sea level. The views are expansive with meadow after meadow enclosed by drystone walls, and trees in the valley bottom concealing where the River Gaunless begins life.

St Mary's Church gazes down the valley from the centre of the village and is distinctly different to most other churches in Durham. Made of corrugated iron sheeting and painted white, it has a pyramidal bellcote and fetching big bell and the church as a whole could be straight out of *Little House on the Prairie*. While there's not a lot to see in Woodland beyond the church, the views of the sub-Pennine landscape are beautiful and even more generous as you follow the B6282 – an awesome, lonely road with snow markers – in a southwesterly direction across **Langleydale Common** where heather moors stretch for miles around.

16 COPLEY & SURROUNDS

As you descend through Copley towards the River Gaunless you'll pass through this long village with bay fronted stone cottages, a few farms and a village **Literary Institute** straddling Sun Road (the B6282). A relic from the 19th century when such libraries-cum-social hubs were found in many mining villages, the institute dates to 1898, as the little plaque on the exterior details. Its community function is unchanged today, operating as a village hall.

Away from the busy village in the valley bottom, it is easy to overlook a cluster of stone buildings whiling away the years where the B6282 is carried over the Gaunless, but do pull over in the little parking area on the south side of the river to take a closer look. What remains of **Copley Smelt Mill** includes the single-story stone building by the road and the larger double-fronted house on the bank side (once the manager's house). A huge smelt chimney is concealed by trees above the parking area. Together they worked as a smelt mill for around 100 years from the late 18th century, converting lead ore (galena) from mines in Teesdale into lengths of iron. Though missing its water wheel that once powered bellows working the furnaces and some other buildings, you still get a sense of how all the landscape features and buildings before you once came together as part of an industrial complex. Even the old packhorse trail running below the manager's house, pleasingly named **Steele Road**, remains intact. Its name is evocative of the fragments of galena (a greyish colour with silvery flecks) that no doubt littered the track where ponies plodded along laden with the ore. An information board in the parking area explains the function of individual buildings.

"Its name is evocative of the fragments of galena that no doubt littered the track where ponies plodded along laden with the ore."

To visit the early 19th-century **smelt chimney**, take some steps leading steeply uphill through woodland from the parking area. You can, in fact, just about see the round column from the parking area but the sandstone blends in so perfectly with the trees that you won't know it is there until it is right in front of you. Poisonous gasses from the smelting process were sucked away from the buildings by the river through an underground shaft and emitted through this chimney.

Only the most determined and adventurous will contemplate the scramble through woods to find the elusive **Jerry Force waterfall**. While I have heard its roar and tried twice to locate it, I must admit that I failed both times. And don't assume the Ordnance Survey map holds the key to its location (you'll see the waterfall is marked across Arn Gill Beck but I am reliably informed it is on Hindon Beck where the 23ft-high fall spills from shelf to shelf like mermaid's hair).

Still intrigued? Here are a few route notes to put you on the right track: from the parking area on the south side of the river by the smelt mill, cross back over the Gaunless and take a track off to your left by the side of a cottage. The path crosses flat ground towards woodland where it merges with another track from the right becoming Steele Road, an old packhorse route. You now have two options: either cross the old stone bridge, which is covered in moss, and follow Steele Road uphill with the wooded gorge of Arn Gill Beck below to your left. The river slips out of view the higher you climb until it is lost altogether. You'll come to the white-washed Steele House Farm and its two horse paddocks at the top of the gorge. A footpath runs through the farm to reach Hindon Beck gorge on the other side of the farm. Descending steeply through trees towards the sound of a torrent of water will likely lead you to Jerry Force but you'll need a good sense of direction and your wits about you for the descent.

Alternatively, back at the moss-covered bridge (with the smelt mill buildings behind you) you'll see a red box attached to a tree. Turn right off Steele Road here, along a well-worn path, following Hindon Beck upstream through woodland carpeted in wild garlic in spring. After ten minutes or so, go through a gate and continue ahead with the beck on your left but now falling away as you climb through the gorge. Continue picking your way through the woods until eventually, I am told, you will reach the fall. Alternatively, you can cross the beck and return on the other side of the river, following it downstream back to the mossy bridge. I continued for some way before the route became too rough and slippery underfoot and I lost my nerve. Good luck dear reader (and do take a compass and map).

17 BUTTERKNOWLE

The Gaunless trickles through woodland on its merry way to Butterknowle, a pleasing name meaning 'butter hill', no doubt because of the production of dairy goods here in times gone by. The tradition was revived in the valley not that long ago by a couple who produce cheese from their farm on the outskirts of the village (between Copely and Butterknowle). **Teesdale Cheesemakers** (page 104) is well worth a stop both to purchase cheeses from their shop and enjoy the valley views from their little café.

Butterknowle itself is a rather rambling **village** standing either side of its main road with long, plain terraces and the occasional farm and pub. The shy Gaunless is nowhere to be seen until you descend to its banks where the B6282 is carried over the stream on the edge of **Cockfield Fell** (page 104), a wild-looking area of common land to the southeast. Anyone interested in bridge architecture or railway engineering should take a stroll to see **Swin Bridge** (page 106), which crosses the Gaunless about a mile or so east of Butterknowle. It holds the title as the world's first railway skew bridge, built 1830. A couple of footpaths converge at the crossing and are walked in little over a mile or so from access roads close to the northern side of Cockfield Fell.

¶¶ FOOD & DRINK

Teesdale Cheesemakers Pond Farm, 11 Copley Ln, DL13 5LW ✆ 07887 676397 ⊘ teesdalecheesemakers.co.uk ⊙ 09.00–16.00 daily (till 21.00 Fri). Husband and wife team Jonathan and Allison continue a family tradition in the farming area of Butterknowle, producing soft, blue, goat and hard cheeses on their 8ha smallholding. Their 'cheese-centric café' with indoor and outdoor seating is a lovely spot to sample their produce over a coffee (roasted in nearby Mickleton): breakfast rolls (the bacon and sausages are produced with rare-breed pork from the farm), cheese boards, burgers, toasties, scones and cakes. Check online for upcoming dairy tours and cheese-tasting events. You can also hire glamping huts for overnight stays on-site.

18 COCKFIELD VILLAGE & FELL

Cockfield is a busy old village stretched out over a mile or so with a long, sloping green and some fascinating history. At the eastern end is a cluster of historic buildings worth exploring, including **St Mary's Church**, bits of which are early 13th century (the east wall of the chancel and south wall of the nave) but mostly dates to a rebuild in 1911. One of its most curious features is a 14th-century stone effigy of a girl who, legend has it, drowned in the moat of **Cockfield Hall**. The outline of the moat remains but the manor was replaced in the 17th century by the current hall and farm. Public access is permitted from a farm track running down the side of the church boundary.

"Even without the industrial archaeology, the fell is a very fine place for a windswept walk."

While Cockfield is a pleasant enough place to wander round, it's the namesake fell bordering the village to the north which really is of huge historical interest, with its old tramways, coal pits and medieval rabbit warrens. Even without the industrial archaeology, the fell is a very fine place for a windswept walk.

One of England's largest Scheduled Ancient Monuments, **Cockfield Fell** is an extraordinary expanse of lowland fell about two miles across which is full of bumps, pits and relics from mining, quarrying and farming over the last several hundred years. This being common land, livestock and horses wander freely, grazing on the rough grasslands and among the gorse bushes; note too the ramshackle pigeon crees.

An anti-clockwise **walk** from Cockfield village across the fell to the River Gaunless and back (a circuit of around 3½ miles) will reveal many of these fascinating landmarks. You'll need ✳ Ordnance Survey map 305. Once you reach the Gaunless, via some fell cottages, turn upstream through the wooded valley. The view is made all the more picturesque by the giant legs of **Lands Viaduct**, built in 1862 by Thomas Bouch (of Scotland's Tay Bridge fame), which once carried steam engines across the fell on their way to Barnard Castle from Bishop Auckland. Strewn up the bankside are the blown-apart remains of the rest of the viaduct, destroyed after the crossing closed in the 1960s. Under the viaduct ran a branchline of the historic Stockton & Darlington Railway, the Haggerleases Line, which is still visible as a straight grassy channel along the north side of the river.

TWO COCKFIELD BROTHERS & A WHOLE LOT OF JAZZ

Cockfield was the birthplace of two remarkable men born in the 1730s: George and Jeremiah Dixon, the ingenious sons of a wealthy coal miner. The elder brother, **George Dixon**, was an early inventor of coal gas and experimented lighting his house (which stands to this day on Garden House Lane) using gas piped into his home, until he caused an explosion. He also attempted to construct a canal on Cockfield Fell to transport coal to the Tees, but the project proved too expensive to complete, and his canal was abandoned (though, delightfully, reeds grow on the site of his experimental canal to this day).

Meanwhile, George's younger brother, **Jeremiah Dixon**, an astronomer and surveyor, was on the other side of the Atlantic working alongside another surveyor, Charles Mason, to establish the disputed boundary line between Pennsylvania and Maryland, known to this day as the Mason–Dixon Line. Their work founded the demarcation between the southern and northern states and gave rise to the term Dixieland to describe the (slave) states south of the line and, later, the famous eponymous jazz music coming out of New Orleans.

During his time in North America, Jeremiah was said to have turned on a slave owner he came across one day who refused to stop beating a woman, giving the man a good whipping himself. The weapon, so the story goes, stayed in Jeremiah's possession and was kept in his Cockfield home until his death.

Nearing Butterknowle, the track crossed the river at an angle, over a bridge still standing today and known as **Swin Bridge**, said to be the world's first railway skew bridge, built 1830. Constructing the bridge at an angle – or skew – was necessary because the railway does not meet the Gaunless dead on. If you crouch down and look under the arch, you'll see the stonework appears fanned or twisted which gave the bridge the strength to carry the weight of the railway.

On the return south back to the village via one of the many grassy tracks over the fell, you'll pass an Iron Age settlement as well as the remains of old tramway trackbeds and plenty of depressions where little coal mines – or bell pits – were dug. Two peculiar looking mounds on the west side of the fell are worth explaining. They were once rumoured to be the graves of Roman centurions but are now believed to be artificial medieval rabbit warrens, known as 'pillow mounds', created to provide a ready supply of game for human consumption.

19 WEST AUCKLAND & ST HELEN AUCKLAND

The Gaunless River bisects two substantial 'Auckland' villages a few miles upstream from the rather more well-known Auckland, Bishop Auckland ('Auckland' is Old English for 'land of the oaks' or 'oak-land').

West Auckland is a large, bustling place with a busy mix of old and new arranged along a long and spacious centuries-old green. A number of buildings on Front Street are more than three or four hundred years old, including **Old Hall**, a wide two-storeyed house with a prominent central porch on the south side of the street, dating to the 1600s; and the **Manor House** (now a spa hotel), said to have been one of King Henry VIII's hunting lodges. While its frontage and H-plan design is arresting, there's more from the period round the back, specifically a late medieval brewery, albeit with alterations from over the centuries since its construction.

Football fans may enjoy paying homage to **West Auckland FC**, winners of one of the first ever international football competitions – or, if you will, the first ever football World Cup – held in Turin in 1909. A popular account of why the lowly team of Durham miners ended up playing – and winning – against a Swiss team rests on a clerical error resulting in the Durham team being called to play instead of Woolwich Arsenal (which also holds the initials WAFC). Whatever the reason, the underdogs managed to defend the title two years later with a 6-1 win against Juventus and securing their place in footballing folklore. A sculpture depicting the team's unlikely victory stands in the village.

St Helen Auckland shares its name with the venerable parish church standing by the side of the main road through the village. It is an unusual squat-looking church, striking for its lack of a tower. It also has one of the oldest doors in the county, dating to the church's original construction in the 12th century. Another church dating to the same time, **St Andrew's**, in the nearby village of South Church, is Grade-I listed and is thought to be the largest parish church in Durham.

20 BISHOP AUCKLAND

Regeneration money has poured into the historic market town of Bishop Auckland in recent times – and it shows. In the handsome, spacious centre with its fine run of period buildings, new galleries and visitor experiences add to the list of reasons to spend a day in 'Bishop'. There's a lot to pack in: outstanding art galleries; Auckland Castle and historic parkland; woodland and riverside trails; a tremendous 250-year-old walled garden; Auckland Tower and the spectacular Kynren outdoor summer shows (page 109).

While it is true that the tired shopping streets behind tell a different economic truth, from a visitor's perspective you will probably centre your visit around Market Place, the castle and parkland. If you do venture down **Newgate Street**, the main shopping precinct, note its long, straight length, this being the old Roman highway, Dere Street. A few vintage shopfronts here take you back to a different era, including the Grade II-listed old McIntyre shoe shop dating to 1900, still with its unchanged signage, bow windows, Art-Nouveau detailing and mosaic flooring. Further down Newgate Street, at number 105, is **Gregory's Bakers & Deli**, also listed by English Heritage. Once a butcher's, opened in the late 19th century, Gregory's retains many original features from its Edwardian refit, including stained glass and some wonderful decorative tiles inside depicting rural scenes.

"Regeneration money has poured into the historic market town of Bishop Auckland in recent times – and it shows."

Taking centre stage in **Market Place** is the modern, 95ft-high **Auckland Tower** (Market Pl, DL14 7NJ ✆ 01388 743750 ☉ Feb–Dec 11.00–16.00 Wed–Sun (winter to 15.00) ♿), providing visitors with a view of the castle, town centre, parkland and wider countryside from a viewing platform 50ft from the ground (reached by steps or the lift). It's a good place to start your visit, first to orientate yourself and map all the attractions, but also to find out about the Prince Bishops (you'll be hearing a lot about them as you tour the town) and pick up leaflets and information about what's on. A small shop sells gifts and useful guides and maps on Durham.

A few paces away from Auckland Tower is the stirring **Mining Art Gallery** (Market Pl, DL14 7NJ ✐ 01388 743750 ☉ Feb–Dec 11.00–16.00 Wed–Sun (winter to 15.00) ♿) housing works by nationally recognised Durham miner-artists, including Norman Cornish, Bob Olley and Tom McGuinness.

"The stirring Mining Art Gallery houses works by Durham miner-artists, including Norman Cornish, Bob Olley and Tom McGuinness."

Through the dark, dirt and dangerous tunnels, men toiled underground in coal mines across Durham, and so we see a lot of muscle, sweat and rock depicted in their paintings; but as much of this important gallery, arranged over a few floors, is devoted to the miners' lives above ground: the streets where their children played, the pubs where they drank after shifts, their hobbies and everyday goings-on in the terraces where they lived.

A video of Cornish painting in his hometown of Spennymoor gives insight into the painter and his connection with mining families. He said of his works: 'I paint human beings, I paint their hopes and their shapes and their attitudes and the feelings I have when I look at them. The images come from the people. They create them. I am just the medium'. Indeed, there's much humour, community and humanity here and even those without any interest in the mining heritage of the North East will find the art accessible and engaging.

One of Cornish's most celebrated works, the *Gala Mural*, is housed in the **Town Hall** (Market Pl, DL14 7NP ✐ 03000 269524 ☉ 10.00–16.00 Mon–Sat ♿) round the corner from the gallery (you can also see many other of his works in Spennymoor's Town Hall gallery, pages 115 and 117). A Gothic-style building of considerable size, the Town Hall dominates the head of Market Place, providing a spacious modern meeting place for visitors and locals in its central café-cum-gallery. It also hosts comedy nights, gigs, theatre shows, children's events and cinema screenings.

RENAISSANCE TOWN

Bishop Auckland's transformation into a culture hub was fuelled over the last 10 to 15 years by a number of sources but a name closely associated with the town's revival is Jonathan Ruffer, a financier, art collector, philanthropist and Durham local on a mission to revitalise the town, largely out of his own pocket. He is said to have spent over £100 million to date and is responsible for The Auckland Project galleries and developments you see around the town.

It started with his interest in a series of 12 Zurbarán paintings hanging in Auckland Castle, which were due to be sold ahead of the castle being put on the open market. 'I went to buy some paintings and ended up buying a castle as well,' he says of the purchases. Ruffer then went on to make future acquisitions around Market Place, opening galleries and filling them with his astonishing private collection of Spanish art – hence the Spanish Gallery (see below) – as well as financing the construction of Auckland Tower and the Faith Museum. It is hoped that the injection of capital into the centre will feed a wider regrowth of the town over the coming years.

Norman Cornish's *Gala Mural* is on permanent display, a treasured work commissioned by Durham County Council in 1962, for which Cornish had to take unpaid leave from the coal field for a year to fulfil. Across the 30ft canvas, he brings to life the energy, excitement, colour and coming together of miners, their families (dressed in their Sunday best) and colliery musicians arriving for the annual Miners' Gala celebration: the colliery banners like sails on masts pulling the crowds across the canvas. It's well worth seeing.

On the northern outskirts of the town, open grassland provides the location for **Kynren** (Flatts Farm, DL14 7SF ⌀ 11arches.com/kynren ☉ Jun–Sep eve Sat & Sun ♿), a spectacular outdoor show narrating 2,000 years of English history in 90 minutes during weekend nights in summer. A cast of 1,000 volunteers and crew put on a superb family event under the gaze of Auckland Castle, spanning from Boudicca to the Viking raids; the Norman Conquest to the Industrial Revolution. Stunts, fireworks, charging horses, a recreated Viking boat – I could go on. Make sure you book in advance for the hugely popular shows.

The Spanish Gallery

Market Pl, DL14 7NJ ⌀ 01388 743750 ☉ 11.00–16.00 Wed–Sun (winter to 15.00) ♿

This distinguished gallery houses the UK's largest collection of Spanish art outside of London. Allow a couple of hours to take in the four

LAND OF THE PRINCE BISHOPS

There are two kings in England, namely the Lord King of England, wearing a crown in sign of his regality and the Lord Bishop of Durham, wearing a mitre in place of a crown, in sign of his regality in the diocese of Durham.

Steward of the Bishopric William de St Botolph, 1302

'County Durham: Land of the Prince Bishops' is a road sign you will encounter while touring the region, but who were the Prince Bishops? To make sense of Durham's history and built heritage, it helps to know a little about these powerful men who ruled large areas of the North of England for centuries from the time of the Norman Conquest.

Unable to protect England from repeated invasions north of the border, the Norman kings of England granted exceptional secular privileges to the Bishop of Durham, whose diocese extended across the region then known as Northumbria to the frontier with Scotland, on condition he protected the interests of the Crown. Successive bishops became known as the 'Prince Bishops', who ruled almost autonomously from Durham Castle and their main country residence at Auckland Castle with the authority to levy taxes, mint coins, issue charters and appoint sheriffs. They even had their own army. And they lived like royalty, owning hunting forests, manor houses and castles.

By the end of the 11th century, the bishops' rule was restricted to the land largely between the Tyne and Tees – an area that became known as the 'County Palatine of Durham' – but they were still hugely powerful, second only to the king. Fast forward to the Reformation and the Prince Bishops found they were rather less influential when their civic powers were much reduced under Henry VIII and again following the reform acts of 1832 when they were fully restored to the Crown. Despite the loss of regal authority, Durham Castle remained a ceremonial centre of power (now under the ownership of Durham University) with their main residence at Auckland Castle, which to this day is often referred to as Auckland 'Palace'.

floors of Spanish Golden Age art: largely oil paintings from the 16th and 17th centuries, much of it religious, as well as medieval sculptures and artefacts. There are surprises too, like the top-floor gallery that immerses visitors in Moorish ceramic art with its walls and terracotta floors covered with exact replicas of tiles from Seville, and decorative carved archways.

Francisco de Zurbarán's original *Benjamin* (from the series *Jacob and His Twelve Sons*) greets visitors on entering the gallery. *Benjamin* has been on quite a journey since he came to life on canvas in the 1640s; and the reunification with his brothers in Bishop Auckland (the other

12 portraits have hung in the castle's Long Dining Room since their purchase by Bishop Trevor in 1756. Incidentally, the *Benjamin* in the castle is a copy) has come to signify a new start for the town because it was the purchase of the set in 2011 that sparked the current regeneration of Bishop Auckland – and the creation of this gallery. For this reason alone, it is worth visiting the castle (see below) before the gallery to place all of this in context (though please note *Benjamin* is currently on loan).

Elsewhere, visitors are treated to works by Murillo, Valázquez, Ribera and El Greco (his early 17th-century *Christ on the Cross* is one of the gallery's most treasured masterpieces). If you're new to Spanish art from this era, you'll find the curators have done a skilful job at narrating the significance of particular works in the context of the Spanish Golden Age and bringing them together in a way that is meaningful to someone with little or no knowledge of this flourishing period.

Auckland Castle & Deer Park

DL14 7NR 🖉 03000 269524 ⊙ Feb–Dec 11.00–16.00 Wed–Sun (winter to 15.00) ♿

The ruling prince bishops of Durham established a hunting lodge high above the River Wear and in a loop of the River Gaunless some 800 years ago but it wasn't until 1832, when Durham Castle – once the main seat of the bishops of Durham – was given to the university, that Auckland Castle became the bishops' principal residence. Today, the castle (sometimes referred to as 'Auckland Palace' or 'Bishop's Palace'), parkland and walled garden is under the stewardship of The Auckland Project, a privately owned regeneration organisation (page 109). For many, a visit here will be the highlight of a trip to Bishop Auckland.

"Two neat rows of whitewashed Georgian cottages flank the dramatic 18th-century Gothic entrance to Auckland Castle and Deer Park."

Two neat rows of whitewashed Georgian cottages flank the dramatic 18th-century **Gothic entrance** (the gatehouse with a clock tower) to Auckland Castle and Deer Park, which is reached off Market Place. While touring the parkland and buildings, keep in mind the tremendous power and wealth held by the prince bishops who would have hosted lavish ceremonies here, all funded through taxes, the church and profits from local mines.

On stepping into the grounds, you'll first come to one of the newest buildings in The Auckland Project's portfolio: the **Faith Museum** – a

church-like structure (under construction at the time of writing) made almost entirely of sandstone (incidentally quarried from the same location as stone for Durham Cathedral) that explores the development of faith in the British Isles.

Opposite the Faith Museum, the land occupied by the castle's huge 17th-century **walled garden** falls away steeply to the River Gaunless. Ahead, mature parkland slopes towards the confluence of the rivers Gaunless and Wear offering several miles of walking trails within the 320ha wooded **Deer Park** (DL14 7NR ✐ 03000 269524 ☉ dawn till dusk; free entry). An 18th-century stone bridge spans the water but the most celebrated feature in the grounds is an unusual Gothic Revival **deer shelter** dating to 1767. Part folly, part animal enclosure, the arcaded quadrangle created for use by the prince bishops who once used the semi-wooded parkland for hunting and recreation, also seems to catch the eye of passing children. 'It's very giant', I overheard an impressed toddler remark. He later asked his mother why there are so many castles here. I think what he rightly observed is the extensive castellated walls and towers seen throughout the estate, which seem to fire the imagination of youngsters and add to the adventure-playground appeal of the parkland.

But now, let's turn to the **castle**, really an embattled manor, and its adjoining chapel. Access is through a gateway in a castellated screen which is the work of 18th-century architect, James Wyatt, whose Gothic style continues inside.

Interior highlights are the **state rooms**, including the Long Dining Room with its collection of Francisco de Zurbarán portraits (page 110) of *Jacob and His Twelve Sons* dating to the 1640s. The dining table has been laid as if part-way through a meal (the realistic fake food was created by art students at Durham). The Throne Room is of palatial proportions and boasts a vaulted ceiling, the bishop's wooden throne and portraits of the prince bishops from centuries past.

Much of what you've seen by this point dates to the 17th and 18th centuries, but when you enter the splendid **St Peter's Chapel**, said to be one of the largest private chapels in Europe, the clocks rewind

◀ **1** Mining Art Galley, Bishop Auckland. **2** Kynren narrates 2,000 years of human history. **3** The interior of Auckland Castle. **4** Auckland Tower. **5** The Spanish Gallery, Bishop Auckland.

several hundred years to the 12th century. St Peter's started life as a banqueting hall but was rebuilt in the 1660s, after the Civil War, for Bishop Cosin, who died several years after its completion (his body is interred in the nave, marked by a marble grave slab). The interior is much celebrated on account of its size, height, use of Frosterley limestone, and intricately carved woodwork. The panelled ceiling is brightly painted with eagles, lions and mitres – a reoccurring motif. A few very fine wood carvings of note: decorative pew ends and the reredos behind the altar.

¶¶ FOOD & DRINK

A scattering of cafés front Market Place in the centre of Bishop Auckland including Fifteas Tea Room (see below) and **Breaking Bread** (8 Market Pl ✐ 01388 608770 ☉ 09.00–16.00 Tue–Sun), which was doing a busy morning trade when I visited. The surroundings are unremarkable, but the food was fine, particularly the home-baked sourdough. Another option is the somewhat trendy **Fox's Tale** (2–4 Newgate St ☉ 09.00–17.00 Tue–Sat) also serves good breakfasts (full English and the like) and modern lunches. The **Bishop's Kitchen café** inside the castle is useful for those on tours. Also consider the Mediterranean offerings in tapas restaurant **El Castillo** next to the Spanish Gallery.

The Copper Mine Bar & Eatery 26 High Jobs Hill, Crook DL15 0UL ✐ 01388 76333. Five miles north of Bishop Auckland on the outskirts of Crook, The Copper Mine is a rare find in an area with few decent pub restaurants. It's a bit out of the way (but only ten minutes by car from Bishop Auckland) but the views of the sub-Pennine landscape on the edge of Weardale are rather enticing. Meat eaters are well catered for in this modern restaurant (wood floors and furniture and laid-back atmosphere) with a selection of steaks, stews, Sunday roasts, pies and chicken dishes (chicken souvlaki is their signature dish) on offer alongside pizzas, fish and chips and a couple of vegan options (mushroom stroganoff and a vegan burger). Local beers always on tap with Durham Brewery and Allendale regularly featuring at the bar. Friendly, dog-welcoming, inexpensive and good food – so many reasons to seek out this pub.

Fifteas Tea Room 9 Market Pl ✐ 01388 304886 ☉ 09.30–17.00 daily ♿. With nods to the mid 20th century in the décor and staff uniforms, and a washing line with a corset, underskirt, hats and stockings, is this snug café where families and friends consume a lot of cake. Also serving decent breakfasts and lunches.

Gregory's Bakers & Deli 105 Newgate St ✐ 01388 602024 ☉ 08.30–14.30 Tue–Fri, 08.30–13.30 Sat ♿ small step to shop. Once a Victorian butcher's, Gregory's shop front and interior retains many decorative features from the early 1900s. Now trading mainly in bakery and delicatessen produce, including made-to-order sandwiches, pastries, quiches, bread and cakes, though the tradition of meat sales continues with their offerings of pies and sausage rolls, all of which are made on-site. Their speciality is the Bishop Auckland Pork Dip sandwich (slices of pork with stuffing, pease pudding and an onion dip).

SOUTH DURHAM

🏠 **Blackwell Grange Hotel** (page 309), **The Pickled Parson** (page 309), **Rockliffe Hall** (page 309)

Undulating farmland criss-crossed by old railway lines characterises much of the landscape between Durham and Darlington, an area celebrated for its railway heritage and some prominent old towns, notably **Sedgefield**. Those with even a passing interest in the art of coal miners such as Norman Cornish should make a diversion to the Town Hall gallery in **Spennymoor**.

21 SPENNYMOOR

> Spennymoor has all that a painter needs in order to depict humanity
>
> Norman Cornish, quoted in Durham County Council's Norman Cornish Trail leaflet

The Norman Cornish connection makes a visit to Spennymoor worthwhile. A town once ringed by collieries and now with a number

NORMAN CORNISH

'I got myself a couple of pints of Dutch courage… and I went to the colliery and asked for a minute's notice. There I was finished with the mine.' After working as a coal miner for 30 years, since the age of 14, Norman Cornish set out to fulfil his artistic ambitions by becoming a professional artist and lecturer at Sunderland Art College in the 1960s. He painted intimate scenes of everyday life in the pit village of Spennymoor where he lived: miners at the start of their shift; women chatting on street corners; children going to school; the local horse-pulled cart doing the rounds; and men crowded in pubs. In every canvas the viewer is pulled into Cornish's world of hard work and community – a world he was so intimately connected to that he was able to paint these scenes as if he was a part of the crowd. What connects all his works is a sense of humanity, something that was fundamental to Cornish and is felt in every piece.

A large collection of Cornish's paintings hang in **Spennymoor's Town Hall** (page 117) and the **Mining Art Gallery** in Bishop Auckland (page 108). One of his largest and most famous paintings, of the annual Durham Miners' Gala, is displayed in **Bishop Auckland's Town Hall** (page 108).

ROB ATHERTON/S

JOHN B HEWITT/S

MIKE KIPLING PHOTOGRAPHY/A

of budget shops and take aways facing its long through road, it nonetheless has some historical gems hidden here and there: an old-fashioned sweet shop next to the Town Hall and, opposite, a superb ironmongers with a vintage shopfront that can't have changed in over half a century. But it is the **Town Hall** (you can't miss its tall clock tower on the main road) that's worth your time. Upstairs is the wonderful **Bob Abley Art Gallery** (DL16 6DG ✆ 01388 815276 ☉ 09.00–17.00 Mon–Fri, 09.00–16.00 Sat & Sun; free entry), housing a permanent collection of **Norman Cornish** paintings including *The Lollipop Man*, an everyday

"Next door to the Town Hall is the John Kitson Archway, displaying some of Cornish's best-known works backlit on glass panels."

scene at school home time; and *Pit Road* in which we follow miners trudging to the colliery, a subject Cornish depicted many times over his life. Also here is the painter's studio which was carefully reconstructed here from his home on Whitworth Terrace some years after his death in 2014.

A number of original Cornish paintings are for sale alongside works by other notable artists including Bob Olley, Swin Tempest and Tom McGuinness, all of whom capture the lives of miners and their communities with sensitivity and affection. Note too the long 'Mouseman' table and chairs in one gallery and the wonderfully unchanged council meeting rooms (once a court room).

Next door to the Town Hall is the **John Kitson Archway**, an enclosed walkway connecting High Street with a car park, displaying some of Cornish's best-known works backlit on glass panels. The Town Hall is the starting point of an **art trail** leading visitors to places in Spennymoor painted by Cornish (pick up a leaflet in the Town Hall).

22 KIRK MERRINGTON & WESTERTON

A Norman church once crowned the top of the unassuming village of **Kirk Merrington**, a couple of miles south of Spennymoor. **St John's** was rebuilt in the mid 19th century and, while not particularly noteworthy architecturally (though, please do admire the grotesque stone corbels), it does boast a superb view of the county from its churchyard: from the Pennines to the North Sea, with Durham Cathedral peeping through

◀ **1** Hardwick Park. **2** Locomotion, Shildon. **3** Sedgefield town centre.

trees in the middle of the panorama and, further north, Penshaw Monument on the outskirts of Sunderland.

The far-reaching views did not go unnoticed by the 18th-century astronomer, Thomas Wright, who built an observatory in nearby **Westerton**. The cylindrical stone tower, also known as **Wright's Folly**, stands by the side of the main road through the small village.

23 SEDGEFIELD

Even without its famous racecourse, historic parkland and rural traditions, the town's spacious Georgian centre, large greens and medieval church make Sedgefield (pronounced with a silent 'g') conspicuously appealing. Despite its Georgian streets and heritage sites, however, Sedgefield remains somewhat off the tourist trail.

Much praised for its 17th-century interior woodwork, including a highly decorative chancel screen, **St Edmund's Church** stands in the centre of the town, flanked by Front Street and Rectory Row, and dates to the mid 13th century. For the most part, the church is Early English in style though its tower was constructed a few hundred years later at the end of the 15th century.

Opposite St Edmund's on Rectory Row is **Ceddesfeld Hall** (TS21 2AE ⌘ sedgefieldsca.org.uk ⌖), which goes by the Anglo Saxon name for Sedgefield. Once a rectory but now owned by the council and operated as a community hall (and a grand one at that), the Georgian mansion was built in 1792 on the site of a medieval rectory that had burnt down. Gardens to the rear, known simply as **Sedgefield Park** today, were laid out as an 18th-century pleasure ground with open lawns studded with trees leading to ornamental ponds. You can access the parkland freely from surrounding streets and visit the hall for public events including summer concerts and the like.

"The town's spacious Georgian centre, large greens and medieval church make Sedgefield conspicuously appealing."

Far better known for its Georgian landscaping is the popular **Hardwick Park** (Sedgefield TS21 2DN ⌘ 03000 262899 ⌖), a large historic parkland west of Sedgefield enclosing a Georgian manor, now the Hardwick Hall Hotel. Reached in half a mile from the town centre by following a footpath through the Hardwick Arms Hotel archway on North End, the 18th-century pleasure grounds were designed by James

SHROVE TUESDAY FOOTIE

On Shrove Tuesday, a notoriously fierce game of mob football begins at 13.00 from Sedgefield's village green. A small leather ball is passed through the bull ring opposite the Black Lion pub and then tossed into the rowdy crowd of men who spend the next few hours kicking and throwing the ball (and each other) about town until at 16.00 someone wins the ball by returning it to the bull ring. The origins of the game go back several centuries, possibly a millennium. Traditionally it was played between countrymen and tradesmen but now anyone joins in.

Paine who was responsible for the serpentine lake, hall and follies, including a leaning tower and sham ruined gatehouse. A network of paths run by the council wind through trees leading to all these places from a modern visitor centre (♿), and car park (clearly signed from the A177 and just a few minutes drive from the A1). There's a little café at the visitor centre plus toilets and a playground.

¶¶ FOOD & DRINK

If you're looking for a drinking hole, there's quite a choice in Sedgefield, though they can be a bit noisy. That said, I enjoyed a beer outside the **Dun Cow Inn** (43 Front Street), made famous when Tony Blair popped in with the then US President, George W Bush in the 1990s. It's popular with locals and, though a little tired inside, there are many old photos on the walls to catch your eye. On the food front, things look up somewhat with a couple of decent places to eat. Also consider **Herd & Herb** (1 North End, TS21 2AZ ✆ 01740 622305), annexed to a boutique hotel; a feast of above average-priced meat and fish dishes with some vegetarian options and a kids' menu.

No 4 4 High St, TS21 2AU ✆ 01740 623344 ☺ daily. The reason many people are drawn inside this friendly little café is for the sweet offerings in the patisserie (meringues are their speciality – as are afternoon teas) but there's also an extensive sandwich and jacket potato menu and home-cooked pies to heat at home, which may be useful if you're self-catering. A beef rosti, and cottage pie piled with lumpy, cheese-crusted mash looked delicious when I visited.

The Pickled Parson 1–2 The Sq, TS21 2AB ✆ 01740 213131 ⬦ thepickledparson.co.uk ☺ noon–15.00 & 18.00–21.00 Wed–Sat, noon–17.00 Sun. The curious name of this old hotel building, now a restaurant with modern rooms above, recalls the tale of a local clergyman said to have been preserved by his wife on his death in order that she could continue drawing an income from local residents. Chapel chairs inside are about the only reference to anything ecclesiastical in this smart but informal restaurant with dark blue walls and modern lighting. The menu is pretty standard: posh burgers, and some fish and meat dishes as well as Sunday lunches. I enjoyed a good fish sharing platter with whitebait, mackerel pâté, goujons, smoked salmon and three different breads for around £12 per person.

24 LOCOMOTION & SHILDON

Locomotion, Shildon DL4 2RE ✆ 03300 580058 ⊘ locomotion.org.uk ⊙ 10.00–17.00 Wed–Sun (winter to 16.00); free entry ♿

Shildon, just southeast of Bishop Auckland, claims to be the world's first railway town. Before the age of steam, this was a small village with a population of around a hundred but that all changed with the development of the Stockton & Darlington Railway (S&DR), which saw Shildon rapidly expand to a community of several thousand by the 1840s, reaching nearly 8,000 at the turn of the 19th century, with over a third of its population employed by the railway. Shildon's railway works closed in the 1980s but the town's railway legacy continues to draw visitors who mainly come for the fantastic railway museum, **Locomotion**, that occupies the sidings on the original line of the S&DR.

Over 70 historic engines are housed here, mostly indoors within a huge modern engine shed (to be replaced by a new exhibition hall in autumn 2023). They include: steam and diesel engines; the *Deltic Prototype* – with eye-catching mid 20th-century styling; Queen Alexandra's Royal Saloon carriage and a late 19th-century snow plough. For many, the highlight will be Stephenson's *Locomotion No. 1*, built for the opening of the S&DR and the first steam engine to pull a train carrying people. Imagining Stephenson driving his locomotive on its inaugural trip on 27 September 1825 with a few hundred passengers crammed into coal wagons is terrifically romantic. A local newspaper recorded the event:

> Astonishment, however, was not confined to the human species, for the beasts of the field and the fowls of the air seemed to view with wonder and awe the machine... The whole population of the towns and villages within a few miles of the Railway, seemed to have turned out, on this occasion, and we believe we speak within the limits of truth, when we say that not less than 40 or 50,000 persons were assembled to witness the proceedings of the day.
> *The Durham County Advertiser*, 1 October, 1825

Special events are held throughout the year (the *Flying Scotsman* was wowing visitors on one of my previous visits and, on a different occasion, the museum had brought together all the surviving *Deltic* locomotives). At the historic end of the site, reached on a short **walk** (&) past a playground, is a very rare **coal drop** where wagons would refuel steam engines by tipping their load from above. **Timothy Hackworth's cottage**, keeping alive the memory of the famous S&DR engineer whose name is stamped all over Shildon (I counted three streets named 'Hackworth' as well as the local park, school, pub and various other buildings), stands at the end of Hackworth Close on the other side of the line. A goods shed, railway cottages and various other buildings relating to the famous railway are dotted about this area (ask in the museum for a map of locations).

Mention the name Stephenson to staff and they'll give you a good-humoured grumble. During the famous Rainhill trials engine competition of 1829, Hackworth's engine *Sans Pareil* (housed in the museum) lost to the Stephensons' *Rocket*, and some locals haven't forgotten this – or the reason why they think his engine exited the race early (see below).

RAINHILL TRIALS

The date was October 1829; the location: Rainhill, Lancashire. The objective: to impress the directors of the new Liverpool and Manchester Railway with designs for the best locomotive to pull trains on the new passenger line. The prize was £500 – and guaranteed prestige. There were five competitors: a horse-powered machine and four steam engines.

Timothy Hackworth and George and Robert Stephenson knew each other well from their days at Wylam in Northumberland and had worked together on engineering projects, but for the nine-day competition at Rainhill they were rivals. The event was witnessed by thousands of people (which must have pleased the railway's bosses who gained valuable PR for their new venture). Problems with Hackworth's engine, *Sans Pareil*, ensured a win for the Stephensons' *Rocket*, which powered into the pages of newspapers and history books thereafter. The potential for steam engines to revolutionise passenger transport and drive the Industrial Revolution was realised from this moment on. Robert Stephenson observed, 'The trials at Rainhill seem to have sent people railway mad'. Timothy Hackworth was also driven to distraction when he discovered a crack in *Sans Pareil's* cylinder casting, which had been built at the Stephensons' Newcastle workshop. This led some to charge the Stephensons with foul play, though there was no evidence of this.

25 HEAD OF STEAM: DARLINGTON RAILWAY MUSEUM

North Road Station, Darlington DL3 6ST ✆ 01325 405060 ⊘ head-of-steam.co.uk ⊙ Apr–Sep 10.00–16.00 Tue–Sun; Oct–Mar 11.00–15.00 Wed– Sun ♿

The famous railway town of **Darlington**, just south of Durham's border, boasts a wonderfully spacious and pedestrianised centre with many 18th- and 19th-century buildings, including a restored Victorian market hall and clock tower (1864) that bears a resemblance to Big Ben – even the bells were made by the same company. But it's the town's fantastic railway museum that I couldn't resist highlighting in this guide. At the time of writing, the area around the museum was being transformed into a much larger heritage attraction due to open in 2024 ahead of the 200th anniversary of the Stockton & Darlington Railway (S&DR) – the first passenger line in the world.

At the current **Head of Steam museum**, just north of the town centre, visitors are transported to the age of steam travel on the route of the historic S&DR. Here, you can take in the wonderfully preserved station dating to the 1840s, still with its original footbridge, Victorian loos, booking office and platform, and several steam engines. Authentic railway posters, leather suitcases on trolleys and vintage signs are wonderfully evocative of the early days of railway travel.

Train buffs may also like to pay homage to Darlington's *Mallard* – a brick sculpture of the famous 1930s engine – unveiled in 1997 near the A66 made with 182,000 bricks. It's a bit odd and has received a fair amount of ridicule over the years but it holds some affection for locals these days. Access is from Morrisons supermarket in the Morton Park Industrial Estate.

123

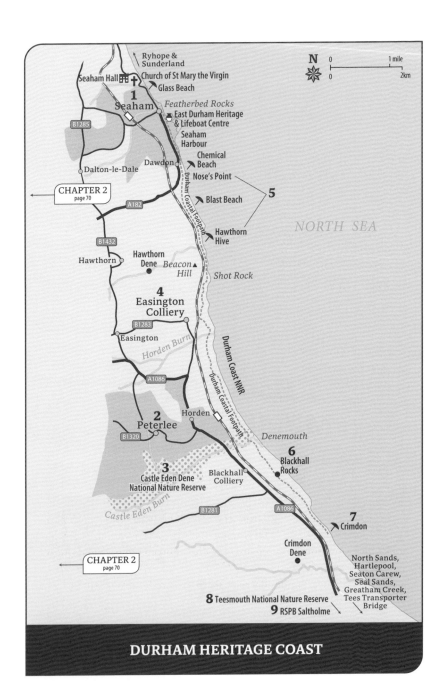

DURHAM HERITAGE COAST

3

DURHAM
HERITAGE COAST

Durham offers some of the most outstanding coastal scenery in the country: towering limestone cliffs draped in greenery above pebble-strewn shores; the luminous North Sea stretching to the horizon like a sheet of aluminium. On the cliff tops, wildflower meadows attract many butterflies and birds, but the most distinguishing features of Durham's coast between Sunderland and Hartlepool are the steeply sided wooded gorges or 'denes' formed by glacial meltwater eroding finger-like channels in the limestone escarpment. Now important refuges for rare plants and ancient trees, a network of paths allow walkers to explore these treasured nature reserves that open to the sea offering an unusual diversion away from the shoreline.

An 11-mile **coastal footpath** connects Seaham with Crimdon – the scope of this chapter – much of which passes through nature reserves. It's a challenging and exhilarating linear walk (though shorter, less strenuous circuits are possible) up and down the denes, across rare wildflower meadows and through saltmarshes on raised boardwalks but, for most of the way, walkers are elevated 100ft high on the clifftops, taking in the glinting North Sea and expansive views. Below, long, rolling waves cleanse the beaches; and with every tide, the sea steals more buried pieces of waste from the coal mines and glass works that once framed the headland, rounding the edges of hundred-year-old bricks and smoothing fragments of 19th-century coloured glass into beads for local craftspeople to work into jewellery.

'Eldon', 'Lumley', 'Londonderry' – the names of local pits still visible on bricks poking through the sand – are a striking reminder of the mining heritage of East Durham and the *Get Carter* (1971) days of the latter half of the 20th century when Durham's 'black beaches', as they were then known, were coated in colliery debris. Colliery villages developed along the coast with the opening of coal mines in the 19th century and while the housing stock has altered since the mines closed, the familiar utilitarian red-brick terraces stay true to their original design in places, particularly at **Easington Colliery**. Elsewhere, like at **Seaham** – a lively harbour town with many sea-fronting cafés, a popular promenade and plush spa hotel – the community seems to have moved on from its mining days, though relics are proudly displayed here and there. Commemorative pit wheels appear at Horden and Seaham, and the names of local bays and landmarks are hugely evocative of this heritage: Blast Beach, Shot Rock and Chemical Beach; but perhaps most poignant is the pit shaft cage on a hill at Easington Colliery. It stands alone facing the sea and is one of the most moving reminders of Durham's industrial legacy.

As for the blackened beaches, they were extensively cleaned over the course of a decade at the turn of the 21st century and are now a very special place for wildlife and people. Soft dunes and family-friendly **beaches** appear in a few places, at Seaham and Crimdon, but mostly visitors are drawn to Durham's coast for the clifftop walks across **flower meadows**. Where mines once stood, skylarks sing all spring long above grasslands coloured with bird's-foot trefoil, knapweed, small scabious, cowslips and several varieties of orchid. A butterfly count in summer could reach upwards of 15 species, perhaps including the rare Durham Argus (a local variety of the northern brown Argus). There are many reasons why this coastal strip is so wildlife rich, but in a large part it's down to geology, specifically the **magnesian limestone** at your feet – a

CLIFFTOP WILDFLOWER MEADOWS

Some 295 million years ago, a north–south reef stretched from the Tyne to the Tees inhabited by tropical sea creatures whose shells and skeletal remains accumulated over time to form a lime-rich mud on the seabed that hardened into limestone. This so called 'magnesian limestone' is what the grey-white cliffs and rock stacks you see all the way along Durham's coastal strip are made of and why this is such an important place for wildlife.

Where the rock breaks the surface it supports a lime-loving assemblage of plants including common rock rose, cowslip, wild marjoram, knapweeds, salad burnet, small scabious, bird's-foot trefoil, blue moor grass and several orchids (fragrant, pyramidal and bee). Also look out for the rare dark red helleborine. Particularly rewarding sites include **Blackhall Rocks** (page 147), **Hawthorn Meadows** (page 128), **Wingate Quarry** and **Cassop Vale** (both inland between the A1 and A19).

TOURIST INFORMATION

Though lacking in official tourist information offices, there are a few places to go for informal local advice, including the **East Durham Heritage & Lifeboat Centre** (page 132) at Seaham Harbour which is run by volunteers with a huge amount of knowledge of the area. Rangers at Castle Eden Dene's **Natural England offices** (Stanhope Chase, Peterlee SR8 1NJ ✆ 07584 144564) are similarly helpful.

habitat famed for its rare plants that is almost exclusively found on the Durham coast and nowhere else in Britain.

GETTING AROUND

Travelling to the coast from Durham city is straightforward by **car** (half an hour) with car parks dotted along the clifftops above all beaches and in coastal towns and villages. **Bus** services are somewhat limited: from Durham to Seaham takes an hour (Go Northeast service 65 Arriva 22, Durham–Seaham), and a few buses shuttle between villages described in this chapter, including Easington Colliery and Peterlee.

With **train** stations at Seaham and Horden (also Seaton Carew, Hartlepool and Sunderland), you'd think there'd be a direct service from Durham but unfortunately you have to go via Newcastle, a one-way trip of an hour. Where the stations come in useful is to facilitate the return leg of a linear coastal walk. **Seaham station** is at the north end of the coastal path, **Horden** roughly at the mid-way point, and **Hartlepool** just south of Crimdon not far from Hartlepool Marina.

Cycling along the coast is not as joyous as elsewhere in the county, despite long stretches on disused railway lines (the north–south NCN Route 1 makes use of railway paths but is mostly set far back from the sea). While there are short stretches of the coastal path you could easily cycle, it is not possible to ride the full 11 miles owing to steps up and down the denes.

WALKING

The 11-mile **Durham Coastal Footpath** (page 144) makes for a superb, albeit quite long, linear day walk (take a taxi for the return leg; see page 128), but there are plenty of shorter routes that can be tailored into a loop by walking on the clifftop coastal path one way and along the beach the other (facilitated by steps). A favourite circuit in the Seaham area is from **Nose's Point to Hawthorn Hive** (page 143), a four-mile round trip across National Trust wildflower grasslands, returning along Blast Beach or continue through Hawthorn Dene and return by bus from Hawthorn village. In the other direction (north) from Seaham Hall there's another beautiful return walk also of around four miles from **Glass Beach to Ryhope** on the outskirts of Sunderland and back via Ryhope Dene, again making use of the clifftop path and beach.

One of several wooded gorges on the coast, **Castle Eden Dene** (see page 137) offers several miles of enchanting woodland walks in this beautiful National Nature Reserve well-known for its rare plants and ancient trees. Combined with a hike to nearby **Blackhall Rocks** and its grassland nature reserve, this is the ultimate Durham coast route for variety of scenery – a walk of five miles return.

TAXIS

These are all friendly taxi firms, mainly based in Seaham but they will transport you right along the coast and further afield. A trip from Crimdon to Seaham (for the return leg of the coastal walk) will cost just under £20.

COASTAL HIGHLIGHTS

Pebbles and beachcoming: Blast Beach (south of Seaham) and Glass Beach (north end of Seaham).

Rock pooling: Rocky shores feature at the ends of bays right along the coast but some of the best are at Blackhall Rocks, Featherbed Rocks (by Seaham Harbour) and Nose's Point (south of Seaham).

Sand dunes: Crimdon and Seaton Carew (Hartlepool).

Sandy beaches & swimming: Crimdon and Seaham Marina in the shelter of the North Pier.

Wildflowers and butterflies: Hawthorn Meadows (clifftop grasslands either side of Hawthorn Dene), Hawthorn Hive bay and Blackhall Rocks nature reserve. Cassop Vale and Thrislington National Nature Reserves (NNRs), around ten miles inland are also special reserves.

Woodland: Castle Eden Dene, Crimdon Dene and Hawthorn Dene.

Blueline Taxis Peterlee & Hartlepool ✆ 0191 5865737
Hamlet Taxis Seaham ✆ 0191 5811652 ♿
Jaffa's Taxis Seaham ✆ 0191 5814569
Kileys Taxis Seaham ✆ 0191 5816708
Seaham Taxis ✆ 0191 5816143

SEAHAM & SURROUNDS

🏠 **No.16** (page 309), **Seaham Hall** (page 310)

The most northerly town on Durham's coast, six miles south of Sunderland, Seaham pulls in the crowds with its lively mix of sea-facing cafés, beaches and promenade focused on and above the harbour area.

Take a short stroll north out of town and you'll reach **Seaham Hall**, an impressive Georgian mansion (now a hotel) and Anglo-Saxon treasure, church of St Mary's. Together these buildings tell the story of Seaham's beginnings and provide a pleasant retreat from the bustle around the harbour. Below Seaham Hall is **Glass Beach**, so named for its pearls of sea glass buried in the sand. Collecting these little wave-worn jewels is a local obsession and I urge anyone visiting the area to head down to the beach first thing in the morning to join in the beachcombing.

Seaham merges into Dawdon at its southern end where the first of Durham's stunning clifftop meadows is encountered on the coastal footpath. A walk from **Nose's Point** to local beauty spot **Hawthorn Hive** comes highly recommended (page 143).

1 SEAHAM

> Upon this dreary coast, we have nothing but country meetings and shipwrecks; and I have this day dined upon fish, which probably dined upon the crews of several colliers lost in the late gales.
>
> From a letter penned by Lord Byron during his year-long stay in Seaham Hall in 1815

Seaham is the most-visited destination on the Heritage Coast, enticing locals and holidaymakers to its beaches, historic marina, spa hotel and unpretentious run of bistros, chip shops and ice-cream parlours. While the lively seafront lacks the Victorian grandeur of seaside holiday resorts elsewhere on the northeast coast, Seaham does boast a scattering of historic buildings – and much natural architecture in the form of limestone rock stacks, cliffs and caves.

Old Seaham

Farming communities likely inhabited this area from the Bronze Age and the Romans almost certainly settled here but little remains from this time except for pieces of pottery and coins found over the years and some Roman stones in the walls of **St Mary the Virgin Church** (Church Ln, SR7 7AF ☉ summer Wed & Sat), a wonderful Anglo-Saxon church at the north end of Seaham. Access is from the B1287 coast road but you can walk from North Beach Car Park or Seaham Hall hotel by crossing a meadow. It is one of only a small number of pre-Viking churches in the country and well worth seeking out. Its long nave and chancel and embattled tower have changed over the centuries but much of the nave's masonry is 8th century, as too are some of the windows. The chancel and west tower were added in the 13th century.

A short walk from St Mary's is the exclusive **Seaham Hall hotel**, built in the late 18th century as a family home and boasting a fine Georgian frontage with four Tuscan columns supporting a porch. It is best known for its connection to the poet **Lord Byron** who married the daughter of the estate's owner, Anne Isabella Milbanke, in the drawing room of Seaham Hall in 1815. Their union was short-lived they had one child, the pioneering computer programmer, Ada Lovelace. The Byron legacy is celebrated in the town with various places bearing his name and a commemorative statue of the couple (pointedly facing away from each other) by the Byron Place shopping centre opposite the harbour.

Seaham Harbour

Seaham Hall was sold to the Londonderry family in 1821, a pivotal moment for the estate and the wider area which was rapidly expanding from the small community around its Anglo-Saxon church into a thriving town built around a new port, a mile south of the church, becoming the harbour town you see today. Financed by Irish nobleman, Charles William Vane (who took his wealthy wife's name and later became the 3rd Marquess of Londonderry), the first shipment of coal from nearby mines departed his docks in 1831 (to much fanfare) signalling a new era for Seaham.

---

1 The beach at Seaham. **2** The *George Elmy* lifeboat. **3** Sculpture of World War I soldier, 'Tommy'. **4** Chemical Beach. **5** A beachcombing haul from North Beach (also known as Glass Beach). ▶

VISIT COUNTY DURHAM

VISIT COUNTY DURHAM

DAVE HEAD/S

VISIT COUNTY DURHAM

Industrial output from nearby coal mines, glass bottle works and iron foundries accelerated, facilitated by the new railways that allowed larger quantities of minerals to be shipped out of the port. Incidentally, the South Hetton to Seaham line, which opened in 1833, was one of the very first railways in the world and the impact it had on the town cannot be understated. Staithes enabled coal wagons to efficiently tip their load onto waiting colliers in the harbour below, thus increasing exports from nearby mines. Today, a small colony of kittiwakes use the surviving wooden struts as nesting ledges but if you want to get a better idea of what the docks used to look like, the wonderful **East Durham Heritage & Lifeboat Centre** (Seaham Harbour Marina, SR7 7EE ☉ Apr–Oct 10.30–15.30 Thu–Sun; Nov–Mar from 11.00) in the harbour displays a few black and white historical photos, among other artefacts relating to Seaham's industries. Run by volunteers, the heritage centre's flagship attraction is the *George Elmy* **lifeboat**. The tragic history of the vessel, its loss in the 1960s and eventual discovery on eBay in 2009 (page 134) is an engaging saga fondly recounted by staff.

The harbour area serves a very different public today to during its industrial heyday and you'll find the cafés and gift shops around the lifeboat heritage centre overlooking the **marina** are thronged with visitors at the weekend. A **watersports activity centre**, Adventure Access, operates from behind the lifeboat museum (☏ 0191 5814391 ⌘ adventureaccess.co.uk) offering paddleboarding and kayaking sessions for children and adults, and there's an early morning open-water swimming scene from the **beach** below the North Pier that is also popular with families.

"On the nearby green by the promenade is a rather moving modern sculpture of a World War I soldier by a local sculptor."

On the clifftop above the harbour is the **Londonderry Office** building, once the headquarters of the Marquess' mines and railways, which remains the centrepiece building in the heart of Seaham with its prominent clock tower and bronze statue of the Marquess of Londonderry. On the nearby green by the promenade is a rather moving modern sculpture of a World War I soldier by local sculptor Ray Lonsdale, known simply as '**Tommy**' and, opposite, North Terrace with its mix of bistros, shops and take-aways.

Gone are all the heavy industries that once fuelled the local economy but they survive in the memories of local people, many of whom worked in the coal mines until their closure in the late 1980s and early 1990s, and those related to the 190 men killed in two explosions at Seaham Colliery in the late 19th century; and of course in the striking place names: Glass Beach, Chemical Beach and Blast Beach, all of which are easily reached on foot by following the clifftop promenade south out of town.

Seaham's beaches

Within a short walk of St Mary the Virgin Church at the north end of Seaham is **Glass Beach** (reached from North Shore car park off the B1287), famous for its pearls of sea glass – a reminder that Seaham was the largest glass bottle manufacturer in Britain between the mid-1800s and 1921. On sunny weekend mornings, locals go beachcombing for these tiny fragments of frosted waste glass glinting in the sand in many different shades of blue, green, clear and amber. It's obvious who are the treasure seekers: they're the ones walking heads down, slowly meandering across the beach, pausing every now and then to extract beads from the sand. When I visited at nine o'clock in the morning there were already at least a hundred or so people collecting these glass jewels – a highly addictive pastime, as I found out. 'This is nothing,' a local lady with her grandson told me, 'in a few hours, this beach will be heaving.'

Glass Beach, as it is known to many – though officially it's North Beach – is famous for its 'multies' containing several shades in one piece. You can scour the beach simply by searching with your eyes but I was told

BUTTERFLIES

Butterflies thrive in Durham's coastal grasslands because of the variety of flowering plants; on warm summer days, the keen-eyed may spot up to 15 species. Red admiral, peacock, ringlet, meadow brown and common blue are relatively abundant during the summer, but you may also see scarcer butterflies like the small copper, large and small skipper or even the rare Durham Argus, a locally endemic subspecies of the northern brown Argus, because it is found on the county's magnesian limestone grasslands and nowhere else; the caterpillars exclusively feed on rock rose, which grows extensively over the cliffs. Look for a small brown butterfly with orange spots around the edges of its wings and a white border. Hawthorn Hive and the clifftop meadows hereabouts are reliably good spots for a butterfly hunt.

the best technique is to shift the sand with your foot to reveal beads hidden below the surface. Local jewellery makers work the glass into necklaces, rings and bracelets to sell online (see ⊘ seahamwaves.co.uk for example). It's not just glass fragments that will fill your pockets, however, this beach also has an array of coloured pebbles: sandstone, granite, limestone, shale and whinstone are just some of the stones you may find.

Just north of Seaham Harbour is **Featherbed Rocks**, a favourite bay to go rock pooling at low tide but also with lots of sand for bucket

LOST AT SEA: THE *GEORGE ELMY* LIFEBOAT

'It was a Sunday evening and I was searching on eBay for things relating to Seaham,' recounts Brian Scollen, a local heritage enthusiast and one of the founders of the East Durham Heritage & Lifeboat Centre in Seaham harbour (page 132). His search under the word 'Seaham' would often throw up artefacts, old photographs and so on, but on this occasion, a fishing boat was pictured for sale described as the 'George Emily' [sic]. 'I couldn't believe it,' says Brian, who immediately recognised it as Seaham's old lifeboat. He contacted the seller who verified the boatmaker's stamp, 'G & G 504', on the bow, which unequivocally identified it as the *George Elmy*, lost for over half a century following a tragic mission to save the crew of a fishing coble one Saturday afternoon in 1962.

Having initially rescued four men and one nine-year-old boy from the stricken fishing boat, the five-man RNLI crew and five passengers attempted to return to Seaham harbour, the lifeboat battling against a fierce sea; close to the harbour entrance, however, the *George Elmy* capsized. Lifeboats from Sunderland and Hartlepool, a search plane and hundreds of locals came to help, but all those on board were lost except for one fisherman who survived by clinging to the upturned hull.

The *George Elmy* was extensively damaged and little is known about what happened to her in the years following the disaster until she re-entered service with the RNLI in Poole on the south coast; she was then decommissioned in 1972 and became a fishing boat (changing her name multiple times in the process: *Gabrielle*, *Samantha*, *Ellen Louise* and then *Miza* – the latter the name that Brian saw for sale on eBay). With local support, funds were secured to purchase the *George Elmy*, which returned to Seaham in May 2009 before undergoing restoration on the Tyne by a well-known traditional boat restorer, Fred Crowell at South Shields. Four years later, on 23 June 2013, the gleaming lifeboat, with a new mahogany cabin, motored home to Seaham to a rapturous welcome. She's now brought out on Seaham Lifeboat Day in late June, but for most of the year the *George Elmy* is on display in the 1870 boathouse, now wonderfully renovated to house a little museum.

and spade fun. Sandy bays are a rare sight on the Durham coast so the little bay called **North Pier** beach, between Featherbed Rocks and the marina, is one of the most popular places for families and swimmers.

🍴 FOOD & DRINK

The main coast road through Seaham becomes North Terrace above the harbour where a long strip of cafés, restaurants, take-aways and ice-cream shops draw the crowds at the weekend. A lively hub of bistros is centred around the marina and lifeboat heritage centre. For fine dining, your best bet is **Seaham Hall hotel** (Lord Byron's Walk, SR7 7AG ✆ 0191 5161400 ♿) both for its Ozone Asian restaurant in the spa and plush Dining Room in the Georgian hotel. A quiet bar and lounge is also open to non-guests, serving drinks, sandwiches and bowls of chips in modern surroundings.

Clean Bean Restaurant & Bar 22 North Tce, SR7 7EU ✆ 0191 4474748 ◷ 09.00–16.00 Sun–Thu, 09.00–22.00 Fri & Sat. A modern restaurant with a select menu of international dishes: all day traditional English and vegan breakfasts; mussels and sourdough, steak sandwiches, Mexican tacos, Japanese noodles, curry and Sunday lunch (usual meat roast plus a nut roast) later in the day.

Downey's 5 North Tce, SR7 7EU ✆ 0191 5130213 ◷ 11.00–20.00 Mon–Sat, 11.00–17.00 Sun. One of the most popular fish and chip restaurants in Seaham. Dine inside or take your food to the green opposite.

Flamingo Café Seaham Harbour (behind the lifeboat heritage centre), SR7 7EE ✆ 07399 067840 ◷ 10.00–14.00 Mon & Tue, 10.00–15.00 Wed–Sun. Youthful vibe and sought-after tables on a sunny terrace above one of Seaham's rocky beaches and next to the activity centre. It's all very wholesome, chic (and pink) in here and you'll find a lot of avocado, oats, tofu, edamame, seeds, nuts and eggs on the extensive (and not inexpensive) breakfast and lunch menu – a nourishing array of fancy sandwiches, protein shakes, bowls of granola, porridge and salads. There's a special 'pups' menu for dogs.

The Lamp Room 20 North Tce, SR7 7EU ✆ 0191 9033797 ◷ 09.00–16.00 daily, plus 17.00–21.00 Thu, Fri & Sat ♿. When choosing a location for breakfast one morning, this modern place on the sea-facing road through the centre of Seaham caught my eye largely because it was packed, the coffee looked strong and the breakfasts a stomach-filling plate of quality items (chunky sourdough bread, on the vine tomatoes, local black pudding and bacon). Eggs Benedict lovers will appreciate the multiple varieties on offer, including the tempting Miners Benedict (poached eggs on sourdough with black pudding and parma ham). The lunch and dinner menu is a dizzying selection of seafood, burger, salad and posh sandwich options with the addition of tapas and a lobster menu in the evenings. And let's not forget Sunday lunches.

Lickety Split 13 North Tce ✆ 0191 5810719 ◷ 11.00–17.00 Mon–Fri, 10.00–18.00 Sat & Sun. There's no shortage of places to pick up a cone or lolly in Seaham, but this diner-themed café specialising in sundaes and shakes has the most extensive menu. Their signature namesake sundae contains five scoops of ice cream, bananas and Amarena cherries, dribbled with toffee and chocolate sauce or you could try Chocolate Overload (does what it says on the tin) or Chantilly Glace, made with Durham clotted cream ice cream.

PETERLEE & EASINGTON COLLIERY

⋀ **The Barn at Easington** (page 310)

The sprawling modern town of **Peterlee** and the red-brick terraces of **Easington Colliery** will in all honesty hold little appeal for anyone visiting the Durham coast, but they do have places of historical and nature interest worthy of a diversion including Peterlee's *Apollo Pavilion*, the enchanting **Castle Eden Dene National Nature Reserve** and Easington Colliery's wildflower grasslands, mining memorials and monuments. Visit on a Sunday evening – rehearsal night for the Easington Colliery Brass Band – and you might just hear the musicians' wonderful tunes on the wind as you approach the village from the coastal path. There can be few more stirring experiences on this coast.

2 PETERLEE & THE *APOLLO PAVILION*

Let us, therefore, close our eyes on the nineteenth century degradation and squalor, and let us only look with unseeing eyes on the sordid excrescence of the first decade of this century, let us blind ourselves to the septic and ugly building wens and ribbons perpetrated and planted on us between the wars, but let us open our eyes and look brightly forward and onward to the new town, the new living... Peterlee.
C W Clarke, *Farewell Squalor*, 1946

There are few compelling reasons to visit Peterlee – a busy modern town built between the 1950s and 70s with a shopping centre and several supermarkets at its concrete heart. The Krankies used to live here. You won't find any remnants of a quaint older village, no views of the coast nor even of beautiful Castle Eden Dene Nature Reserve (see opposite), which ribbons along the southern edge of the town. So why visit? Well, it turns out that Peterlee, named after a celebrated local miner and trade union leader, Peter Lee, has a fascinating story to tell of post-war urban planning and Corbusier-inspired design with one architectural jewel worth visiting: the *Apollo Pavilion*. Described by English Heritage as 'an absolutely unique work of considerable international importance', those with even a passing interest in modern design will find a diversion to this Brutalist piece of public art in a housing estate worthwhile.

Apollo Pavilion

Oakerside Dr, Peterlee SR8 1LE ☉ 24hr

Part sculpture, part bridge, the Grade II-listed *Apollo Pavilion* spans a small lake forming the centrepiece of the Sunny Blunts housing estate in Peterlee. Built by abstract artist Victor Pasmore at the time of the first moon landing in the summer of 1969, he hoped the concrete walkway would provide an 'emotional centre' to the estate, a place in 'which to walk, in which to linger and on which to play'.

Clearly Brutalist in its aesthetic, the *Apollo* has attracted a predictable amount of controversy over the years and, for a long time, stood vandalised, its murals covered by spray paint; many called for its demolition. 'All people here think of the pavilion is that it is a heap of dirty, slimy concrete covered in graffiti which youths climb up to have sex on, and from which to urinate on passers-by. It should be destroyed and forgotten about, not preserved.' So argued one local councillor who reached out to Prince Charles and even begged the army to blow it up. 'No way' was the response of English Heritage who listed the artwork in 2011 following its restoration. There was no graffiti when I visited and children were enjoying the sculpture and running across its walkway in exactly the way Pasmore had intended.

"Part sculpture, part bridge, the Apollo Pavilion *spans a small lake forming the centrepiece of the Sunny Blunts housing estate."*

3 CASTLE EDEN DENE NATIONAL NATURE RESERVE

Car park: Stanhope Chase, SR8 1NJ; the dene is signed off the Durham Way ✆ 07584 144564

Wooded ravines, called 'denes' and 'gills' appear at intervals along Durham's coast as a result of glacial erosion ten thousand years ago, but nowhere has the limestone eroded quite so deeply and scenically than at Castle Eden Dene – a 3½-mile-long wooded gorge along the southern edge of Peterlee. Dense pockets of ancient yews make some parts feel dark and enchanting; elsewhere foliage cascades from

limestone walls towering over a burn that has carved a sinuous route to meet the sea at **Denemouth**. You can enter the reserve at this point from the Durham Coastal Footpath by passing, rather wonderfully, under a ten-arched **viaduct**; otherwise, there are a few access points from Peterlee including a car park by the Natural England offices and café (see address above).

Some 300 varieties of flowering **plants** grow in this Site of Special Scientific Interest including a few colonies of herb paris (a low-lying plant with a solitary purple flower surrounded by long pointed green petals) as well as 150 species of mosses and liverworts. They sprout from fissures in the limestone and clothe the boughs of old broadleaved trees that have been a part of this extraordinary landscape for a very long time. Indeed, Castle Eden is said to be the largest remaining semi-natural woodland in North East England. Some of the venerable **yew trees** in the gorge – of which there are an astonishing number – started life during Saxon times if not earlier. We know this because the Saxons called the gorge 'Yoden' meaning Yew Dene (a word that lives on in a number of local street names and as a fish and chip shop in Peterlee) – and because of the sheer girth of the oldest specimens.

Spring is a rewarding time to visit, when wood anemones, bluebells, violets and swathes of wild garlic are in bloom. A single specimen of Britain's rarest plant, the lady's slipper orchid, grew here until one day in 1926 when a policeman plucked its only flower and gave it to a young woman studying botany.

"Spring is a rewarding time to visit, when wood anemones, bluebells, violets and swathes of wild garlic are in bloom."

Castle Eden Dene was privately owned for 250 years (until the 1940s) by the Burdon family who lived in the nearby manor house (or 'castle'), built in the latter half of the 18th century, and used the dene to entertain visitors. That explains the grottos, ornamental shrubs, old footbridges and the wide paths once used by carriages carrying finely dressed day trippers. If you are imagining a romantic 18th-century woodland garden, you're on the right lines: it's all hugely atmospheric and ripe for folklore. Legends abound in Castle Eden, hence all the curious names including Devil's Lapstone, Pegjellima's Cave and Bruce's Ladder. One involves a man called Gunner who broke a pact he had

◀ **1** *Apollo Pavilion*, Peterlee. **2** Castle Eden Dene NNR. **3** The red-brick terraces of Easington Colliery.

FAREWELL SQUALOR

There was no escape... It was coal all the time
C W Clarke, *Farewell Squalor*, 1946

Peterlee was founded in response to a post-war council report titled 'Farewell Squalor' which envisioned a new, modern town for miners that would alleviate overcrowding and break with the traditional 19th-century pit village design with their neat rows of red brick terraced houses and Aged Miners' bungalows. To this end Berthold Lubetkin, a pioneering modernist architect (of London Zoo's Penguin House fame), was instructed as chief planner. His utopian Corbusier-inspired vision for Peterlee looked skywards – to high-rise tower blocks, recreational areas and, yes, even a zoo – but his plan was rejected by the National Coal Board and Lubetkin departed the project with Peterlee leaders fearing their bold dream for the future of east Durham would result in the 'descent from the spectacular to the nondescript'.

In 1955 Victor Pasmore, a pioneering abstract artist, joined the Peterlee development board. His brief was simple: 'do what you like but don't do what we have done before'. His influence in Peterlee is felt today in the layout of housing areas connected by pedestrian walkways and fluid grasslands, and the Cubist design of houses: flat roofs, large windows, and timber and concrete detailing. Though the housing stock has changed in places and many homes now have pitched roofs, you get a strong sense of his artistry, particularly in the Sunny Blunts estate which holds at its centre the *Apollo Pavilion* (page 137).

made with the devil. His corpse was found in an eerily dark pool under an iron bridge that bears his name to this day.

Castle Eden Castle is a privately owned Georgian mansion on the southern edge of the woods (glimpsed through trees) whose drive connects with the old village of Castle Eden (signed off the B1281 west of Hesleden). Though just a single road, known simply as **The Village**, the facing rows of cottages make for a picturesque diversion. Not far beyond the houses, through open land, the prominent lead spire of **St James's Church** appears above the canopy. It dates to 1764 but note the medieval masonry in its west-end walls and tower.

¶¶ FOOD & DRINK

Café in the Dene Oakerside Tea Rooms 1 Stanhope Chase, SR8 1NJ ⊙ 10.00–16.00 daily ₺. Convenient café (and toilets) by the Castle Eden Dene car park in Peterlee, offering a small selection of hot and cold food including fish fingers, scones, cakes and hot drinks. Sunny outdoor seating area to the rear. One entrance to the dene is a few steps from the café.

Castle Eden Inn Stockton Rd, TS27 4SD ✆ 01429 800287 ◷ noon–20.30 daily. Popular family friendly old inn south of the National Nature Reserve serving decent pub food: roast meat and veg, steaks, fish and chips, burgers, pasta dishes and so on.

4 EASINGTON COLLIERY

Along the Durham coast you will find reminders here and there of the region's industrial heritage – memorials to pit disasters; winding wheels; sculptures; remembrance gardens; murals – but at **Easington Colliery** it feels as though entire parts of the village are the monument with terraces arranged in a grid design (the streets are divided into blocks and all begin with the same letter), houses with plain frontages, back lanes and the odd coal shed standing in yards. Elsewhere in the village, pubs, schools, churches, shops and allotments were built to service the mining community. All these elements come together to make Easington Colliery very distinctly a Durham pit village.

From when coal was first drawn in 1910 and for the next 80 years, life revolved around the colliery, the working patterns of men (3,000 at the colliery's peak in the 1930s), many of whom were underground before the sun rose, and the women who toiled above ground, caring for children, cleaning clothes black with coal dust and ensuring food was on the table when their husbands returned home. Some had paid jobs too. To juggle this much was only possible with the help of neighbours and a sense of shared experience that bound mining families together.

"When Easington Colliery closed in 1993, 1,400 men lost their jobs – almost an entire community out of work at the same time."

When Easington Colliery closed in 1993, 1,400 men lost their jobs – almost an entire community out of work at the same time. I once got chatting to an elderly ex-miner who told me about working in water up to his knees every day. I asked what he did after the mine closed, to which he replied with a grin 'I took early retirement'. You can imagine the impact on the whole of this area when one by one the collieries closed, and it is no surprise that walking round the streets today, a number of properties are boarded up. Victorian terraced houses sell for £30,000.

On the corner of Crawlaw Avenue and Ashton Street, the old colliery pay office (Easington's only remaining colliery building) now houses the **Easington Colliery Brass Band**. It looks out over the coalfield itself at the north end of Office Street and it is here that the band meet on Wednesday and Sunday evenings from 19.30 (you can pop in if you want to see them perform or just listen from outside). On four days of the week, the building operates a community café (see opposite). If you follow a footpath north across the coalfield (signed from Crawlaw Avenue) after ten minutes or so you'll come to the site of a mine shaft where one of the most poignant monuments to those men who worked – and died – extracting coal hundreds of feet below ground now stands. The lone steel **pit shaft cage** (a lift shaft) faces the sea on a hill and has become a landmark on the coastal trail. It is deeply moving. **Wildflower grasslands** (now a local nature reserve) surround the site that affords broad views of the sea and coastline. You can also park in the Easington Colliery Coastal car park, accessed off Crawlaw Avenue.

THE EASINGTON COLLIERY PIT DISASTER

The Queen and I have learnt with the deepest distress of the explosion at Easington Colliery and of the severe loss of life there. We send our heartfelt sympathy to all those who have lost husbands or sons. — George R

All colliery villages experienced the trauma of losing men underground, and Easington Colliery was no exception. A look through lists compiled by the Durham Mining Museum of deaths at Easington pit reveal the names of 181 men – and boys – who died from when the first pit was sunk in 1899 to 1993 when the colliery closed. Among the scores of young, middle-aged and elderly miners crushed by machinery or buried under falls of stones, are the following entries registering the deaths of some of the youngest: 'Elliot, Arthur, 20 May 1953, aged 15, head caught by lift cage'; 'Mackin, Thomas, 18 Mar 1927, aged 14, Landing Lad, fall from rope'; 'Turner, George G., 03 Oct 1929, aged 15, Engine Lad, wrapped around the winder'.

Most names, however, are suffixed by '29 May 1951, 4.35am' – the date and time of one of the worst pit disasters in Durham's history when sparks from a cutting machine ignited gas in one of the seams, causing an explosion that entombed 81 men 900ft uderground. Two rescuers also died. A Grade II-listed stone carving of a miner carrying a Davy lamp commemorates the tragedy in a remembrance garden within **Easington Colliery Cemetery** (main entrance on Crawlaw Road, SR8 3LP), where most of those killed are buried: the majority were young men in their twenties but some were elderly men, including the oldest, Frederick Ernest Jepson, aged 68. Miners' lamps, a coal cutter machine, picks and a coal wagon also feature in the garden.

Inland from Easington Colliery is the old village of **Easington** which is worth visiting on your way to or from the coast to see **St Mary's Church** on the main road, Hall Walks (the B1283). For the most part, the church is Early English dating to the 13th century, but the tower is Norman. Internally there's a fair amount of 17th-century woodwork but note too the Frosterley marble in places. On the other side of the main road is a striking limewashed manor called **Seaton Holme**, the former retirement home a Durham bishop and also medieval in origin.

¶¶ FOOD & DRINK

Pay Note Café 1 Ashton St, SR8 3QQ ✆ 07369 234847 ⊙ 10.00–14.00 Mon, Tue, Thur & Fri. Housed in the old colliery pay office on the corner of Aston Street and Crawlaw Avenue, about 500yds from the coastal footpath, this simple, modern and inexpensive café is a welcome sight for anyone visiting Easington Colliery or walking along the clifftop. Breakfasts cost under £5 and sandwiches and toasties are a couple of pounds.

DURHAM COAST NATIONAL NATURE RESERVES

Dunescapes feature along Durham's coast, notably between Crimdon and Hartlepool Headland, but what makes the county's seaboard really special is less to do with sand and more to do with rock, specifically the magnesian limestone that forms the towering cliffs and deep gorges or 'denes' for which this coast is famed. On the clifftops, the meadows supported by this unusual outcrop are fantastically species rich and host an array of insects and a large population of skylarks. The most special reserves are found between Dawdon's Nose's Point and Crimdon – the area described here. For Castle Eden Dene NNR, see page 137.

5 NOSE'S POINT TO HAWTHORN HIVE

A mile south of Seaham at Dawdon are two beaches, **Blast Beach** and **Chemical Beach**, separated by the well-known headland, **Nose's Point**. Now under the care of the National Trust, their names recall the chemical and iron industries (where there were 'blast' furnaces) that once prospered here and, along with Dawdon Colliery, blighted the beaches with spoil before a mammoth five-year clean-up operation in the late 1990s. The once industrial landscape provided the eerie backdrop to the opening scenes in the film *Alien 3* (1992), but it's a very

THE DURHAM COASTAL FOOTPATH

Well-signed along its entire 11-mile length, the **Durham Coastal Footpath** from Crimdon to Seaham ribbons along a grassy, windswept headland, mostly across nature reserves. The path is up and down much of the way on account of all the rivulets and denes that are so prevalent along the Durham coast; some you can skirt round, but others involve a hike down to the shore and back up the other side. The route is easy to navigate, however, and could be done in walking shoes or trainers. You can start your walk at either end (I recommend walking north for the promise of fish and chips in Seaham, but you can also pick up food in the sea-facing car park café at Crimdon). The start and end points of the trail, as well as the villages in between, are serviced by buses from Hartlepool, Durham and Sunderland but you can also arrange for a taxi pickup at Seaham (page 128).

At **Crimdon**, butter-coloured dunes slope gently on to the beach where children play in the summer months and throw pebbles into the sea. In the 1920s Crimdon was a well-known holiday spot, as the information boards tell you. As you walk north, the beach becomes rockier and there are good places to search for sea creatures in the many pools.

Blackhall Rocks Nature Reserve (page 147) is a mile ahead and another well-known spot to go rock pooling. Treasure hunters will find much to interest on the shore but you can also walk along the clifftop path to take in the botanically-rich grasslands. *Get Carter* fans may want to hunt around for the remains of the colliery conveyor featured in the end scenes of the film (a long channel is what you're looking for, north of Blue House Gill at ♥ NZ463399).

The headland path continues past some allotments and descends to **Denemouth** beach at the opening of the **Castle Eden Dene National Nature Reserve** (page 137). A walkway leads across the mouth of the gorge by a reedbed and under the arches of an early 20th-century viaduct. The beach here is not so appealing as elsewhere on the Durham coast and you'll notice if you walk to the shore that a compacted shelf of stones, coal fragments and bricks with the names

different place today, albeit still with a noticeable 'shelf' of compacted stones and spoil. Towering above the pebbly sands are the cream-coloured limestone cliffs, rock stacks and wildflower grasslands that make Durham's coast so distinctive. Fulmars and kittiwakes nest on rocky ledges during the summer months and from May to August the meadows on the clifftop are filled with buttercups, clovers and grasses with the odd flush of orchids here and there; spring skies tinkle with the song of skylarks.

A circular **walk** of around four miles from Nose's Point (where there's a car park) to Hawthorn Hive and back via Blast Beach takes of local collieries runs the length of the bay. Over time, this ridge will erode away and eventually the sea water will reach higher up the shore, restoring the marshland habitat.

Back on the headland, press on to **Horden** – once a popular spot for bathers and daytrippers in the early 20th century before one of the biggest coal pits in the country was sunk here. There are some beautiful meadows close to the coastal footpath. On the cliffs note the rock rose (yellow flowers) and bloody cranesbill (purple) flowering in many parts. You may also see orchids.

Scenes in *Billy Elliot* were filmed in **Easington Colliery** (page 141), a couple of miles ahead. If you detour off the coastal path to the village, you may recognise the red-brick terraces and back lanes from the fictional village of 'Everington' in the 2000 film. Continuing north along the path, a footpath off to the left (over the railway line) enables access to the stunning grasslands and coastal views from the high vantage point of **Beacon Hill** (the coast path itself skirts round the hill, beyond Shot Rock).

For the next mile, the footpath stays close to the railway line before descending into **Hawthorn Dene**, a wooded gorge with ancient ash and oak trees, as well as two lime kilns. In early spring the ground under the railway viaduct is covered with ramsons that scent the air with garlic as you walk. Bluebells fill the gorge in April. **Hawthorn Hive** (page 147) is a rocky cove at the mouth of the dene with caverns and wildflowers growing from the cliffs in abundance in summer.

The final leg of the coast path continues along the clifftop, skirting more meadows and with views of **Blast Beach** (page 143) below. An alternative route is to walk the length of Blast Beach using the steps at its southern end but the walk along the shore is tiresome because of all the stones and it's a difficult climb back up to the headland at the northern end because of a steep, rocky bank.

Nose's Point (page 143) is a well-known vantage point between Blast Beach and Chemical Beach offering long views of the sea and coastline. Rock stacks are the last arresting coastal feature before you walk into **Seaham**.

in the best of the natural scenery and wildlife. You can walk one way across the National Trust clifftop grasslands and the other along the beach (access via steps) or stay on the headland, forming a circuit of sorts by walking both sides of the meadowlands. And don't become confused by all the paths across the headland – they all follow the same southbound trajectory and will lead you to **Hawthorn Dene**, a semi-ancient, wooded ravine with wildflower meadows managed by Durham Wildlife Trust. (An alternative return to Seaham is to walk through the dene to Hawthorn village and return by bus.) The woodland opens quite marvellously to the North Sea under the brick arches of **Hawthorn**

CETACEANS

Pods of bottle-nosed and white-beaked dolphins are fairly frequently sighted along the North East coast and Durham's headlands are a good vantage point from which to watch them swimming across the bays. You're most likely to see them in August, but May is a good time too. Lone harbour porpoises and minke whales occasionally make an appearance.

Viaduct. At its mouth is **Hawthorn Hive**, a beautiful bay with little caves formed in the limestone cliffs colonised by many butterflies and wildflowers. A little further on, set back from the clifftop, is **Beacon Hill**, the highest point on the coastal trail at 285ft above sea level.

6 BLACKHALL ROCKS

If you've seen the 1970s gangster film *Get Carter* starring Michael Caine, you might know that the coastal scenes were filmed hereabouts with Blackhall Colliery's aerial conveyor featuring memorably in the climactic closing shots (page 144). Round and round it goes, tipping huge bucket loads of pit waste on to the shores below. Durham's 'black beaches', as they were then known, are remarkably different today, however: skylarks sing all spring long and kestrels hover over the sloping limestone cliffs now dotted with cowslips and primroses. I once watched a barn owl working its way along the many folds in the Blackhall Rocks cliffs. Later in summer, the grassland **nature reserve** on the headland erupts into flower, drawing an astonishing variety of butterflies. From this expansive vantage point, it's worth scanning the sea for porpoises, dolphins (bottlenose and white-beaked) and minke whales, especially during May and August – the peak months for sightings.

Many visitors enjoy the views from the coastal path that winds its way along the headland, but the **shore** is easily accessed from Blackhall Rocks car park via a footpath and is well worth exploring to go rock pooling and see the many pits and caves formed in the limestone cliffs. Treasure hunters will find it hard to walk along the stone-strewn beach and ignore the many curious objects protruding from the sand: pebbles, worn colliery bricks and so on.

◀ **1** View across Blackhall Rocks. **2** Bottle-nosed dolphins can be seen along this stretch of coast.

7 CRIMDON

Photographs from the 1920s and 30s show Crimdon's sandy beach thronged with holidaymakers, its soft dunes dotted with little makeshift cabins where local families would enjoy some time off from colliery life. Today, you won't find quite as many people but the sands here are some of the most appealing on the whole of the Durham coast. Access to the beach is from a car park on the headland (just south of Crimdon Dene Holiday Park caravan site) where you can also pick up take-away food, teas and ices from a modern, purpose-built café (&)– and use the loos. Steps wind down the dunes to the shore.

"Today, you won't find quite as many people but the sands here are some of the most appealing on the whole of the Durham coast."

For a **walk** of a few miles, head south from the holiday park to the mouth of Crimdon's wooded dene. The **viaduct** spanning the limestone gorge was built in 1905. Cross a bridge then follow a path through a gate towards the trackbed of a disused railway, passing Crimdon House on your right. Pick up the disused railway line heading northwest; after just over a mile, strike off right through fields and ascend to Benridge Farm eventually meeting with Fillpoke Lane by Tweddle Children's Animal Farm. Turn right on to the lane for the final mile back to the caravan park.

TEESMOUTH & SURROUNDS

Far from the clifftop coastal meadows and colliery villages of Durham's coast and just south of Hartlepool's dunes is Teesmouth, an extraordinary flat expanse of wild grasslands and wetlands where nature flourishes amid one of the most heavily industrialised landscapes you will find along the English coast. Birds love it here, especially in autumn and winter when wildfowl and waders fill the lagoons and mudflats, and raptors patrol the skies. One of the best places to get up close to the birds is from the **RSPB Saltholme**'s bird hides on the north side of the Tees estuary and opposite the Tees Transporter Bridge, but if you want to see the area's population of seals, you'll need to head in the direction of **Seaton Carew** where the mammals rest along tidal inlets at low water.

1 The Tees Transporter Bridge. **2** Seal Sands is a great spot to see grey seals. **3** Teesmouth NNR. ▶

8 TEESMOUTH NATIONAL NATURE RESERVE

Framed by Hartlepool power station, oil refineries and a battalion of electricity pylons, this wetland nature reserve is not for everyone, yet it is fantastically rich in birdlife and wild in its own way. There's a rawness to the landscape that I'm drawn to, making this one of my favourite places to go wildlife watching on the North East coast. I've seen hares sprinting across the rough grasslands, short-eared owls on the hunt for voles, throngs of wading birds dabbling in the tidal creeks, seals hauled up on mud banks and peregrines ready to strike from overhead power lines.

Spread over 865 acres of grasslands, marshes and waterways, the reserve is split into two parts, divided by Hartlepool power station: Seal Sands and North Gare. **North Gare** offers easy access to the dunescape from its namesake car park and is reached by turning off the A178 on to North Gare Road (the car park site is behind the dunes at the end of the road). Look out for owls and hares in the undisturbed grasslands either side of the road, where you may also find marsh orchids during the summer. A walk along the sandy beach beyond the dunes is recommended throughout the year. A colony of little terns nests hereabouts; they are particularly vulnerable so keep dogs on leads in spring and summer.

Seal Sands is the area around Greatham Creek, about 1½ miles north of the RSPB's Saltholme reserve (see opposite). A good place to view the seals (at low tide) is where Seaton Carew Road (the A178) crosses the creek over a small bridge. You can also park in the Seal Sands car park, a few minutes' walk south of the creek, to access a viewing hide. Shelduck arrive here in large numbers during the winter, accompanied by teal and wigeon. Curlews, redshanks, lapwings and oystercatchers are also always nearby. Peregrine and merlin strike unexpectedly so keep a look out for those moments of panic when a pandemonium of wildfowl and waders take to the air.

Those curious to experience Teesmouth's industrial landscape (the same skyline that provided Ridley Scott with the inspiration for some of the dystopian scenes in *Blade Runner*), should follow the road signs for Seal Sands at a prominent roundabout less than half a mile north of RSPB Saltholme on the A178. Use your car as a wildlife hide as you drive along the loneliest of roads by the side of a ghostly railway line. Pipes trail through the grasslands for a few miles and spill out of swimming pool sized cylinders like spaghetti out of a pan. It is the strangest of places – and perfect for evening hare and raptor watching.

9 RSPB SALTHOLME

Seaton Carew Rd, TS2 1TU ℘ 01642 546625 ⊙ 09.30–17.00 daily ♿

On the north banks of the River Tees opposite Middlesbrough, this wonderful RSPB reserve with a visitor centre and café is a more accessible way to experience the area's wildlife than picking around the wider wetlands that fall within the Teesmouth National Nature Reserve. A rough path (gravelly in places but suitable for pushchairs and wheelchairs) provides rewarding views of a central lagoon and outlying wet grasslands that are thronged with birds throughout the year.

TEES TRANSPORTER BRIDGE

℘ 01642 727265 ⊘ teestransporterbridge.com

One of three remaining transporter bridges in Britain, the longest of the 11 surviving bridges of its type in the world and one of the great experiences of a jaunt into the industrial north, the Transporter Bridge just had to be mentioned in this book, despite its location in Middlesbrough. It is, however, very much a part of the landscape of Teesside and the Teesmouth and Saltholme nature reserves. If you are travelling north on the A1, you'll find it half hour drive east of Darlington, or a 15-minute walk north of Middlesbrough railway station.

The landmark Grade II-listed crossing, which carried its first passengers in 1911, has the appearance of two cranes facing each other with their brilliant blue arms meeting some 160ft above the middle of the Tees. Its cantilever construction allows a platform – or gondola – suspended by steel cables to efficiently cross the river without really restricting the movement of boats.

The journey is over too quickly (in just two minutes 30 seconds) but for 70p (£1.50 for those with cars) it is what you might call a cheap thrill.

In 1931, in the days before strict safety controls, my grandmother, aged 11, walked across the top of the bridge with her father. 'It was quite an event and I was very excited,' she told me. 'We climbed the staircase up the tower and then followed the walkway across the length of the bridge. When the platform below started moving across, the whole bridge shook and I thought I'd fall!' On reaching the other side, they returned to Middlesbrough in the conventional way which cost, she remembers, a penny. Today, a glass lift operates six times a day, providing access to the upper walkway where you can enjoy superb views. Note that, however, at the time of writing, the bridge was closed owing to lengthy ongoing restoration works; check the website for up-to-date details.

Winter sees the arrival of large numbers of shelduck, wigeon and teal, among other ducks, which join swelling flocks of lapwing, golden plover and curlews that are here from autumn. Just wait until a peregrine falcon or marsh harrier flies by and the whole grassland erupts with the wing beats of hundreds of birds. Late on winter afternoons, set yourself down in **Paddy's Pool hide** to watch the birds grazing greedily around the lake under the distant gaze of the Tees Transporter Bridge.

As the cold days lengthen, breeding common terns (one of the UK's largest populations) nest on the cockleshell islands created in the central pool in front of the visitor centre and sand martins return to nesting holes created in an artificial bank. You can view the birds coming and going from the visitor centre café. They will stay here throughout the spring and summer, along with lapwing, yellow wagtail (several pairs breed annually in surrounding meadows) and a number of other birds.

Tables for picnics can be found in a small sheltered **walled garden** planted by celebrity gardener Chris Beardshaw as a haven for butterflies and other invertebrates.

The award-winning Slow Travel series from Bradt Guides

**Over 20 regional guides across Britain.
See the full list at bradtguides.com/slowtravel.**

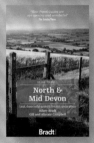

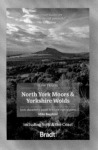

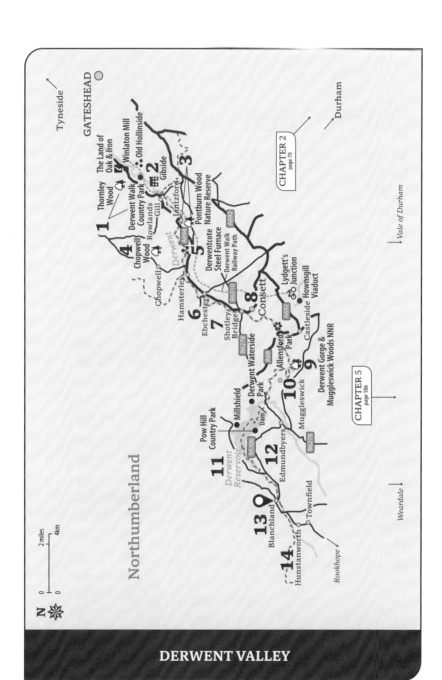

DERWENT VALLEY

154

4
DERWENT VALLEY

Thickly wooded along much of its 30-mile course to the Tyne, the beautiful River Derwent forms the Durham–Northumberland border and today is a place of recreation; a home to otters, red kites and ancient trees; and a community bound through history to its landscape: to iron, coal, wood and water.

From the 17th century, the Derwent countryside was transformed into a powerhouse of iron and steel production that lasted for the following 300 years. Even as recently as the 1980s, the belching steelwork chimneys and skies red with iron oxide above Consett formed a striking horizon visible for many miles around but, as elsewhere in Durham, the economy pivoted in the latter half of the 20th century and the furnaces, forges and mines closed one after another. Today those industries are evoked by a handful of relic buildings and in street names, public art, monuments and memories, but the woodlands are flourishing and the river still flows vigorously, a reminder of where the Derwent's industries began.

Rekindling interest in the region's industrial legacy today is **The Land of Oak & Iron** ($\mathit{\hat{\diamond}}$ landofoakandiron.org.uk), a valley-wide heritage project on the outskirts of Tyneside at Winlaton Mill, facilitating access to and appreciation of the Derwent's past. A modern visitor centre (page 156) serves as a good starting point for trips through the valley.

The **Derwent Walk Railway Path** is one of the best ways to explore this area; once it leaves behind the Tyneside fringes at Swalwell, the landscape becomes increasingly rural with former colliery villages appearing every few miles and then – rather wonderfully – the Derwent curls round the Georgian pleasure grounds of **Gibside**, a landmark National Trust property in the region.

Tree coverage increases on travelling upstream and westwards through the valley following the Derwent in the shadows of **Chopwell Wood**,

17th-century **Derwentcote Steel Furnace, Ebchester, Shotley Bridge** (of historic sword-making fame) and the one-time steel-manufacturing town of **Consett**. It is here we are most reminded that this whole area prospered not just because of its minerals, workforce and proximity to a powerful river, but because of the network of railways developed to transport raw materials and goods. Such is the extent of the coverage of these lines, now converted to leisure trails, that you can travel from Tyneside, through the Derwent Valley to many corners of Durham without crossing a single road. On the outskirts of Consett, four of these old railways converge at **Lydgett's Junction**.

West from Shotley Bridge, the landscape of the **Upper Derwent Valley** steps up a gear, becoming increasingly remote with some heavy moors and ancient woodland habitats, particularly at **Derwent Gorge** and **Muggleswick**. **Edmundbyers** is a lovely old village worthy of a break on your travels, perhaps on your way to **Derwent Reservoir** where the river swells to become one of the largest manmade lakes in the North East, enticing sailors, anglers, walkers, cyclists, wheelchair users and families who make good use of its perimeter mixed-use trail.

Historic **Blanchland** huddles under an amphitheatre of moors not far from the infant Derwent and, while the village itself sits on the Northumberland side of the border, it is included here for being simply one of the most alluring places in the whole of Derwentdale. 'No other spot brings me sweeter memories,' wrote the poet W H Auden of Blanchland.

---

i TOURIST INFORMATION

The Land of Oak & Iron Heritage Centre Winlaton Mill NE21 6RU ✆ 01207 524898 🖰 landofoakandiron.org.uk ◷ 09.00–16.00 daily 🔩. The Industrial Revolution is celebrated at this modern, purpose-built heritage centre, community space and café by the river in the Derwent Walk Country Park (accessible from the railway path or riverside footpath). Providing local information, maps, guides, history of the valley and leaflets, making this your first stop on travels in the Derwent Valley is a must.

Always busy with visitors and locals because of the lovely café with indoor seating and sheltered courtyard tables (plenty of grassy play areas for children too) and a lively calendar of events: folk music, bird walks, craft days. Live music and pizza nights on the last Friday of the month. Also see food & drink listing on page 160.

RAILWAY PATHS

Connecting Swalwell in Gateshead with Consett is the **Derwent Walk Railway Path** (page 160), a 12-mile former railway line providing easy access on two wheels to towns and villages in the Derwent Valley. Wide, flat and wooded for much of its length, the trail follows the course of the river, first travelling through the Derwent Walk Country Park with its colourful woodland canopy in autumn and spectacular views from the Nine Arches Viaduct before entering Durham around Rowlands Gill and Gibside. Westwards from here, the towns and villages along the southern edge of the Derwent come every few miles: Lintzford, Hamsterley Mill, Hamsterley, Ebchester, Shotley Bridge and finally Consett where the path terminates at **Lydgett's Junction**. At this important railway junction, an array of signs point in all directions along more old trackbeds: the **Waskerley Way** (page 173), **Lanchester Valley Railway Path** (page 85) and the **Consett & Sunderland Railway Path**; this is also an important intersection for the **Coast-to-Coast cycleway**. The question, really, is where next? Sunderland, Weardale or Durham city?

GETTING AROUND

Travel through the Derwent Valley from the east is quick and straightforward as far as Consett, but as the scenery becomes more remote, the roads become more fiddly and everything slows down as the Pennine hills gather around.

By **car**, accessing all of the places in this chapter is easy on the main A694 that stays close to the River Derwent as far as Consett; continuing westwards, smaller B roads and unclassified lanes connect to the likes Edmundbyers and Blanchland.

Bus travel is again very efficient as far as Consett, with regular Red Kite Ranger 47 buses (⊘ gonortheast.co.uk) shuttling through the valley from Newcastle to Consett via Winlaton Mill, Chopwell and Shotley Bridge. The same bus company operates the frequent X45 along roughly the same route. From Consett to Blanchland a very infrequent Weardale bus (773) makes three daily trips via Edmundbyers.

WALKING & CYCLING

The **Derwent Walk Railway Path** (above and page 160) runs right through the valley, connecting Tyneside with Consett via many of the towns and villages described in this chapter, making travel by bicycle a breeze. At Consett's Lydgett's Junction, a meeting of four old railway paths, you can continue your journey into Weardale or south towards Lanchester and Durham city, almost completely off road. For travel to Derwent Reservoir and Blanchland, you'll need to use the roads, some of which are peaceful but all involve some steep climbs and descents.

Riverside walks are limited to a few stretches around the historic Derwentcote Steel Furnace, Gibside, Ebchester, Allensford and a longer stretch east of the Derwent Walk Country Park towards Newcastle – a popular route. The Derwent flows under Blanchland on its way to Derwent Reservoir, offering walkers the chance to trace its course for a few miles on public rights of way that stay close to the riverbanks. I've described a short circular route on page 184. The Red Kite Ranger bus (page 157) can help with return journeys if on foot.

Hill walks are most rewarding the further west you go, especially above Blanchland. From Castleside (on the outskirts of Consett) and south of Edmundbyers, bulging moorland offers tantalising glimpses of the high Pennines above Weardale, with much to offer the experienced hiker, as well as cyclists on the **Coast-to-Coast** long-distance route in the Waskerley area.

Walks and cycle rides in the Forestry Commission's **Chopwell Wood** (just north of the Durham border) are hugely popular on a network of well-maintained paths. The other notable woodland for walkers is **Derwent Gorge and Muggleswick Woods**, a National Nature Reserve, but you really are on your own here, forging a route through the trees by way of an informal network of paths.

Derwent Reservoir is a hot spot for jaunts into the countryside with its lakeside trails, clear and accessible to all.

CYCLE REPAIRS

Steel Town Cycles Unit 4, 25–27 Derwent St, Blackhill, Consett DH8 8LR ✐ 01207 258270, 07429 421066 ⊙ 09.00–17.00 Mon–Sat (16.00 on Sat & later some days). Repairs and shop in a useful location for railway path and Coast-to-Coast cyclists. Will come to you within a ten-mile radius.

TAXIS

Jackson's Taxis Consett ✐ 01207 502277
Jays Taxi Consett ✐ 07745 747805
Local Taxi Winlaton ✐ 0191 4620060
Swans Taxi Consett ✐ 07500 804779

THE LOWER DERWENT: GATESHEAD TO CHOPWELL

⋀ West Wood Yurts (page 310)

With your back to the urban fringes of Gateshead, the valley becomes increasingly green with a mosaic of grasslands and woods lining the valley sides, and settlements appearing every few miles. **Thornley** and **Chopwell** woods are treasured recreation areas and popular with locals for their network of walking and mountain-biking trails. The renowned 18th-century landscaped grounds of **Gibside**, one of the National Trust's landmark properties in the North East, occupies a natural shelf above the Derwent and offers many more miles of woodland walks.

1 DERWENT WALK COUNTRY PARK & THORNLEY WOOD

An area of grass, woodland and wetlands between Swalwell in Gateshead and Rowlands Gill on the edge of Durham draws family groups over the weekend to its visitor centres, bird hides, riverside meadows, lakes and woods, which are all connected by a series of marked trails. Derwent Walk roughly follows the course of the river so the park is somewhat linear in nature until it blends into Thornley Wood which bulges across the A694 to occupy the hillside on the northern slope of the valley. The park's most striking feature is the dramatic Nine Arches Viaduct (page 160) which strides across the wooded gorge and from where there are tremendous views of red kites soaring above the treetops.

The **Land of Oak & Iron Heritage Centre** (page 156) is reached off the A694 and provides a good starting point for exploration of the riverside, accessing the Derwent Walk Railway Path and **Old Hollinside**, a Grade I-listed medieval fortified manor house on the south side of the Derwent. The ruinous building dates to the 13th century and stands in an isolated spot at the top of a steep grassy slope.

Thornley Wood (Lockhaugh Rd, Rowlands Gill NE39 1AU ☏ 01207 545212 ○ 10.00–16.00 daily) and its friendly visitor centre is a little further up the valley and also reached off the A694 or on foot by following the riverside path. Its sculptures and network of trails through the trees makes this a popular spot with families, and there's also a café.

THE DERWENT WALK
RAILWAY PATH TO GIBSIDE

A recommended family-friendly walk or cycle ride from Tyneside to Gibside is from **Derwent Walk Country Park** (pages 157 and 159) along the old trackbed of the Derwent Valley Railway. Opened in 1867, the railway now operates as a 12-mile leisure trail from Swalwell to Consett's Lydgett's Junction where it connects with a number of other railway paths for onward travel through Durham.

The **Land of Oak & Iron visitor centre** (page 156) and car park at Winlaton Mill on the north side of the Derwent is a good place to start the linear 2½-mile journey to Gibside, or you can park at **Thornley Wood** (page 159), half a mile upriver from Winlaton Mill, which also has facilities.

The route is very well used; flat, wide, wooded for much of its length and offers glimpses of historic monuments and buildings as it shadows the Derwent upstream, the river twinkling through the leaves of birch and oak trees in the vale below. **Nine Arches Viaduct**, an awesome crossing spanning 500ft, offers aerial views of the treetops below where red kites soar. These semi-urban birds of prey with a prominent forked tail were reintroduced to the Derwent Valley in the early 2000s and are now a frequent sight in the lower reaches of the valley.

When you reach a road, either follow the signs to **Gibside** (see opposite) or take the fiddly, though more off-road route, by crossing the A694 and following a grassy footpath through houses (you may need to refer to an OS map for this bit).

It's possible to continue beyond Gibside, where the line offers glimpses of medieval **Friarside Chapel**, once the chapel of a leper hospital, and runs through **Pontburn Wood Nature Reserve**, an ancient tract of woodland close to the stone hamlet of **Lintzford** (page 165), before crossing open countryside above **Ebchester** and continuing round **Shotley Bridge** to **Consett**.

⅋ FOOD & DRINK

In addition to The Land of Oak & Iron Heritage Centre (see below), you can also pick up simple hot dishes and take-away sandwiches from the café in the **Thornley Wood Visitor Centre** (page 159). For pub food and Sunday roasts, you could try the **Red Kite Pub** in Winlaton Mill (✆ 0191 4140673).

The Land of Oak & Iron Heritage Centre Winlaton Mill NE21 6RU ✆ 01207 524898 ⌖ landofoakandiron.org.uk ⏱ 09.00–16.00 daily ♿. A lively spot offering visitor information (page 156) by the River Derwent, with direct access to the paved footpath by the river and the railway path above the opposite banks (reached by a footbridge). There's indoor seating in the modern café (take a board game to your table) but it's the outdoor tables in the suntrap horseshoe courtyard that get snapped up quickly on bright days. Breakfast baps (meat, veggie and vegan options) and a cuppa are a great way to start your day in the Derwent Valley for little over £5. For lunch, it's sandwiches, toasties, jackets, fish-finger buns, chips and cakes. Great coffee here too. The last Friday of the month is an ever-popular pizza and live music night.

2 GIBSIDE

Near Rowlands Gill NE16 6BG (signed off the A1) ✆ 01207 541820 ◷ Apr–Oct 10.00–18.00 daily; Nov–Mar 10.00–16.00 daily (but check online as times vary) ♿ some paths bumpy; all-terrain electric wheelchairs for hire (book ahead by calling the above number); National Trust

> **[The Hall] stands in the midst of a great wood of about 400 acres,
> through which there are a great many noble walks and rides
> intersperse'd with fine lawns, with a rough river running thro' it, on
> each side of which are very high rocks, which gives it a very romantick
> [sic] look.**
> Edward Montagu, local colliery owner, in correspondence with his wife in the mid 1800s

Raised above the heavily wooded Derwent, its Chapel and Hall perched on the edge of the steep-sided slopes of the valley, and the 140ft Column to Liberty pointing skywards on a hill in the distance, J M W Turner's watercolour of Gibside captures the romance of the Derwent landscape in 1817. But gone is the admired half-mile long Avenue of oak and lime trees, the estate having been laid to waste following a period of decline in the late 18th century, Under the ownership of a prominent coal-mining baron, George Bowes (ancestor of the late Queen's mother), the gardens were landscaped in the 1720s to a design by Stephen Switzer and transformed into an aristocratic pleasure ground, but it later suffered under the ownership of his daughter, Lady Mary Eleanor Bowes, whose husband forced the sale of many of the trees and allowed the buildings to decay.

MARY ELEANOR'S DAFFODILS

If visiting in early spring, take a walk to the Hall to admire the daffodils. There are a number of varieties but the one to look out for is the pale yellow double daffodil known as the 'Gibside Daffodil'. It was planted by Mary Eleanor in the mid to late 18th century and discovered not long ago by estate workers who noticed it among an area of overgrown scrub and believe it may have been growing continuously ever since the Georgian era.

When the National Trust became involved in the upkeep of Gibside in 1965, much of the estate lay in ruins from over 150 years of repeated periods of neglect, but the Palladian Chapel – the crowning feature of Gibisde – was still intact and well-preserved owing to regular use through the 19th and 20th centuries. Once the Chapel was under the Trust's wing, they later took on more of the wider grounds and buildings until Gibside resembled the landscaped parkland envisioned by George Bowes.

Today the 720 acres of woods and open grasslands radiate all the 18th-century grandeur of its past with eye-catching monuments, classical architecture and a reinstated avenue of trees, now nearly 200 years old. The **Jacobean Hall**, built by earlier occupants of the estate, the Blakistons, and the **Orangery** remain what you might call 'picturesque ruins' but, overall, the spirit of Gibside, founded as a pleasure ground, is restored.

Work began on Gibside's treasured Georgian centrepiece, the **Chapel** (May–mid-Oct 10.00–17.00 daily; mid-Oct–Apr 10.00–16.00 Sat & Sun; service 15.00 Sun; choral evensong & prayer 15.00 first Sunday of the month ♿ using a side ramp), in 1760 to a plan by renowned architect of the day, James Paine. George Bowes didn't live to see the completion of the exterior of his mausoleum nine years later (which was converted into a church in 1809). Constructed using a cream sandstone, the swags on the dome, row of urns on the balustrade and fine carvings on the portico columns are much admired. Many decades would pass before the interior of Bowes' classical masterpiece would be unveiled to reveal its exquisite, intricately carved plasterwork, unusual three-tiered pulpit and finely curved pews made of bright cherry wood.

A stroll from the Chapel along the tree-lined **Avenue**, where once Bowes likely ran his racehorses, to the **Column to Liberty**, is wonderfully romantic, especially in autumn when the intensity of light and colour is spectacular. Heavy industry once surrounded the estate, but Gibside was something of an exclusive hideaway for Bowes and even today that sense of being cut off from the urban landscape on its doorstep is felt by many Tynesiders who visit here in large numbers at the weekends.

You can cycle (or walk) to Gibside from Tyneside in four miles by following a railway path (page 160).

---

1 Gibside Chapel. **2** Chopwell Wood. **3** Derwentcote Steel Furnace. ▶

GIBSIDE'S TRIALS & TRAGEDIES

Architecture and gardens aside, Gibside has a gripping human story to tell as it passed hands from George Bowes, the coal titan, to his only child, **Mary Eleanor Bowes**, an intellectual and botanist and once the wealthiest heiress in Georgian England. Her personal life was marred by two disastrous marriages: the first ended with the death of her husband abroad; the second in the downfall of both countess and estate before she was finally granted a divorce (which incidentally paved the way for reforms of divorce laws in England).

Mary Eleanor never returned to Gibside and to her beloved Orangery and the estate fell into the hands of her eldest son, **John Bowes**, the 10th Earl of Strathmore, who set to work restoring the ruinous grounds, re-gilding the Column to Liberty, repairing buildings and planting new woods. One day before his death in 1820, John Bowes married his mistress and housemaid who had nine years earlier given birth to his only child, also called John, who went on to marry a French actress and amass a tremendous collection of art for their new purpose-built museum, the Bowes Museum of Barnard Castle (page 242).

Through the war years, Gibside again underwent a period of decline, buildings were dismantled, and the Forestry Commission replaced many of the broadleaved trees with conifers. They planned to transform the landscaped garden into a plantation woodland, but at this point the National Trust stepped in, saving Gibside as a complete Georgian estate.

Much of the focus for a day out is centred around the two extreme ends of the estate: the area around the Chapel where there's a café, Walled Garden, second-hand bookstore, shop, vegetable stall and, a short walk away, a large adventure playground known as **Strawberry Castle**; at the other end of the Avenue is the unusually grand **Stables** with more offerings of cakes, and artist studios and trails into the surrounding conifer woodland.

¶¶ FOOD & DRINK

All the usual National Trust offerings (light lunches, cakes and scones) served in a **café** with outdoor seating in a lovely spot near the Chapel. Close by is a little honesty stall with vegetables for sale grown in the restored 18th-century Walled Garden.

At the far end of the Avenue, within the wind-sheltered stables' courtyard, is the **Carriages café** (⊙ 11.00–16.00 daily). From the end of May until early October, **The Garden Tap** brewery and pub (⊙ noon–18.00 Wed–Sat; until 21.00 on Fri, last entry 20.00) opens its doors in the old bakery. Log braziers and beers brewed on site, plus pizzas on Fridays and Saturdays.

3 LINTZFORD & PONTBURN WOOD NATURE RESERVE

Picturesque **Lintzford** is cupped by the meandering River Derwent and is reached across an elegant Georgian bridge humped over the rushing water. The hamlet's detached, multi-bedroomed stone houses about a green and enclosed by the craggy gorge walls of the Derwent appear to have been left behind in the 18th century when the river worked a paper mill on the site of an old corn mill. An ink works occupied the area much later.

From the hamlet, if you continue up Lintz Green Lane you will reach the Derwent Walk Railway Path by the old station platform and bridge and can walk as far as you wish: east towards Rowlands Gill or to **Pontburn Wood Nature Reserve**, a quarter of a mile west along the trackbed. Here you will come to the first of two **railway viaducts**; the largest ten-arched crossing dates to the late 19th century and stands 120ft tall. Pontburn Wood is under the stewardship of the Woodland Trust and is one of a number of patches of old native broadleaved woodlands in the valley, inhabited by all the usual birds you'd expect including woodpeckers, nuthatch, thrushes and tits. Though well used by locals, the woods are peaceful and this is a quieter place for a woodland walk than nearby Thornley or Chopwell woods (see page 159 and below) which have more in the way of infrastructure.

4 CHOPWELL WOOD

High Spen NE39 1LT; road access to the car park is from Hooker Gate (High Spen), off the B6315; footpath access from a few places including Chopwell. There's a useful bus stop at Hooker Gate with connections to Newcastle (Go Northeast bus 47) and Consett (bus 45 or 46 can connect with route 47 at Rowlands Gill).

Miles of footpaths and mountain bike trails criss-cross this popular 900-acre forest just north of the Durham border, managed by the Forestry Commission. The landscape is hilly in places, offering plunging views of the Derwent Valley from the three main trails (one of which is wheelchair accessible).

The Forestry Commission are gradually thinning out the conifers and replacing them with broadleaved trees such as oak, beech and ash so that the landscape better resembles the forest that once covered the valley. This should increase the diversity of wildlife seen in the woods; that said, despite the dominance of conifer trees at the moment you are never far from deer, red kites and all the usual woodland birds. Red squirrels used to live here but are a very rare sight today.

Chopwell

Brick terraces in this old mining village on the western edge of Chopwell Wood stack one above the other on a hillside overlooking the Derwent Valley. At the top of the village, extending away from Hall Road, they run in long uniform lines, divided by back lanes or greens. Encroaching new housing threatens the vernacular architecture but, for now, many of the streets stay true to their original Victorian form.

Marx and Lenin terraces keep alive the memory of when Chopwell was nicknamed 'Little Moscow' in the early 20th century for its support of the Communist Party. During the General Strike of 1926, the Union Jack was removed from council offices and replaced with the Soviet flag. The miners' union banner famously displays the faces of Marx, Lenin and Keir Hardie, and is paraded through the streets during the Durham Miners' Gala (page 61) in July. Chopwell's mining past is also recalled on Derwent Street where the old colliery wheel now stands as a monument.

⫴ FOOD & DRINK

The Feathers Inn Hedley on the Hill, NE43 7SW ✆ 01661 843607 ⊘ from noon Thu–Sat, noon–19.00 Sun (food till 16.30). People travel from miles to this multiple award-winning pub in Northumberland, four miles northwest of Chopwell, which is why I've included it here. A lovely old stone inn with snug dining rooms (each with a log burner) and outdoor seating. Boards inside list the local growers, producers and foragers behind the ingredients on your plate (almost everything is sourced from the North East) and so you'll find roe deer from nearby woods, beef from Haydon Bridge, Slaley Wood mushrooms, halibut, crab and lobster landed at North Shields and Sunderland, and cheeses from Northumberland. While the menu is not extensive, the plates of food are more interesting and upmarket than your average gastro pub.

5 DERWENTCOTE STEEL FURNACE

Forge Ln, NE17 7RS ⊘ all times; parking and picnic area (signed) on the far side of the A694; free access (outside only); English Heritage

From the 1700s, the Derwent Valley was at the heart of the British steel-making industry until Sheffield became more dominant in the following century. The furnace on the southern edge of Chopwell Wood, built in the 1730s, is the earliest and best example of its type in Britain; complete and very distinctive. There's no general public access inside (except on special guided tours around once a week at 11.00 in summer – less frequent in winter – see English Heritage website for days) but you can walk up to it by following a track downhill towards woods.

Iron was converted into steel in stone chests located below the conical beehive chimney that stands between two stone buildings. Iron bars imported from Sweden were packed into these cavities with charcoal and then heated to 1,000ºC until the charcoal diffused into the iron, making steel. To do this, the furnace had to be fed with coal every few hours for at least a whole week. Ten tons of steel were manufactured here every month by two workers. The raw steel was then taken to a forge to be worked, after which the furnace is said to have taken a week to cool down. It ceased production in 1891.

EBCHESTER, SHOTLEY BRIDGE & CONSETT

🏠 **Bonners Lodge** (page 310), **Derwent Manor Boutique Hotel** (page 310) ▲ **Hidden Retreat Glamping** (page 310), **Starlight Camping & Caravanning** (page 310)

The mid-Derwent Valley is heavily populated, with the old steel town of **Consett** dominating the landscape to the south which merges into the village of **Shotley Bridge**, nestled by the river. Largely built of sandstone, Shotley Bridge is a worthy detour on your travels through Derwentdale with a few pleasant cafés for lunch. Nearby, **Ebchester** boasts a very old church and countryside walks from the **Derwent Walk Railway Path** that crosses open land above the village, offering fine valley views.

6 EBCHESTER

Roman stones (and even the remains of a bath house) were discovered in the gardens of this small, unassuming village on a main thoroughfare three miles north of Consett. Such finds reveal that Ebchester overlays a Roman fort (Vindomora).

On pausing in Ebchester on your travels through the valley, you'll find a pleasant run of old stone cottages leading away from the post office and a very old church built in part using recycled Roman stone. The oldest walls of **St Ebba's** date to around 1100 and include a Norman chancel arch, while the base of the font is thought to be an old millstone, which could be Roman. To the rear of the church is the headstone of 'Jos. Oley' who died in 1896, 'the last of the Shotley Bridge sword makers' as the inscription details – look for a large arched stone roughly opposite the rear door.

A useful **village store** opposite the church is well stocked with provisions and has a few fresh cakes and snacks to take-away, as well as selling papers and guides to the area. You could take your lunch to the open countryside above the village, reached from Shaw Lane. From the church, the residential street curls away steeply uphill from the village, soon becoming a country lane. The entrance for the **Derwent Walk Railway Path** is half a mile from the church, up this road.

7 SHOTLEY BRIDGE

It is surprising that renowned German-British architectural historian, Nikolaus Pevsner, should find Shotley Bridge 'devoid of buildings of special architectural merit' when he travelled through the town in the mid-20th century, visiting a terrace of stone cottages built by the famous German sword makers in the late 17th century. He even quotes the inscription found on one door mantle in his *The Buildings of England: County Durham* (1953):

> **Des Herren Segen machet reich**
> **Ohn alle Sorg, wan du zugleich**
> **In deinem Stand treu und fleissig bist**
> **Und duest was dir befohlen ist. 1691**

It roughly translates as: 'The Lord's blessing will make you rich and without worries, if you persevere, are faithful and hardworking and if you follow his command.' Nonetheless, it would seem officials felt similarly to Pevsner when they authorised the demolition of the three-storey buildings on Wood Street within years of Pevsner's visit, the same street, incidentally, where the famous 'Pitman Poet', Tommy Armstrong was born in 1848 (page 74).

The history of Shotley Bridge is tied to the late 17th-century sword-making industry (page 170), a legacy recalled in the name of the pub, the Crown and Crossed Swords, street names Oley Meadows and Cutlers Hall Road, and the modern Swordmakers Apartments. Only

---

1 Ebchester. **2** Hownsgill Viaduct. **3** *Terra Novalis* sculpture, Consett.
4 Countryside around Consett. ▶

THE SHOTLEY BRIDGE SWORD MAKERS

Some say the 19 immigrant sword-making families from Solingen in Germany settled in the Derwent Valley because they were fleeing religious persecution; others believe they were lured by the secluded location and soft water of the Derwent, good for tempering steel. Whatever the reason, it was an unlikely beginning for a Durham village in the late 17th century.

Two of these families, the Oleys and Moles (anglicised from Ohlig and Mohl), became known for producing some of the finest weapons in the country, which were used by the English army during the Napoleonic wars. The trade died out in the mid 19th century when Sheffield and Birmingham developed stronger steel industries than in the Shotley Bridge/Consett area. The Moles moved to Birmingham and continued in business, eventually becoming part of the razor-making firm now known as Wilkinson Sword.

one original building survives from the period: **Cutler's Hall** (22–24 Cutlers Hall Rd), built for William Oley and his wife, Ann, in 1787, as is dated above the doorway alongside the initials 'W & A O'. The date is significant: the Napoleonic wars had started two years earlier and the Shotley Bridge sword makers hit boomtime, such was the demand for their swords, but by the end of the wars in 1815, the industry was in terminal decline and the last sword mill closed 1840.

"The old bath house, saloon and circular stone spa well (once covered with a conical thatched canopy) remain in situ on Spa Drive."

Today, Shotley Bridge's remaining old stone terraces, wooded setting and hillside aspect make it one of the most attractive towns in the Derwent Valley and certainly, if you've travelled here via neighbouring Consett, it's quite a surprise to come across such tall, affluent-looking houses. A long winding throughfare runs through the **town centre** dotted with a few cafés and pubs. There's also a large number of beauty salons, which I like to think continue the tradition of grooming and health instilled in Shotley Bridge ever since it became a **spa town** in 1838. For over 60 years, visitors enjoyed the complex, set in ornamental gardens where the cricket ground now stands. The old bath house, saloon and circular stone spa well (once covered with a conical thatched canopy) remain in situ on Spa Drive by the riverside. Charles Dickens visited and is said to have remarked the spa water tasted like 'poison'.

¶¶ FOOD & DRINK

Pubs and cafés are dotted about the centre of Shotley but there are a few choices just out of town including **Knitsley Farm Shop** (page 172) serving fantastic breakfasts and lunches.

Isabella's 8 Front St, DH8 0HH ✆ 01207 655100 ☉ Tue–Sat. The best cakes, brownies, flapjacks and scones for many miles around – all freshly baked; you can sample them over an afternoon tea (ideally book ahead). Lunches are that bit superior too, making use of local ingredients including cheese from Northumberland. Also, special evening nights such as Italian and tapas (call to check and to book).

Sale Pepe 10-11 Front St, DH8 0HH ✆ 01207 509969 ☉ 17.00–23.00 Wed–Fri, 16.00–23.00 Sat, noon–21.00 Sun; last orders 2hrs before closing. Reliably good Italian (pizza, pasta, risotto, fish and meat dishes, as well as Sunday roasts).

8 CONSETT

Steel was everything to Consett. Even today, despite the loss of industry in 1980 (and nearly 4,000 jobs), the town is synonymous with the metal, having grown around the burgeoning industry in 1840. Consett's proximity to five abundant resources: iron ore, coking coal, limestone, railways and river made this an unbeatable location for the Derwent Iron Company's furnaces and rolling mills. While the area had had a long association with iron foundries on the Derwent since the early 1700s, and with

"Gifted to the public by the Consett Iron Company, the Victorian pleasure ground remains a popular open space with families."

iron works already established at nearby Winlaton Mill by industrialist Ambrose Crowley (a name you see stamped about a bit in these parts), the valley only reached the soaring output of the late 19th century due to the advent of the railways.

Thousands of workers moved into the area occupying stone terraces built by the ironworks, some of which still stand, including an unchanged block around St Aidan's Street opposite the **Blackhill & Consett Park**. Gifted to the public by the Consett Iron Company in 1891, the Victorian pleasure ground remains a popular open space with families, and now has play areas and a café.

While the town has a fascinating social and economic story to tell (who knew the Eiffel Tower was constructed with Consett steel?) and some curious firsts (home to the earliest Salvation Army band in the world), Consett is not somewhere many people visit. But if you are in the area, perhaps pedalling through on one of the railway trails or the Coast-to-Coast cycleway which passes through the town on the Consett & Sunderland Railway Path, look out for industrial relics including a huge 25-ton 'ladle' on rails at **Lydgett's Junction**, once used for transporting molten iron between blast furnaces. *Terra Novalis*, meaning 'new made land' is a landmark sculpture by Turner Prize-winning artist, Tony Cragg, on a hillock overlooking the railway path and the site of the former steelworks. Also close by and well known to cyclists is the arresting **Hownsgill Viaduct** of 1858, built for the famous Stockton & Darlington Railway, and best viewed from the road. Its 12 arches rise to 150ft, towering over Knitsley and High House Woods.

Allensford Park

Consett is connected to the River Derwent at the popular picnic and swimming area at **Allensford Park** and along footpaths through **Deneburn**, a wooded beck passing under Hownsgill Viaduct and connecting with nearby Castleside. Allensford is a pleasant spot and the site of a few historic buildings reminding of the early ironworks in the area, including a 17th-century farmhouse on the north side of the bridge and, in nearby woods, a blast furnace dating to a similar period. Research by Newcastle University reveals it was last used in the mid 1700s. From the picnic site, a popular footpath trails the wooded **Wharnley Burn** to an old footbridge and waterfall.

¶¶ FOOD & DRINK

You'll find plenty of pubs, take-aways and a few cafés along Consett's Front Street.

Knitsley Farm Shop & Granary Café East Knitsley Grange, DH8 9EW ✆ 01207 592059 ⊙ 09.00–16.00 Tue–Sat (café closes at 15.00). Surrounded by grasslands on a working farm between Consett and Lanchester is this fantastic farm café, butcher, shop and well-stocked deli run by the sixth generation of farmers. Almost everything for sale once walked the fields outside the courtyard café or grew nearby, and the owners are passionate about the quality and provenance of their meats and produce. And so you will find one of the best stocked butcher's counters in the region with around a dozen different sausages, all made on-site from rare breed pigs, plus homemade burgers, pies and their signature cured bacon, produced with black treacle, beer and spices.

Breakfasts are a feast of quality items. For lunch, there's more in the way of – yes, you guessed it – meat: ham broth soup; ploughman's lunch served with ham, pork pie

WASKERLEY WAY

Forming an arc across one of the most remote tracts of upland terrain in England, this former railway now makes for a stunning ten-mile cycle ride and wonderful introduction to the North Pennine moorland landscape.

Turning your back on the old steel-making town of Consett on the outskirts of Tyneside, cyclists pick up the Waskerley Way at a famous intersection of four old lines, **Lydgett's Junction**, and its 12-arched **Hownsgill Viaduct**. The urban fringes peter out quickly and the landscape becomes green with a mix of grazing fields, woodland and parkland, becoming increasingly more remote from Healeyfield as you peddle on over the heather plateau above **Muggleswick Common**, avoiding collisions with free-ranging sheep

and passing a nest of three remote reservoirs: **Smiddy Shaw**, **Waskerley** and **Hisehope**. You feel on the rooftop of England up here and the views are terrifically generous all around with Derwentdale to the north and Weardale before you to the south.

Picnic areas break up the route at useful intervals, with the most famous being at **Parkhead** (page 201), once a remote Victorian station and now a popular refuelling point for Coast-to-Coast cyclists. The café building and trackway recalls the boom years of the 19th century when wagons trundled across these hills, transporting lead ore, limestone and coal. Many cyclists will continue south from Parkhead on an exhilarating 2½-mile stretch of tarmac into Stanhope.

and a Scotch egg; sausage and mash; Aberdeen Angus steak sandwiches served in local 'stottie' bread (a slightly sweet bread special to the North East). Meat-free options include sandwiches, jacket potatoes and quiche.

Maddison's 26 Front St ✐ 01207 583318 ☉ Mon–Sat. Friendly, somewhat funky café with a popular breakfast menu (eggs every way and waffles). For lunch: soup, salads, toasties, crêpes and a large selection of cakes and scones.

UPPER DERWENT VALLEY

🏠 **Derwent Arms** (page 310), **Lord Crewe Arms** (page 310), **Low House YHA & campsite** (page 310)

Far away from the urban centres lower down the valley, the upper reaches of the Derwent are flanked by green hills dotted with historic ruins and 18th- and 19th-century stone villages making the area between **Consett** and **Blanchland** very appealing to walkers and cyclists. Below **Derwent Reservoir**, the only place in the area attracting anything resembling a crowd, the Derwent flows under the boughs of ancient trees in its namesake gorge – an important refuge for rare birds in the valley.

9 DERWENT GORGE & MUGGLESWICK WOODS NATIONAL NATURE RESERVE

Ancient oak woodland cloaks the tightly ribboned River Derwent between Allensford and Derwent Reservoir, which is best visited in spring when an understorey of bluebells, wild garlic and wood sorrel are in flower and migratory songbirds have returned to breed. They include the well-known trio associated with very old woods: redstart, wood warbler and pied flycatcher, but also look out for those shy river birds: the kingfisher, dipper and goosander. Unlike other tracts of oak woodland along the Derwent, the lack of infrastructure and relatively remote location makes this a rather special place for those who delight in solitude and would relish the opportunity to listen undisturbed for the unmistakable coin-spinning notes of the wood warbler.

While lacking in official **access** points and parking areas, there are occasional lay-bys along the road between Muggleswick and Castleside, including about half a mile west of Comb Bridges where a descending footpath connects with the Derwent. A longer **walk** taking in the expansive views and moorland scenery above the river before entering the woods is from the hilltop hamlet of Muggleswick or, from the northern side of the Derwent in Northumberland, from Crooked Oak, reached at the end of the Wallish Walls Road (park carefully here to allow farm vehicles to pass). A number of unofficial tracks wind through the woods so it's a case of taking a map and having a good sense of direction.

10 MUGGLESWICK

An intriguing name and nothing to do with *Harry Potter*, in case you were wondering (despite Royal Mail forging a connection with the hamlet with a gift set of Potter stamps featuring 'Muggleswick' on the franking mark). 'Wick' is a common Old English suffix meaning dairy farm, but the 'Muggle' bit is unclear, a likely corruption of the farm's owner. But let's forget about the name and enjoy the hilltop setting with outstanding moorland and pasture views all around, and the extensive ruins of a Grade I-listed **monastic grange** dating to the 13th century, built for the priors of Durham. Records from 1464 record a hall, chapel, farm and dairy on the site, which today is situated in the grounds of

---

1 Muggleswick. **2** Derwent Gorge. **3** Countryside around Muggleswick.
4 The upper reaches of the Derwent are prime otter country. ▶

Priory Farm and can be viewed from the main lane through the hamlet, just beyond some cottages and below the church. Most impressive of the surviving masonry is a very tall wall with turrets and a tracery at the highest point.

All Saints Church stands alone in a field and dates to the early 18th century with 19th-century alterations. Services are held on the first Sunday of the month at 15.00.

Muggleswick is a rewarding destination for a **hill walk** or **cycle ride** from Edmundbyers (page 178), making use of tracks across the moors as well as a paved lane (with wandering sheep and very little traffic) along the fellside offering superb views of the countryside. Derwent Reservoir appears as a streak of blue across a broad sweep of greens and yellows: all meadow, fell and forest.

11 DERWENT RESERVOIR

Derwent Waterside Park Visitor Centre, DH8 9TT ✆ 0345 1550236 ♿

The River Derwent's journey from the Pennine moors to the Tyne is halted by the two-mile-long Derwent Reservoir – one of the largest reservoirs in the North East, straddling the Northumberland–Durham border – a popular recreation area with local families, anglers and boat-owners.

A visitor centre, café and shop selling snacks and knick-knacks for children operates from the north side of the dam, about a mile northeast of Edmundbyers, reached from the B6278. This is the main hub, with a large playground, but there are a number of other quieter picnic and parking sites around the water with less infrastructure.

"A four-mile mixed-use path curls halfway around the lake between the visitor centre and Pow Hill Country Park via the dam wall."

A four-mile mixed-use path curls halfway around the lake between the visitor centre and Pow Hill Country Park via the dam wall, gaining views of sailing dinghies on the water, wildfowl in the shallows, and the surrounding upland meadows and fellsides sloping to meet the water's edge. The surfaced paths are largely wheelchair and pushchair friendly, though they can be a little muddy and bumpy in places. Picnic tables on grassy areas overlook the water close to all parking areas.

Two of the busiest spots are the **Pow Hill Country Park** (for the Boat Shack Café) and the area around the visitor centre, marked on local maps as the **Derwent Waterside Park**. Both sites become very busy on sunny weekends and during the school holidays when there are long queues to buy ice creams and food. A quieter area with picnic tables and toilets but no café is **Millshield** on the north banks of the water, not far from the sailing club.

¶¶ FOOD & DRINK

You can pick up coffees, ice creams, snacks and burgers at the **Boat Shack Café** in Pow Hill Country Park (DH8 9NU ✆ 01207 255117 ☉ 10.00–16.00 Thu–Sun, till 19.30 Sat & Sun) on the southern shores of the reservoir, and at the main visitor centre at **Derwent Waterside Park** (DH8 9TT ✆ 0345 1550236 ☉ daily) on the north side of the dam, but for a proper sit-down meal and good plates of food, consider the **Derwent Arms** (page 178) in Edmundbyers, 1½ miles south of the visitor centre.

12 EDMUNDBYERS

Tales of witches and apparitions permeate this old village a mile south of Derwent Reservoir famed for the 17th-century trial of several local women accused of holding meetings, bewitching livestock and other acts of maleficium. The last of Edmundbyers' witches was said to be Elizabeth Lee who, having never been found guilty, eventually passed away at the old age of 87 in 1792, as her gravestone in the parish church of St Edmund's details. Why it was later brought to hang inside the church we do not know, but the placing of the stone close to a protective stained glass 'Eye of God' window may be deliberate. Her burial plot in the churchyard is a mystery but the profusion of wild garlic scenting the grounds in spring ought to help keep away any harmful spirits. As for ghosts, talk to those who run Edmundbyers' YHA about sightings of former resident, Ann Elliot, murdered on the moors in 1785, and who is said to haunt the village.

St Edmund's Church sits at the foot of the village, enclosed by a wooded churchyard. Evidence of its Norman beginnings are clear in the windows of the chancel, though some historians have suggested its origins are much older owing to some pieces of masonry and a few windows showing similarities with Saxon churches elsewhere. Victorian restorers tinkered with the building over the years replacing the Norman chancel arch with three bows, but they also uncovered the church's original altar stone and returned it to the chancel, and inserted new stained glass into the windows including the unusual 'Eye of God' in the west wall, said to be Masonic. Note too the priests' grave covers in the porch. They are some 700 years old and picture a chalice, identifying the deceased as clergymen. Before you leave the churchyard, take a look at the rudimentary faces carved on the stone corbels.

Away from the sheltered surroundings of the church, Edmundbyers' long **village green** (behind the pub) with its old stone trough and open aspect on a hillside is altogether a sunnier, livelier spot. A steady stream of cyclists pass through the village or stop to rest their legs in the Derwent Arms' bright beer garden, joining a merry crowd of locals and families on country outings. Also serving drinks is the diminutive drinking hole annexed to the quirky **YHA** just down the road. The cottages date to the 1700s but the hostel itself is one of the oldest in the region, first welcoming guests in 1936.

Visits to Derwent Reservoir are possible from Edmundbyers in a little over a mile's **walk**, descending from the north edge of the village through field after field on foot to Pow Hill Country Park. **Cyclists** should follow the B6306. A longer walk could lead you up on to the grouse moors over Edmundbyers Common along a bridleway (part of the long-distance Lead Mining Trail) high above the Burnhope Burn and past Cuthbert's Currick and returning via College Edge with wonderful valley views in eight miles, or a linear route to Blanchland in five.

"A steady stream of cyclists pass through the village or stop to rest their legs in the Derwent Arms' bright beer garden."

ⓘ FOOD & DRINK

The Baa Low House YHA, DH8 9NL ☎ 01207 255651 or 07884 969725 ⓘ 16.00–21.30 Mon–Thu, noon–23.30 Sat & Sun. I love this little pub annexed to the youth hostel. It draws a jolly crowd of locals, cyclists, hostel goers and, well, anyone passing into its little 18th-century cobble-floored room with a wood burner. Local ales, and pizzas served until 20.00.

The Derwent Arms DH8 9NL ☎ 01207 255545 ⓘ 08.30–late daily, food till around 20.45. The best place for a substantial meal or Sunday roast in the village and for many miles around, unless you'd rather somewhere even more upmarket (in which case, the Lord Crewe Arms a few miles down the road in Blanchland will welcome you). Inside, the Derwent Arms is a fairly smart, though laid-back, country pub with dark wood panelling and tartan fabrics. The beer garden catches the sun and all the goings on in the village. On the menu (breakfast, lunch and dinner) is great pub food: the usual burgers and fish and chips, steak, stews, curry and a couple of vegetarian options including pasta. Their lighter 'sandwiches' are very good value for a bun filled with fish goujons, sausage or cheese and served with chips and salad for under £10. Local beers include those from Allendale and Hadrian Border Brewery.

13 BLANCHLAND

> I rode to Blanchland, about 20 miles from Newcastle. The rough mountains round about were still white with snow. In the midst of them is a small winding valley, through which the Derwent runs. On the edge of this the little town stands, which is little more than a heap of ruins. There seems to have been a large cathedral church by the vast walls which still remain. I stood in the churchyard [and] all the congregation kneeled down on the grass. They were all gathered out of the leadmines... A row of little children sat under the opposite wall, all quiet and still. The whole congregation drank in every word with such earnestness in their looks, I would not but hope that God will make this wilderness sing for joy.
>
> John Wesley's account of preaching in Blanchland in April 1747

Hunkered in a hollow by the wooded River Derwent and seemingly unchanged for several hundred years, Blanchland is the most historically alluring village in the Derwent Valley – and far from the ruinous settlement it may have been when Wesley visited. On summer's evenings the sandstone houses and little humpback bridge spanning the Durham–Northumberland border are soaked in ochre sunshine, providing one of the most intact 18th- and 19th-century vistas you will find anywhere in England. But, for me, Blanchland is at its most

"Seemingly unchanged for several hundred years, Blanchland is the most historically alluring village in the Derwent Valley."

timeless in winter when the smell of coal wafts through the village, luring ramblers off surrounding fells and towards the yellow glow from the Lord Crewe Arms.

Blanchland almost certainly gets its name from the French white-robed Premonstratensian Canons who established an abbey here in 1165 (hence the white letterbox in the village). Almost everything else you see grew around the abbey in the centuries following the Dissolution of the Monasteries and particularly in the 18th century. The outer court became the **village square** with cottages around three of its sides and the monastic church became the parish church. **The Lord Crewe Arms,**

ROAD WITH A VIEW: BLANCHLAND TO ROOKHOPE

This awesomely remote road climbs on to some of the most isolated moors in the Pennines, offering spectacular views of Weardale as you make the descent into Rookhope. Owing to the altitude and steep decline from the moors, it's important not to attempt this route in poor weather; snow markers edge the road for a reason.

Bid farewell to Northumberland as you depart **Blanchland** in a westerly direction along Clap Shaw lane. Soon after crossing the River Derwent, take the turning on the right (continuing straight on here, incidentally, will take you on an equally thrilling ride across the moors to Stanhope via Dead Friar's Bank and Stanhope Common) and begin the climb out of the Derwent Valley to **Hunstanworth** – of architectural note for its Victorian cottages and church (page 184).

At first the landscape is all open farmland with woodland marking the course of the Derwent in the gorge below but the scenery quickly steps up a gear and becomes more remote and wild-looking from Hunstanworth onwards. By the time **Townfield** is behind you, heather becomes dominant, the skies huge and the lane, interrupted here and there by cattle grids, offers stunning vistas across **Hunstanworth Moor**. After the highest point, at 1,666ft above sea level, the thrilling descent into Weardale awaits. From **Lintzgarth**, the road flattens and follows the stony burn on its merry way through the famous lead-mining village of **Rookhope** (page 203) with much in the way of industrial architecture and rural charm. If you want to see the famous **Rookhope Arch** (page 205; an old smelt mill flue – now a monument to the 18th- and 19th-century lead-mining industry), turn right at the T-junction on your descent from the moors into Lintzgarth and away from Rookhope. You can't miss it, by the road a couple of hundred yards ahead.

If you're still thirsty for altitude and thrilling descents, another road connecting the Derwent Valley with Weardale and offering a similar combination of expansive views, moorland scenery and a large shot of solitude is found on the B6278 **Edmundbyers–Stanhope** road crossing Muggleswick Common. It's best travelled in this direction for the final few heart-racing miles of descent off the moors. Waskerley Way cyclists joining the road for the final run into Stanhope will find it exhilarating, if not terrifying. Note the 'escape lanes' and warning signs asking drivers to check their brakes.

once the Abbot's lodge, kitchen and guest houses, was remodelled into a family home, also in the 18th century, but much original stonework survives in the building's complicated arrangement of rooms. It's now an expensive hotel, restaurant and bar so you can navigate its stairways and corridors to inspect all its nooks, quirks and very old masonry at leisure. The rear beer garden was once the cloisters and retains its original quadrangle layout.

St Mary's Church, hidden by trees just beyond the embattled gatehouse, is hugely atmospheric inside, built out of the ruined abbey with a soaring archway and lancet windows of the Early English style; the rest was reconstructed in the 18th century. A stained-glass panel high above the altar shows a white-robed monk, the folds of his cloak just visible.

According to folklore, during the turbulent centuries of cross-border fighting the monastery almost evaded plundering by the Scots who had lost their way on the fells in heavy fog. Unfortunately, the untimely ringing of the bells announcing it was safe to emerge from hiding revealed the abbey's whereabouts to the invaders. Blanchland later suffered under Henry VIII following the Dissolution of the Monasteries and the abbey closed in 1539. Over 170 years passed before it eventually came into the ownership of Lord Crewe, Bishop of Durham.

Blanchland is a wonderful setting for a snail's-pace wander and those with a nose for anything of antiquity will find much to catch the eye, from the striking **gatehouse** with its arched passageway (15th century but, again, altered in the mid-18th century), the **pump house** or **pant** commemorating Queen Victoria's Diamond Jubilee opposite the post office, and more prosaic buildings: the intact run of Victorian privies, sheds and coal holes at the back of Shildon Road; and the cart shed, pigsties and farm buildings nestled by the banks of the Derwent.

Once you've explored the centre and admired the stone square of cottages, visited the church, gift shop, tea rooms and fetching post office-cum-village shop (note the **white letter box** built into the window – a rare 'Ludlow' design), you might consider a stroll down to the river (page 184) or up the lane north out of the village to the ruins of a lead mine. After half a mile, you'll pass some stone cottages and then, ahead, the **Shildon lead-mining engine house**. It dates to the early 1800s and once housed a steam-powered pump that drew water out of a nearby mine. Continue ahead

"A wonderful setting for a snail's-pace wander and those with a nose for anything of antiquity will find much to catch the eye."

for a longer and more strenuous circular **walk** via Pennypie House and then west over grouse moors (Burntshieldhaugh Fell), following the old packhorse track, the Carriers' Way. The obvious return is via Birkside

Fell, Newbiggin Fell, Newbiggin Hall and Baybridge, with its old chapel, before returning to Blanchland by the side of the Derwent. You'll need OS Explorer map 307 for this route of six miles.

The annual **Blanchland & Hunstanworth agricultural show** (⌂ blanchlandshow.co.uk) is held over the August Bank Holiday, bringing together local communities and the best farm animals and produce in the region for some good traditional fun.

¶¶ FOOD & DRINK

If you can't get a lunch reservation at the Lord Crewe Arms (booking ahead strongly recommended) but would like more of a substantial meal than what they offer at White Monk's tea room, consider the short drive or cycle ride to Edbundbyers (page 177) where you have more chance of an on-spec table. For a casual drink mixing with locals, the informal community pub in the old sports club adjoining the Village Hall, **The Felons Bar**, is open on Friday and Saturday evenings (◷ 18.30–23.00 Fri & Sat) for drinks, a game of pool and live music sessions.

Lord Crewe Arms The Sq, DH8 9SP ✆ 01434 677100 ⌂ lordcrewearmsblanchland. co.uk ◷ daily ♿ downstairs eating areas only. Well known as a luxury hotel and a very good place to dine from breakfast to evening meals and everything in between (lunches, afternoon tea, light bar bites and Sunday roasts). Once a guest house associated with the abbey, the Lord Crewe exudes antiquity and the hotel makes much of its medieval features: enormous fireplaces, rear cloisters (now an outside drinking area but also serving afternoon teas), and vaulted crypt bar.

Evening dinners, where you can expect to pay around £20 for beautiful plates of food, are served in the stripped-back Bishop's Dining Room upstairs. Dishes are fancily described on the menu but are essentially upscaled variations on fish and chips, and meat and veg with some vegetarian options. And so you may find North Sea plaice and chips; venison with red cabbage and a red wine sauce; rack of lamb with pancetta; vegetable Wellington. Look out for grouse and venison from local moors, Durham rare breed pork and salmon (smoked on-site).

White Monk Refectory & Tea Room DH8 9ST ✆ 01434 675044 ◷ 10.00–17.00 Tue–Sun ♿. An easy, relaxed café housed in the old school at the north end of the main street catering well for a passing lunch crowd, and walkers looking for take-away sandwiches of which they have a wide, made-to-order selection. Also on the menu are jackets, quiche, soup, scones and traditional-recipe cakes.

1 Blanchland. 2 Sheep grazing on moorland near Edmundbyers. ▶

Blanchland & the River Derwent

❄ OS Explorer map 307; start: by the humpback bridge on the village side of the River Derwent ♀ NY966503; 1¼ miles; easy.

Though muddy in places, this is a straightforward 1¼-mile riverside trail through gentle wooded countryside (unsuitable for wheelchairs and buggies) that makes for a pleasant evening wander if you're staying in Blanchland.

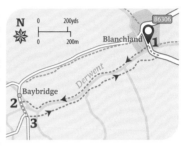

1 By the old stone bridge and with your back to the village, turn right following a grassy track to the **River Derwent**, past a little playground and then over a wooden bridge. There are plenty of places for children to throw stones and a few bathing pools ahead when water levels are high enough. Keep the Derwent on your left, following a well-trodden path upstream through trees (whose raised roots make the trail very uneven in parts) by the side of a drystone wall which is crossed a few times (note the hefty coping stones on some lengths). A fairy waterfall trickles down the opposite side of the gorge to meet the river, where dippers and grey wagtails are a familiar sight. Pass through a couple of gates and walk the length of a boardwalk until you reach a road.

2 Turn left on meeting the road, crossing a bridge over the Derwent (turning right here, incidentally, would take you back to Blanchland via farmland to the north above the village with plenty of views of the stone houses and surrounding countryside).

3 Now on the south side of the Derwent, you'll see the entrance to **woodland** on your left. Follow the trail through dark conifers and then brighter broadleaved trees, and at one point stepping over the aforementioned cascade running down the bank. Return to the village by the hump-backed bridge.

14 HUNSTANWORTH

Remote and presumably quite inaccessible during snowstorms, the intriguing village of Hunstanworth, a few miles south of Blanchland, is dotted about an exposed hillside on the edge of the Pennine moors, high above the Derwent, and is not somewhere you are likely to visit unless you are enjoying a scenic route to Weardale or heading off for a walk in the hills around Blanchland. It immediately catches the eye with its period houses, outwardly unaltered stone farm, striking church and nearby Methodist chapel. Architecturally harmonious even to the lay observer, Hunstanworth was the work of showy London architect Samuel Sanders Teulon, who redesigned the village in 1863. His signature use of multicoloured bricks and slates and Gothic accents here and there are scattered about the village but perhaps most noticeably in the diamond patterned roof of **St James's Church**, which is also noted for its pyramidal tower roof.

Those with a fondness for trivia may delight in knowing that Hunstanworth is the only 'Thankful Village' in Durham and one of only around 40 in England and Wales, so named because all their World War I soldiers returned safely home; in the case of Hunstanworth, there were five fortunate men, four of whom were brothers whose service is recognised in St James's.

If you were to continue on your travels south, the road out of the village continues its climb away from the grazing pastures, meadows and woodlands of the Derwent Valley and up on to the heather moors above Rookhope. Snow posts signal you are entering one of the highest and most isolated areas of upland landscape in England. Now brace yourself for the descent into Weardale.

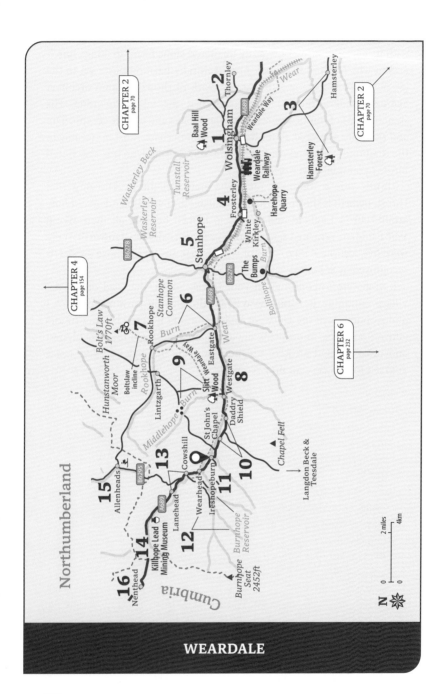

WEARDALE

5
WEARDALE

From the top of the next enormous mountain we had a view of
Weardale. It is a lovely prospect. The green, gently-rising meadows and
fields on both sides of the little river, clear as crystal, were sprinkled
over with innumerable little houses; three in four of which (if not nine
in ten) are sprung up since the Methodists came hither. Since that time,
the beasts are turned into men, and the wilderness into a fruitful field.
John Wesley, founder of Methodism, writing in his journal, June 1772

Weardale, one of the principal Durham Dales, flanked by Teesdale to
the south and Derwentdale to the north, changed profoundly in the
centuries following Wesley's missionary trips in the late 18th century as
lead mining accelerated and workers flooded into the area. A hundred
years later, spoil heaps, fissures and pits littered the valley; the hills
honeycombed for their minerals. When author Alfred Wainwright
walked through Weardale in 1939, the mines had been closed many
decades but he found 'hideous scars' and the 'desolation of abandoned
dwellings' in many places. '[C]rumbling ruins where once was bustling
activity, death where there was life' he wrote. He had few complimentary
things to say of the dale, which he first set eyes on in the rain: 'I was out
of the mist, and looking down on a soaking, bedraggled valley. This was
Weardale, quite the least attractive dale I saw.'

Today, the population of Weardale, which cuts a west–east course
through the heart of the North Pennines Area of Outstanding Natural
Beauty, is a fraction of what it was during the boom years of the 19th
century, and in many ways the valley has reverted to something like it
was in Wesley's day: upland hay meadows and remote farmsteads rising
above trailing villages, hamlets dotted along the Wear, and Methodist
chapels appearing in every settlement and on many a lonely fellside.
Reminders of the mining industries still mark the valley sides, but today
appear as natural features; and where Wainwright saw ruin, destruction
and a grey palette, today's visitor will find the abandoned barns rather

picturesque; discover heritage attractions where once there were mines; beauty in bleakness; and life where there was death.

As you climb out of the valley, the dale appears increasingly unspoiled, wild and remote; it is, in the words of poet W H Auden, 'the most wonderfully desolate of all the Dales'. Stanhope Common, Bolt's Law, Chapelfell Top, Middlehope Moor, Allendale Common and Waskerley are all rich in emptiness – and stunning in the sunshine.

Historic **Wolsingham** stands at the eastern end of the valley and serves as a good base to explore Weardale's hills and one of the largest recreational woods in the North East, **Hamsterley Forest**.

Stanhope, one of the principal settlements in the valley, serves as a gateway to the hills, providing supplies and information. It is also a very pleasant town in its own right and you could easily spend a few hours musing around local craft shops, taking a dip in the heated open-air swimming pool or a ride on the **heritage railway line**.

Attractions in and around the head of the valley, close to the Cumbrian border, include the superb **Killhope Lead Mining Museum** on the site of an old mine, and the historic villages of **Nenthead** (Cumbria) and **Allenheads** (Northumberland) with more in the way of mining heritage.

I've arranged this chapter for visitors entering the dale from the east and described the villages and hamlets encountered as you travel up the valley from Wolsingham, as well as a scattering of places on the fell sides and some recommended half-day walks.

GETTING AROUND

You are going to need your own wheels to explore the dale unless you stick to the villages and towns along the Wear, in which case the useful Bishop Auckland to Cowshill Weardale 101 **bus** (weardale-travel. co.uk Mon–Sat) shuttles through the valley many times a day, stopping at Wolsingham, Frosterley, Stanhope, St John's Chapel, Ireshopeburn, Wearhead and a few other places. The Durham to Stanhope Arriva X46 (arrivabus.co.uk/north-east Mon–Fri) also stops at Wolsingham and Frosterley. Connecting Stanhope and Rookhope, Weardale 102 (Mon–Fri; three times a day) may be of help but you'll need to plan your day around the restricted timetable.

A heritage line, the **Weardale Railway** (page 200), currently operates between Wolsingham and Stanhope with the full 16-mile route between

Bishop Auckland West and Stanhope due to reopen following works (check online for updates) by Easter 2023. While trains are seasonal and only run three times a day, so long as you plan your travels well, you'll find the line useful for return trips when combined with linear walks through the valley, for example, the Weardale Way between Stanhope and Frosterley.

Driving through the valley is a breeze on the A689 but a glance at a road map will reveal a minor paved lane south of the Wear between Stanhope and Ireshopeburn that motorists looking for a quieter, more scenic route, may prefer. **Cyclists** take note, this lane is a wonderfully peaceful route with views of meadows all around and is the obvious – and only sensible way – to pedal through Weardale as the A689 is busy and narrow in places.

WALKING & CYCLING

There are some superb **walks** on to the fells around Rookhope and the old hunting forests (moorland) of the Prince Bishops of Durham above Stanhope and through flower meadows, particularly in Upper Weardale in the vicinity of St John's Chapel and Ireshopeburn.

A string of hamlets and villages along the River Wear make good starting points for hikes into the hills rising out of the dale. In this chapter I've pulled together some of my favourite short walks and village strolls that take in places with geological, mining and wildlife interest, but I have left the long day hikes over the fells to some of the excellent hiking guides to the region, notably Paddy Dillon's *Walking in the North Pennines* (Cicerone).

Jaunts through Weardale by **bicycle** are highly recommended, particularly the leisurely route south of the Wear described on page 202. Strong lungs are needed for any cyclist venturing on to the moors, but once you reach the plateau you'll find miles of open roads and old railway trackbeds offering tremendous views of the North Pennines. The 140-mile **Coast-to-Coast** cycle ride from St Bees to Sunderland passes through Weardale between Nenthead and Stanhope, via Allenheads and Ireshopeburn, on wonderfully high and remote roads as well as making use of the off-road railway trackbed between Rookhope and Rowley. This is a fantastic route with outstanding moorland scenery and views through the dale.

Some of England's highest roads connect Weardale with Teesdale and the Derwent Valley and are very popular with cyclists including the **Blanchland to Stanhope** road via Rookhope (page 180), **Langdon Beck to St John's Chapel** (page 307) and **Westgate to Newbiggin**. It goes without saying that they offer some of the most thrilling descents in the country – as well as really tough climbs, of course.

Mountain bikers are very well catered for in **Hamsterley Forest** with its long-established network of gentle and challenging routes through the trees (page 196).

CYCLE HIRE & REPAIRS

North Pennine Cycles Nenthead CA9 3PF ✆ 01434 341004. Well known to Coast-to-Coast cyclists is this independent bicycle shop and repair workshop in the centre of Nenthead that has been around for years.

Ride Hamsterley Hamsterley Forest Main Car Park, Redford Ln, Bedburn DL13 3NL ✆ 0333 4440629 ⬧ hamsterley.bike/hire-bikes ◷ 09.30–16.00 Sat, 10.00–15.00 Sun. Bikes from £16/adult and £8/child, helmets extra.

TAXIS
Peter's Private Hire Stanhope ✆ 01388 527812
Weardale Private Hire ✆ 01388 537800
Wolsingham Taxi ✆ 01388 526328/07766 491037

LOWER WEARDALE: WOLSINGHAM, FROSTERLEY & STANHOPE

🏠 **Bonners Lodge** (page 310) 🏡 **Bowlees Cottages** (page 310), **Stanhope Castle** (page 310), **Woodcroft Farm** (page 310) ⛺ **Bonners Lodge Caravan Park** (page 311)

Wolsingham's quiet stone streets and location on the eastern edge of Weardale amid rolling hills and popular recreational areas make the town a good base for a jaunt into the surrounding countryside or exploring deeper into the dale. **Hamsterley Forest**, a huge expanse of woodland ten miles south of Wolsingham, is very popular with local

WEARDALE'S COUNTRY SHOWS

Weardale is at the heart of an important hill-farming region in the North Pennines, which is celebrated during the summer at a number of long-established agricultural shows popular with families, visitors and the farming community. Watch the 'best in show' livestock competitions, enjoy regional foods from the many excellent food producers across the North East, and and all the usual – and unique – range of country stalls and events.

Stanhope Unthank Park, Stanhope DL13 2PQ ⊘ stanhopeshow.com. Held over the second weekend in September, this is one of the oldest and largest shows in the North Pennines and features livestock and horticultural competitions, country crafts, equine and vintage vehicle displays and plenty to keep children amused (medieval re-enactments, birds of prey, entertainers). A vintage and handmade fair with antiques, upcycled furniture and local crafts occupies part of the main showfield for one day.

Weardale Show St John's Chapel DL13 1QF ⊘ weardale-show.co.uk. A large show in a small village held on the second to last weekend in August at the heart of Weardale, also known as the Chapel Show, with plenty to entertain visitors: craft and produce tents; a climbing wall for children; all the usual cattle and sheep displays; horse jumping; and many minor competitions such as bale stacking, races, quoits and drystone walling.

Wolsingham Show Scotch Isle Park, Wolsingham DL13 3JG ⊘ wolsinghamshow.co.uk. Durham's largest agricultural show comes together over the first weekend in September and is divided in two: the Agricultural Day on Saturday, and the Country Fair on Sunday, with a huge number of competitions, exhibits, stalls and rides to make for a full day out: cattle, dog, horse and sheep competitions; musicians; falconers; traditional dancers; donkey rides; strongman and farriery competitions; heavy horses; and many regional food and craft stalls.

families and mountain bikers, and, a few miles north of the town, is **Tunstall Reservoir**, a local beauty spot shrouded in trees and offering a few options for walks.

Next upriver are the market towns of **Frosterley** and **Stanhope**, each with their individual character and places of historical interest, but Stanhope really sells itself as a base for tourists, owing to its handsome town centre, useful shops, and central location at the gateway to the wilder, upper reaches of the valley. Both towns are serviced by the delightful heritage railway and are blessed with some beautiful hill and river scenery close by.

1 WOLSINGHAM

Wolsingham is strikingly unchanged (if you overlook the incongruous modern 'Holywood' mansions on a hill above the town), particularly around Market Place where a number of 18th- and 19th-century streets converge, forming one of the most attractive stone centres of any town in the Durham Dales.

A few cafés and pubs, conspicuously the old Black Bull inn, cluster around **Market Place** where you'll also find a couple of shops and a bank machine. River and railway run largely undetected along the southern edge of the village, passing the town's wonderfully intact **Victorian station** (now a private house but you can admire its original station clock, lanterns, canopy and signage from the platform) with heritage steam and diesel trains operating from here on the **Weardale Railway** (page 200).

Two cottages at 27 and 29 Front Street, next to the three-storey Georgian-looking Whitfield House, stand out for being much older, dating to 1677: one has mullioned windows and they both have stone-flagged roofs. If you're taking a stroll around here, at the western end of town, do make a diversion up the lovely sparrow-filled lane that leads to the **church of St Mary's and St Stephen's**. The churchyard is a peaceful

HARPERLEY POW CAMP & WEARDALE CHEESE

A689 between Wolsingham and Crook, about 600yds west of the A68 roundabout

Still with its canteen, theatre and some 40-odd derelict huts, is this prisoner of war camp, a rare survival from World War II between Wolsingham and Crook. On the refectory walls, the paintings of mountains and a boy in lederhosen playing the pipe would have once evoked happy memories of home for the German (and Italian) inmates. The purpose-built theatre even has an orchestra pit. Prisoners worked here as farm labourers and some never left Weardale after the war ended.

Though the camp is not open to the public, you can peer through the wall of conifer trees and just make out the huts, some with moss-covered roofs. One building, number 16, has found a new use as the home of **Weardale Cheese** ($\mathscr{D}$ 07564 196019), a local firm producing seven cheeses including their signature creamy 'Weardale' and a couple of blues, which you may spot for sale in local cafés, shops, farm shops and farmers' markets. In Weardale try Peggotty's in Wolsingham (page 195), Woodhalls Greengrocers or Castle Bank Butchers in Stanhope, or the Chatterbox Café in St John's Chapel (page 210).

spot where a couple of footpaths strike across grasslands to meet with the Waskerley Beck (see below for more details of a short walk). Enjoy, too, the stone faces either side of the lancet windows, including one under the clock tower with coloured eyeballs and another with his tongue out. While the church was significantly remodelled in Victorian times, the arcade inside is 14th century and the lower part of the tower is Norman.

Over the first weekend in September, one of the oldest **agricultural shows** in England takes over grasslands at the eastern edge of Wolsingham (page 191).

Walks direct from the town centre are plentiful, including a half-mile stroll along the lovely **Waskerley Beck** from the **Demesne Mill Picnic Area** at the north end of town (access from the B6296 Tow Law road). A paved path passes some lovely little waterfalls and pools on this roughly square course across fields. After the falls, follow the path as it swings left, then turn left again at a junction with other routes to emerge at the top of St Mary's churchyard. Follow a clear track out of the northeast corner of the churchyard back to the parking and picnicking area.

Tunstall Reservoir & Baal Hill Wood

A few miles north of Wolsingham is the local beauty spot, **Tunstall Reservoir**. Thickly enclosed by broadleaved woods along its eastern edge (Backstone Bank Wood), the tranquil Victorian lake can be walked along a permissive path in 2½ miles. It's a popular route beginning from a parking area in conifers on the western side where there are picnic tables.

You can **walk** to the reservoir from Wolsingham in little over two miles following a footpath from Holywell Farm (♀ NZ076378; not far from the Bay Horse Inn and reached off the B6296; alternatively start from the Demesne Mill Picnic Area where there is ample parking). This route via **Baal Hill House farmhouse** (a 16th-century defensive bastle house) leads through beautiful **Baal Hill Wood**, an ancient woodland once owned by the bishops of Durham during the 14th century. Bluebells, many ferns and carpets of wild garlic emerge in spring under a canopy of oak and birch trees. Look out for rare birds associated with very old woods including red start and pied flycatcher. The onward path to Tunstall Reservoir follows the Waskerley Beck upstream the whole way to the dam. Equipped with Ordnance Survey Map OL31 you can plot your return route across countryside via the reservoir's permissive

path and High Jofless Farm, which completes a circuit of around eight miles (a stiff hike but with wonderful views and a variety of scenery).

¶¶ FOOD & DRINK

For its size, Wolsingham is surprisingly short on places to eat, which makes the good local Italian, **Buon Appetito** (8 West End ✆ 01388 529124 ⊙ Tue–Sun) even more popular with locals. **The Black Bull** (27 Market Pl ✆ 01388 417355 ⊙ noon–late daily) in the centre sees a lively crowd of locals packed into its small front room. The fire was on when I visited on an already warm evening and there was a good deal of banter (and beer) flowing. Expect standard pub grub: burgers, curry and Sunday roast to enjoy inside or in the beer garden to the rear.

For coffees and lunches there are two cafés in the town centre: **No 10** (10 Market Pl ✆ 01388 528714 ⊙ Thu–Tue) serving breakfasts, paninis, jackets, toasties and a few hot dishes including burgers and scampi; and **Peggotty's** (1 Angate St ✆ 01388 527093 ⊙ 09.00–16.00 Tue–Sat), a popular bakery and pantry offering sandwiches, jackets, pies and coffees to take-away. Also consider **Field's Fish & Chips** in East Hedleyhope (page 91).

2 THORNLEY

Only those who make a wrong turn on their way to or from Weardale will find themselves ambling along lanes through this diminutive village on the outskirts of Wolsingham, which I include in this guide purely because it makes a rather lovely diversion on a backroad crawl through the Dales.

A **war memorial** at a triangular green below the old schoolhouse and facing a sloping vale is dedicated to the eight village servicemen killed in World War I, three of whom were sons of the local vicar. To the rear, the cross shaft holds a bronze sword. Thornley's centre is a little further on, past the picturesque Chapel House, where old cottages, a playing green, farms and a Hall dating to the early 1700s encircle **St Bartholemew's Church**, a solidly Victorian centrepiece building with a Gothic spire (and Frosterley marble font inside).

3 HAMSTERLEY FOREST & VILLAGE

Redford Ln, Bedburn DL13 3NL ✆ 01388 488312 ♿

Durham's largest forest blankets nearly 5,000 acres of high moorland between Weardale and Teesdale, five miles south of Wolsingham, and

◀ **1** View towards Stanhope. **2** Hamsterley Forest. **3** Weardale Railway at Frosterley.
4 Danny Hart's Descend Bike Park at Hamsterley. **5** Wolsingham Show.

is best known for its long-established mountain-biking trails (graded according to difficulty) and family-friendly walking trails centred around a main visitor centre car park at Bedburn where there are plenty of play areas and a café. In coming years, a new visitor centre, cabin holiday accommodation and a Go Ape treetop course will increase the infrastructure in the forest (see ⌀ forestryengland.uk/hamsterley-forest for updates).

Walking trails follow **Bedburn Beck** and take in the forest scenery on routes ranging from the 'Gruffalo Trail' and a 1½-mile pushchair and wheelchair-friendly route to some 4½-mile circuits. A scenic four-mile **Forest Drive** cuts through the forest, providing access to some quieter corners – and more trails. There are several places to park along the way.

"A scenic four-mile Forest Drive cuts through the forest, providing access to some quieter corners – and more trails."

The Grove parking area (♀ NZ066298) in the centre of the forest marks the start point of one of the longer walks along Spurleswood Beck, visiting a couple of delightful **waterfalls**: Greenless Hole and Blackling Hole. For direct access to Blackling Hole waterfall, park further west along Forest Drive at ♀ NZ053275.

Well known to mountain bikers are four exhilarating downhill tracks operated by **Danny Hart's Descend Bike Park** (✆ 07882 972982 ⌀ descendbikepark.com ☉ 09.00–15.00 Wed–Sun; book uplifts in advance).

Spread across high ground with generous views and several greens is **Hamsterley village**, a couple of miles east of the forest visitor centre. It's a nice old place with a Baptist Chapel dating to 1774, a pond, and terraces of sandstone cottages. The parish **church of St James** is some half a mile outside of the village and is noted for its Early English architecture and hilltop views.

4 FROSTERLEY

Known for its black 'marble', a limestone containing fossilised sea creatures (page 198), Frosterley is famous throughout the region and much further afield, particularly where fine examples of its polished stone appear on altar stones, effigies, shafts, church fonts and, spectacularly, in Durham Cathedral (page 37), although not, it would seem, in Frosterley itself. However, visitors can see the stone in its raw

METHODIST CHAPELS

With increasing industrialisation and population growth in the region came new forms of Christianity. Methodism had the most profound impact in the North Pennines, and John Wesley, the founder of the Methodist movement, preached in the valleys many times during the 18th century, establishing some of the earliest Methodist chapels here. Today, though a number have been converted into private properties, you'll still see Primitive and Wesleyan chapels in every town and village and scattered on the most remote fells. Few are open to view internally except for High House Chapel (page 210) and the chapel in Nenthead, now The Hive, a wonderful café and community space (page 226). The latter's decorative interior is intact and very similar to the important chapel at Westgate, among others.

Four of the oldest and most important remaining chapels are: **Keenley Chapel**, East Allendale, built 1750; **High House Chapel** (page 210), Ireshopeburn, built 1760; **Westgate Chapel** (page 206), an important place in the development of Primitive Methodism and housing a wonderfully unchanged decorative interior dating to 1871; and **Newbiggin Chapel** (page 291) in Teesdale (now closed) which still houses the pulpit from where Wesley preached in the mid 18th century.

form in the car park adjacent to the village hall where there is a large boulder on display.

Apart from its association with marble, a **heritage railway station** (for rides through the valley, see page 200) and some pleasant routes into the hills, Frosterley is otherwise a rather plain town with a mix of the old and the new, a Co-op food store, a fish and chip take-away (though there are superior chippies not far away in Barnard Castle, Stanhope and East Hedleyhope) and an old pub, the Frosterley Inn (99 Front St ✆ 01388 528493), serving standard pub grub and Sunday lunches. The town just isn't the same without the lovingly restored

"Frosterley is famous throughout the region and much further afield, particularly where fine examples of its polished stone appear."

Black Bull Inn that once served some of the best food in the dale until the Covid pandemic sealed its fate; it's worth checking online, however, in case it ever reopens.

One of the best reasons to visit Frosterley is for the **walking** routes along burns and on to surrounding fells with the Weardale Way providing access to some fine upland scenery in a number of places.

This is particularly true of the countryside south of Frosterley around the medieval settlement of **White Kirkley**, from where you can walk to **Harehope Quarry** along the Weardale Way in a mile or so, enjoying some beautiful woodland and meadow landscapes, a limestone gorge formed by Harehope Gill, and an old lead mine. Wonderful valley views open up by a well-known boot-carved bench on the long-distance path just west of Harehope Gill woods. A there-and-back route is recommended but you can return via woodland along the northern edge of Broadhope Quarry, which climbs to some height above the River Wear – note that this route does require close attention to Ordnance Survey Map OL31.

"Wonderful valley views open up by a well-known boot-carved bench on the long-distance path just west of Harehope Gill woods."

Following the Weardale Way in the other direction (south) from White Kirkley, more in the way of views and hills greet the walker including local landmark, the **Elephant Trees** (♥ NZ040343), a copse on the northern edge of Pikeston Fell seen for miles around.

The Bumps

A popular beauty spot in the area is the **Bollihope Burn picnic area** by an old quarry known locally as **The Bumps** (♥ NZ005349), a few miles south of Frosterley station (by road, follow the signs for White Kirkley

FROSTERLEY MARBLE

Quarried in its namesake Weardale village for centuries, this black marble is distinctive for its numerous white fossilised sea creatures that once swam in the tropical seas bathing the North Pennines 325 million years ago. The marble appears in some important buildings in the North Pennines, as well as churches elsewhere in the UK and even in Mumbai's cathedral in India. It's actually a limestone, polished to great effect to reveal the white skeletons of crinoids and corals and features extensively in the Anglo-Saxon Escomb Church near Bishop Auckland (page 96) and in Auckland Castle (page 111), but most strikingly in the 13th-century Chapel of the Nine Altars in Durham Cathedral (page 37).

You can see the stone in its natural state at **Bollihope Burn**, while for further insight you should head to **Harehope Quarry** environment education centre and nature reserve (Frosterley DL13 2SG ⌂ harehopequarry.org.uk ✆ 07807 002032), signposted off the A689 south of the River Wear.

from the A689 at the western end of Frosterley and follow the lane via Hill End). Now a series of grassy humps between the burn and a lake and opposite some impressive crags, the disused quarry is a pleasant place to have lunch. Many families picnic by the river where the road crosses Bollihope Burn and from where you can access The Bumps and set your children free to run up and down the slopes. You can also walk here from White Kirkley following the Weardale Way upriver for a mile.

5 STANHOPE

The gateway to Upper Weardale is a lively old stone market town with plenty of historic buildings and streets of note, and caters reasonably well for visitors with a few cafés, a Co-op food store, a great butchers and greengrocer, post office and information centre (the Durham Dales Centre; see below and page 201). Cyclists pull up for refreshments outside pubs, there's a constant stream of visitors coming and going from the Durham Dales Centre, and farm trucks laden with livestock and hay bales pass through on the main thoroughfare.

> "The gateway to Upper Weardale is a lively old stone market town with plenty of historic buildings and streets of note."

The parish of Stanhope (pronounced 'Stannup') was hugely wealthy in the 19th century because of a tithe on lead ore claimed by the church; the old rectory (a Georgian mansion on Front Street) is evidence of those heady days.

A good place to start your tour is the **Durham Dales Centre** (Castle Gardens, DL13 2FJ ✆ 01388 527650 ⊙ 10.00–17.00 daily ♿) on the main road just west of the Market Place and the parish church. Arranged around a courtyard with plenty of parking, picnic tables and a tea room, the centre acts as a tourist-information point selling maps but is best known for its local craft shops selling pottery, artworks and handmade cosmetics, children's clothes and toys and so on. Note that the tea room and most of the craft shops close at 16.00.

Stanhope Castle, a late 18th-century, heavily castellated manor (now divided into holiday cottages), is somewhat hidden in the corner of **Market Place**, eyeing Stanhope's principal street lined with stone houses and a police station whose frontage – still with its blue lantern – can't have changed in well over a hundred years (and not since this author's great-grandfather was stationed there).

WEARDALE RAILWAY

📞 01388 526203 ℮ weardale-railway.org.uk ⊙ Apr–Oct Wed & Sat (but check online as this may change), plus additional days in Aug, Easter & Christmas.

Opened in 1847 during the boom years of mineral extraction, this branch line of the Stockton & Darlington Railway was eventually extended to Stanhope and Wearhead but by the time it reached the end of the line in 1895 the lead mining industry was on the wane.

The line closed in 1993 but reopened soon after as a heritage railway with stations at **Bishop Auckland West** (a five-minute walk from the town's mainline station), **Witton-le-Wear**, **Wolsingham**, **Frosterley** and **Stanhope**. At the time of writing, the line was restricted to a six-mile stretch between Wolsingham and Stanhope but by Easter 2023, it will hopefully run for 16 miles between Bishop Auckland West

and Stanhope with the potential to extend to Eastgate in the distant future. Steam and diesel engines run three-times daily when operational, taking in unspoilt valley scenery as they chug above the wooded River Wear. The old station buildings and arched iron bridge at Stanhope are particularly eye-catching, as is the station in Wolsingham (a private house but still with all its original features and signage).

The six-mile stretch of the Weardale Way between Stanhope and Frosterley via Hill End and White Kirkley offers a scenic walk across countryside south of the Wear that can be combined with the heritage railway to make for a rewarding circuit of the two towns.

Opposite the castle is a **market cross** (incidentally, the original medieval shaft stands in the churchyard) and **St Thomas the Apostle Church** (⊙ 09.30–16.30 daily). The stump of a 250-million-year-old **fossil tree** found on moorland rests in an opening of the churchyard wall. More treasures await inside St Thomas's, (including a Frosterley marble font and a Roman altar stone) but before you enter, take in the exterior – specifically the short, sturdy-looking tower, the lower part of which is Norman and contains medieval stained glass in its windows. Much of the rest of the church is 12th century.

Stanhope's **outdoor heated swimming pool** (Castle Park, DL13 2LU 📞 01388 528466 ℮ stanhopepool.co.uk ⊙ May school hols & Jun–Sep), a short walk west from Durham Dales Centre, is gloriously unexpected in this Pennine market town. The 25m pool is run by volunteers and warmed to 27°C. Behind the swimming pool is a playground as well as a picnic area by the Wear where some **stepping stones** provide a tempting way of reaching the southern banks of the river. On your walk to all these places from the town centre, glance over at the premises of the **Stanhope Silver Band** on Cross Street, opposite the Town Hall. The brass band is one of the oldest in England and has been performing at local events for 200 years, including at the annual **agricultural show** on the second weekend in September (page 191).

Family fun can be had by taking a **heritage steam ride** (page 200) from Stanhope's wonderfully restored station on Bondisle Way, reached at the eastern end of the town and signed off the main road.

¶¶ FOOD & DRINK

While there are few places to eat in Stanhope, you will find a Tandoori take-away and fish and chip shop in the centre, and the highly recommended Spanish restaurant, Che (see below), a short walk west out of town. For a light lunch in Stanhope, apart from the Durham Dales Tearoom (see below), there's the **Everyday Café** (27 Front Street ✆ 01388 526013 ⊙ daily; last food orders at 15.00) serving jackets, sandwiches, sausage baps, burgers and fish goujons; and a café on the platform of the heritage train station (**No. 40** Stanhope Station, DL13 2YS ✆ 01388 526203 ⊙ Sat).

Che Horn Hall Farm, DL13 2JR (by the B6278, just off the main A689 through Stanhope) ✆ 07394 635541. A ten-minute walk west out of Stanhope is this authentic restaurant run by a Spanish family, serving many familiar dishes from the Mediterranean: chorizo, meat platters, tortilla, meatballs, seafood, steak, plus vegan options like spinach ravioli and a burger. Leave room for a pudding: Basque cheesecake, churros, Tarta Santiago, lemon mouse or Spanish cheeses. Reservations by text.

Durham Dales Tearoom Castle Gardens, DL13 2FJ ✆ 01388 527650 ⊙ 10.00–16.00 daily &. Convenient and inexpensive café in the Durham Dales Centre, with an outside courtyard. Teas, basic sandwiches, jackets, pies, quiches and toasties.

Parkhead Tea Room Stanhope Moor, DL13 2ES ✆ 01388 526434 ⊙ 10.00–15.00 Thu & Fri, 10.00–16.00 Sat & Sun; last food order 14.30 &. A former station house and now a welcoming high-altitude café three miles north of Stanhope on the route of the Coast-to-Coast and Waskerley Way, Parkhead has served as a refuge for weary cyclists for years. If arriving by bike along the old railway path you will be so pleased for the rest stop on this remote moorland that you'll be more than happy with a no-frills bowl of chips, sandwich, slice of cake and a hot cup of tea, which is good because that's what's on offer. Their speciality is a hot beef roll that comes recommended. And what a great atmosphere, with cheery cyclists coming and going and no finer view in the whole of the dale. If you're staying in Stanhope, it's definitely somewhere you might like to visit even if just for a hot drink and stroll along the old railway trackbed. Also has B&B accommodation.

UPPER WEARDALE

🏠 **Westgate Manor** (page 310) 🏚 **Barrington Bunkhouse** (page 310), **Low Cornriggs Holiday Cottages** (page 310)

Upriver from Stanhope, Weardale becomes increasingly remote and seemingly unspoilt with far-reaching views of villages and hamlets nestled below some hefty moors. A long history of mineral extraction, Methodism and farming permeate through the fabric of streets and across fellsides; spend enough time in these hills and you will soon learn to distinguish between a natural chasm and a manmade hush; a hillock from a grassed-over spoil heap.

Fell-foot hamlets and villages come every few miles: **Eastgate**, **Westgate**, **Daddry Shield**, **St John's Chapel**. Diversions away from river and road reveal minor valleys (many places and their associated burns are suffixed with 'hope' meaning 'valley', including Rookhope, Hollihope and Middlehope) and the miner-farmer landscape of the 19th century. Even just a short climb above the Wear offers a striking panorama of the facing vale, all pleasingly divided into small meadows in the traditional way with drystone walls, and dotted with stone cottages, barns and huts.

If you are not in a hurry (and especially for cyclists), I'd recommend turning off the main A689 and taking the quiet lane along the south side of the Wear from Stanhope to St John's Chapel which winds past old stone farms, cottages, sheep grazing in meadows and the odd stone bridge, and offers much in the way of scenic views of a traditional upland farming landscape. The tranquil unclassified lane on the north side of the Wear between Daddry Shield and Cowshill makes for an equally memorable ride with meadows brimming with wildflowers and wading birds in spring and early summer, and old stone architecture.

6 ROOKHOPE BURN & EASTGATE

Rookhope Burn gushes off the old hunting forest of the bishops of Durham and through the stone hamlet of Eastgate to meet with the Wear, but you'd only know that if you were to trace the waterway upstream in the direction of Rookhope (see opposite). **Eastgate** itself is a quiet stone hamlet straddling the burn with an old pub, the Cross Keys, on one side, and a water mill (its sloping stone-flagged roof suggestive of its 300 years), Wesleyan Chapel and parish church on the other.

There's a rewarding **walk** through woods here and past a number of small falls that can be combined with the Weardale Way to make for a five-mile loop (you'll need ❀ OS Explorer OL31 & 307). The footpath to the burn is reached by following the sound of running water around the back of the mill and across a footbridge where you can follow the aforementioned path upstream to some small **waterfalls**. If you want to make the circular route, continue ahead following the trail as it diverts westwards away from the burn and uphill, eventually meeting with the Weardale Way at Bishop Seat where you turn right towards Rookhope. At Smailsburn, return to the burn, crossing it and then picking up the riverside trail on the east side of Rookhope Burn for the return leg to Eastgate. For a longer walk, continue north from Smailsburn to Rookhope and enjoy more in the way of moorland scenery and the famous lead-mining heritage sites scattered about the village (see below).

¶¶ FOOD & DRINK

In an area with few options for lunch or a drink, **The Cross Keys** (✆ 01388 517234 ☉ food 17.00–20.00 daily, plus lunch Sat & Sun; book ahead for Sunday roasts) stands at a useful place in the valley by Rookhope Burn, which flows past its rear beer garden. Expect all the usual pub favourites on the menu (scampi, burgers, fish and chips, jackets and a few curries). **Horsley Hall** (DL13 2LJ ✆ 01388 517239 ☉ afternoon tea), a mile south of Eastgate, is an impressive 17th-century ten-bedroom country pile, formally a hunting lodge of the prince bishops and now catering for family groups and shooting parties but also serving afternoon tea (sandwiches, cakes, scones and tea) to non-guests in the extensive grounds or inside the dining hall. Booking ahead essential.

7 ROOKHOPE & SURROUNDS

In Rookhope I was first aware
Of self and not-self, Death and Dread:...
There I dropped pebbles, listened, heard
The reservoir of darkness stirred.

W H Auden, *New Year Letter*, 1940

The high-altitude mining village of Rookhope offers spectacular views of Weardale, walks and cycle rides over grouse-filled heather moors and much in the way of industrial archaeology, as well as a few places to stay (but sadly nowhere to eat and drink since the Rookhope Inn closed several years ago).

DUNCAN ANDISON/S

TM66IMAGES/S

JANKO BARTOLEC/DT

Rookhope was a favourite spot of the poet W H Auden, who found much inspiration from the juxtaposition of the natural landscape and industrial machinery; it was his spiritual home, a place of self-discovery for the young man who, as a teenager on holiday, came across an old lead mine shaft (almost certainly Sike Head shaft on Bolt's Law) where he dropped those famous stones, triggering an awakening captured in verse (page 203). When he was writing there were more visible signs of industry than there are today, but there are plenty of lead-mining relics still scattered about: derelict stone huts and miners' cottages; pits and quarries; a winding wheel (by the burn en route to the village of Lintzgarth) and the arresting **Rookhope Arch** (a few hundred yards west of Lintzgarth at ♥ NY92444298), a fragment of a smelt flue that once ran horizontally across the countryside carrying away toxic fumes. Its single arch appears today like an unintentional piece of public art and monument to an industry and way of life that dominated this land for over a hundred years.

A number of these fascinating ruins are easily viewed from a lonely road hugging the burn between Rookhope and Allenheads. Near the farmstead of **Wolf Cleugh** (such an evocative name for these wild parts), two miles west of Rookhope, a row of dilapidated 18th-century lead miners' houses stand close to the south side of the burn (♥ NY902432) and are accessible via a footpath signed off the road.

Cyclists are a frequent sight on the lanes around Rookhope, this being on the Coast-to-Coast route; **walkers** too make good use of an extensive network of trails, especially the Weardale Way that connects Westgate with Eastgate via Rookhope (see page 203 for a suggested walk). Another route up onto **Hunstanworth Moor** offers more in the way of superb heather scenery (page 180).

Stanhope Common

When travelling through Weardale, you will have passed the hamlets of Eastgate and then Westgate and perhaps noted 'Northgate' on a map of the fellside. You may also have wondered where Southgate is and why all these places are known as 'gates'. Well, there is no Southgate but the three 'gates' mark the entrances to an old hunting ground on **Stanhope**

◀ **1** Bollihope Burn, known locally as The Bumps. **2** Derelict miners' cottages at Rookhope.
3 Killhope Lead Mining Museum.

BOLTSLAW INCLINE

The highest standard-gauge railway in the UK, built in 1846 on remote moorland above Rookhope, is now a mix-used trail, but it was here, just below one of the highest places in the Pennines at **Bolt's Law** (at 1,770ft), that wagons once crossed the landscape laden with iron ore, limestone and lead (coal was transported on the return journey). An engine house powered a cable attached to the train that hauled the wagons uphill from Rookhope for about a quarter of a mile; for the onward journey to Tow Law, the wagons were pulled by a steam engine. The line closed in 1923 and all that remains, apart from the trackbed, is the ruin of the engine house at ♥ NY949442. You can follow the line for five spectacularly lonesome miles across Stanhope Common where it connects to the **Waskerley Way** – another old railway line now used for leisure by walkers and cyclists.

Common once owned by the bishops of Durham. Here, the grassy slopes are increasingly dominated by heather the higher you climb away from the river and soon there are hardly any signs of human habitation and you find yourself surrounded by some of the most spectacularly desolate upland countryside in England. At **Bolt's Law** – one of Auden's old haunts – stands 'the finger of all questions' – a lead mine chimney from where you can see five counties on a clear day.

8 WESTGATE

Westgate marks one entrance to the old bishop's hunting ground (see page 205) and is rather unremarkable in comparison to some other more quaint villages in the valley but, as always, you will find things of historical interest if you linger for long enough.

Westgate was an important place in the development of Methodism in the Pennines and here you'll find a beautifully ornate and well-preserved early **Primitive Methodist Chapel** dating to 1871 at the far western end of Front Street (opposite the caravan park). Services ceased in 2007 so access inside is not altogether straightforward (the keyholder, Charlie, lives in the village and can be contacted through a Facebook page called 'Westgate Methodist Chapel') but you can take it from the experts at Historic England that it is of national significance and 'exceptional in its intactness of both its exterior and interior'. Today its upkeep is in

"Internally, the chapel is praised for its decorative upper gallery supported by cast-iron columns and fine carpentry."

the hands of some dedicated local volunteers who do what they can to prevent decay. Internally, the chapel is praised for its decorative upper gallery supported by cast iron columns (painted to look like marble) and fine carpentry with benches curving round the corners of the church.

Other buildings of historical note include an old **Candle House**, once a familiar part of the vernacular architecture in lead-mining villages, this is where miners would collect their candles before going underground. It's the old, somewhat ramshackle barn with a long sloping roof at the junction of Front Street (the main road through the village) and a road signed for Rookhope. The Candle House aptly marks the start point of a fascinating three-mile circular **walk** described on page 208 following **Middlehope Burn** upstream through **Slitt Wood**, taking in a series of beautiful cascades, and artificial features that continue the lead-mining narrative.

¶¶ FOOD & DRINK

Hare & Hounds 24 Front St, DL13 1RX ✆ 01388 517212 ☉ usually from 18.30 daily, plus lunch Sun. Welcoming old-fashioned freehouse with its own brewery (Weardale Brewery), low ceilings, exposed beams and wooden furnishings, serving Sunday lunches and meat and veg dishes for evening meals during the week.

9 MIDDLEHOPE BURN & SLITT WOOD

Middlehope Burn rushes off the moors on its way to meet with the Wear below Westgate, passing through the atmospheric **Slitt Wood**, a Site of Special Scientific Interest (SSSI) woodland with displays of spring-flowering plants clothing the sloping banks of the burn. The beautiful setting is made all the more enchanting by a series of **waterfalls** revealing where layers of limestone, sandstone and shale have eroded at different rates to create natural shelves in the burn. If you get close to the water's edge you can see these different layers in the riverbanks and sift through the stones with your hand to find silvery shards of galena (lead ore) and other minerals like the purple-coloured fluorite deposited when a mine operated in the upper reaches of the valley.

About a mile upstream from Westgate, in a clearing by the water, stand the remains of **Low Slitt Lead Mine** that once worked one of the most important lead veins in the North Pennines. With the assistance of interpretation boards, you can make connections between the stone ruins and recreate how a Weardale lead mine operated. If you've already

METALLOPHYTES

Lead-tolerant plants flourish around old mine workings in the North Pennines where lead and other heavy metals polluted the soil. Many plants are unable to grow on such toxic sites, but a handful of species are remarkably hardy, including the deeply pigmented mountain pansy (the purple variety is the most common in the Pennines), alpine pennycress and spring sandwort, also known as 'leadwort', which is identified by its star-like arrangement of white petals. The old 'washing floors' of lead mines and spoil heaps are good places to look for them in spring and early summer, including at Low Slitt Lead Mine above Westgate.

visited Killhope Lead Mine further up the valley (page 218), you'll find it easier to make sense of the site. Things to look out for: the waterwheel pit (powered by a reservoir on the fell top above the site), mineshop, smithy, bouseteems (a storage area for lead ore – or 'bouse' – divided into compartments by stone walls which would have once had wagon rails running along the top) and the washing floor (where the ore was extracted from rocks and dirt by young lads).

"To enjoy a walk in Slitt Wood and visit the mine, there's a well-trodden route which traces Middlehope Burn upstream."

To enjoy a **walk** in Slitt Wood and visit the mine, there's a well-trodden route of around three miles which traces Middlehope Burn upstream through Slitt Wood and then across open fells (❀ OS Explorer OL31 & 307 ♀ NY901381; park at a lay-by opposite the caravan park in Westgate). To reach this trail, take the Rookhope road (signed) off the main road through Westgate and walk a few hundred yards uphill past houses to a prominent Wesleyan Methodist chapel, now converted into houses but still with its distinctive entranceway. A track off to the left leads to Slitt Woods where you begin your climb alongside Middlehope Burn. The first of a series of falls are just beyond High Mill (originally a corn mill). Half a mile from the mill, the path emerges from the trees at Low Slitt Lead Mine by some ruined bouseteems.

After exploring the heritage site (incidentally, the open space is a nice spot to picnic), you can continue north following the burn upstream which leads on to open fells. At the head of the valley, the trail meets with a lane where you turn right, then right again at a T-junction before the 1½-mile return along the Rookhope road south to Westgate via West Rigg Mine (an old opencast ironstone working, as the information board by the roadside explains), with Weardale laid before you. For a shorter walk, you can make use of a permissive path connecting Slitt Mine with West Rigg (marked on OS maps as a dotted track) and return via the Rookhope road.

10 DADDRY SHIELD & ST JOHN'S CHAPEL

As with many villages in the dale, **Daddry Shield**, half a mile downstream from St John's Chapel, flourished during the lead-mining boom of the early 19th century. The neat rows of miners' cottages facing the main road through the village date to this period. Wild swimmers (and the young who like to throw pebbles into rivers) will find a lovely spot by the Wear where the river sprays over a step into **Ham Pool** which is deep enough for a splash about (roughly 800yds upstream of the A689 road bridge over the River Wear).

The cobbled village centre of **St John's Chapel** with its post office and run of vintage shopfronts could almost be straight out of the Edwardian town at Beamish museum. Nestled in the heart of Weardale, this small village – named after its unusual Georgian church that is entered under a clock tower – sits under some impressive fells that are accessed directly from the village on foot.

The 1752 **church of St John the Baptist** (Hood St, DL13 1QQ ✐ 01388 537063 ☉ Apr–Aug 10.00–16.00 Wed & Sat; services 1st & 3rd Sun of month) replaced an earlier medieval building and provides a focal point in the centre of the village, along with a simple yet moving **war memorial** of a lone World War I soldier.

An impressive road (signed for Langdon Beck, just west of the village centre) connects Weardale with neighbouring Teesdale (page 307), and also marks the start of a **walk** up wooded Harthope Burn that passes some waterfalls. The footpath you're looking for is signed left off the Langdon Beck road after a bridge, by a short terrace of cottages ♥ NY883378). You can return in a loop along the lower reaches of Chapel Fell to Daddry Shield which offers superb views of the dale.

¶¶ FOOD & DRINK

Two pubs stand at either end of St John's Chapel. **The Golden Lion** (12 Market Pl, DL13 1QF ✐ 01388 537231 ☉ 17.00–late Mon–Fri, noon–late Sat & Sun) is a traditional 18th-century pub with low beams, a fire and plenty of local chatter around the pool table. While the menu is not extensive, what they do offer (steaks, pies, lasagne etc) is pleasing enough to accompany your pint from one of several local breweries (this being a freehouse). Best to call ahead to check they are serving food. **The Blue Bell Inn** (12 Hood St, DL13 1QJ ✆ 01388 537256 ⊙ 17.00–23.00 Tue–Thu, 14.00–midnight Fri, noon–midnight Sat & noon–23.00 Sun) is similarly a friendly locals' pub, drawing a merry crowd to the outside chairs on the main street in summer as it catches the evening sun. Inside, you'll find local beers and special food nights (barbeques for example – phone ahead to check).

Chatterbox Café 11 Market Pl, DL13 1QF ✆ 01388 335007 ⊙ 09.00–17.00 daily. This was the only place open early in the morning for many miles around one day on my travels in Weardale and I would have been more than content with a hot cuppa and some toast but I got much more than that on my plate when I ordered the Weardale Breakfast (proper sausages from Stanhope and all the other usual ingredients – no budget supermarket beans here). They also serve a Veggie Weardale and smaller meals (buns filled with any breakfast ingredient). Needless to say, I've happily made subsequent visits here. Lunch options include omelettes, quiche and jackets, but the best by far are the Pitmen Pies and sausage rolls (big meaty affairs made locally). Afternoon tea and cake people take note: they also serve very good flapjacks, chocolate cake, and peanut and caramel slices.

11 IRESHOPEBURN

> **The High House, on a Sunday afternoon is a spectacle worthy of beholding: here you may see assembled from six hundred to one thousand good-looking, fresh-coloured, and well-dressed persons of both sexes.**
> Local historian writing in 1842, quoted in the Weardale Museum

As you travel upstream through Weardale you will enter the trailing stone village of Ireshopeburn by **High House Chapel** (DL13 1HD; currently undergoing restoration). Until 2019, this was the oldest Methodist place of worship in continuous weekly use in the world. The church could be mistaken for a Georgian manor house owing to its considerable size but this important chapel is easy to miss because the front is obscured somewhat by trees. John Wesley preached here 13 times, first by a thorn tree before the chapel was built in 1760. It's the most striking of the early Methodist chapels, both for its size (which tells you something about the burgeoning population during the lead-mining boom of the late 18th century, and the tremendous rate at which Methodism caught

"The former minister's house next door to the chapel (note the fine curved, dressed stone) is now the Weardale Museum."

LEAD-MINING COMMUNITIES

The two big lead-mining companies operating in the North Pennines (W B Lead in the Allendales and Weardale, and the London Lead Company in Teesdale and around Alston) had a tremendous impact on the character of settlements through their promotion of obedience, discipline and education, which is partly why you see chapels, schools, reading rooms and mine agents' houses in many old mining villages.

Lead miners received paltry recompense for the lead ore they dug and for their reduced life expectancy from breathing in dangerous dust, so it became commonplace in the 18th and 19th centuries to supplement their income by farming. Small stone cottages and their associated enclosed fields, known as 'allotments', are a familiar feature on many hillsides to this day. Haymaking was once commonplace across the North Pennines in late summer and this low-intensive farming practice explains why the region remains botanically rich with the most extensive areas of upland hay meadows in England.

hold in the Pennines during this period) and particularly its interior, which has a Victorian organ and pews that wrap round the corners of the room.

The former minister's house next door to the chapel (note the fine curved, dressed stone) was built in 1804 and is now the **Weardale Museum** (Ireshopeburn DL13 1HD ✐ 01388 335085 & 07990 786220 ⊘ weardalemuseum.org.uk ☺ Apr, May & Oct 13.00–16.30 Wed–Sun; Jun–Sep 13.00–16.30 daily ⴅ ground-floor only). This great little folk museum is run by volunteers and packed with many curios discovered in the Dales: Stone Age flints, mineral crystals and many items relating to the social history of the area, the development of the Weardale Railway, and Pennine industries in the 18th and 19th centuries. The focal point is a period living room decorated as it might have looked in Victorian times with a cast-iron range, linen drying over ceiling rails, wooden furniture and everyday domestic items.

If you're interested in the lead mines, there's a lot to work through, including a lead 'pig' marked with the local mine 'W:Blackett' which was found not that long ago on the moors above Rookhope. After the lead was smelted it was cast into lengths – or 'pigs' – about 60cm long. It is a rare find for something once so commonly seen stored by the side of tracks and carried by packhorses (one on each side).

There's also an exhibition relating to John Wesley and the development of Methodism in Weardale, and a fascinating display dedicated to The

Ireshopeburn hay meadows walk

❋ OS Explorer OL31; start: Methodist Chapel, Ireshopeburn ♀ NY872385; 2½ miles; easy

A glance at an Ordnance Survey map reveals an obvious circular walk from Ireshopeburn into the surrounding countryside north of the Wear. It's a beautiful route, both for the dale views and hay meadows brimming with wildflowers from May to August.

1 With your back to **High House Chapel**, turn off the A689 and down a lane signed for New House, crossing the Wear over a stone bridge.

2 Turn right on the riverbank and pick up the **Weardale Way**, following the river downstream for around 500yds towards a junction with a few paths. Turn uphill then right, passing in front of cottages on your left. Trace the drystone wall uphill passing a farm (and over a farm track) to the tarmac lane at the top.

3 Cross the lane by a stone cottage and continue straight uphill, keeping the drystone wall on your left. The path swings in a long arc to the west to meet with another lane, a quarter of a mile uphill. Again, cross straight over this lane and traverse the side of the hill on a track to the farm at **Allercleugh**, keeping the wall on your right and taking in the fabulous meadows below you and the rougher ground above where the curlew cries all spring long.

4 Continue a short way past Allercleugh towards High Whitestones before turning downhill to **Whitestones Farm**. Stay on the farm track until you reach the lane at the bottom.

5 Pick up the footpath signed on the other side of the lane through Low Whitestones and into the field below, descending into the picturesque hamlet of **West Blackdene** by the riverside.

Westgate Subscription Library, founded in 1788. Here's an insightful reference to the library: 'To gain access to this treasury of knowledge; intelligent miners came from great distances impelled by their love of knowledge, they crossed over the mountains from the adjacent valleys and enrolled themselves members of the library in order to pursue at their leisure its literary treasures'.

Don't leave without taking a close look at the tapestries produced by some talented Durham stitchers in recent years. They tell the story of the dale with significant events embroidered in detail. The **Methodist Tapestries Project** is a new endeavour seeking to illuminate the history of Methodism through a series of needlework scenes.

6 Don't cross the charming stone bridge here but instead pick up the Weardale Way by taking the lane off to your left that runs alongside a stone terrace facing the river where the Wear splashes over several little pretty falls. Walk along this lane to another bridge. Continue eastwards (again, don't cross the water), taking the muddy riverside path for the final amble back to Ireshopeburn tracing your steps back over the Wear at the stone road bridge.

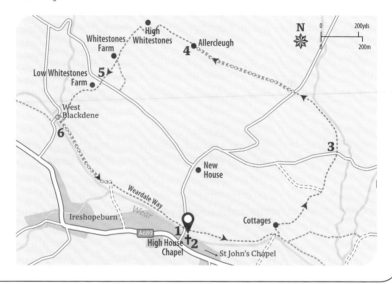

Facing Ireshopeburn above the northern banks of the Wear is the grand façade of **New House**, the headquarters of the mine agent in the 19th century when the industry dominated village life and well over half of all adults in the village were lead miners. According to records held at the Weardale Museum, other professions held in the village included agricultural workers, dress makers, servants, a grocer, butcher, shoemaker, cart man and straw-hat maker. At the back of the complex, which includes a former blacksmith's and workshops, is the old candle house where miners would visit before shifts. There's no public access so you're best viewing the buildings from afar, but if you did want to have a closer look, turn off the main A689 just west of the

Methodist Chapel on to a lane signed for New House, which crosses the Wear and climbs up the facing bank.

12 WEARHEAD & BURNHOPE RESERVOIR

A picturesque stone bridge carries the main road through the valley into the centre of Wearhead – a village that holds much rural charm with its stone terraces, riverside setting and surrounding meadows and moors. If only Wearhead had more in the way of facilities it would be a very fine place to base yourself for a visit to Upper Weardale. That said, it's still worth exploring and you will find plenty of hiking opportunities around here; just make sure you pick up supplies in St John's Chapel, Nenthead or Alston beforehand.

As its name implies, the village marks the source of the Wear which is formed a little way upstream from the aforementioned road bridge at the confluence of two burns: Burnhope and Killhope. A public footpath takes you in a loop of all three waterways in under half a mile which makes for a pleasant **village stroll**. From the south side of the road bridge, a lane splinters off in a westerly direction to Burnhope Reservoir. Take this lane and then, in a few paces, follow the footpath signed off to the right into a field. Follow Burnhope Burn upstream for a quarter of a mile then cross the water over the footbridge. Continue straight ahead, then turn right along a path that skirts the edge of the primary school, crossing Killhope Burn by a stone footbridge, and return to the village along Front Street (15yds or so along Front Street, a signed bridleway on your right by a postbox leads back to the start via the Wear).

Wearhead sits under some bulky hills which drain from the southwest into **Burnhope Reservoir** (DL13 1DJ), created in 1937 at the loss of some remote farms. A few trails connect Wearhead with the isolated water, offering an ever-widening aperture of the dale as you climb out of the valley; alternatively, take one of two pretty lanes and park by the lakeside. Access is either from Wearhead (follow the lane on the southside of the road bridge that carries the A689 over the Wear) or Cowshill (page 217), a wonderfully **scenic route** with wading birds nesting in rushy pastures, wildflower meadows, stunning valley views of

---

1 Burnhope Reservoir. **2** Detail from the Methodist Tapestries Project at Weardale Museum. **3** Middlehope Burn. ▶

the hillsides divided by stone walls, and old farmsteads like **Blackcleugh Farm** dating to the late 17th century (a public footpath allows closer inspection at ♥ NY850397).

Burnhope Reservoir's bleak water is thickly wooded with conifers around much of its perimeter and can be **walked** in under three miles along a quiet permissive footpath devoid of other souls. From the car park on the northern side of the dam, the path is wide and clear to begin with (suitable for wheelchairs) but from the westernmost edge and along the southern side of the water, it winds in and out of the forest.

Hill walkers may want to extend this route onto the moors. **Burnhope Seat** is a well-known remote hiking destination above the reservoir at 2,452ft and is the highest point on a tough ten-mile circuit from the northern end of the reservoir. The usual way up is via the summit of **Dead Stones** before tracing the Cumbrian border to the top of Burnhope Seat and returning via Scaud Hill and Ireshope Moor. It goes without saying that you'll need all the right gear (gaiters a must), OS Explorer 31, good fitness and compass skills to complete the strenuous hike which is largely across Open Access land.

"Burnhope's bleak water is thickly wooded with conifers around much of its perimeter and can be walked in under three miles."

13 COWSHILL & LANEHEAD

The inhabitants of this district, which is wild and little cultivated, are principally engaged in the mines, making a livelihood by having a few acres of fell land upon which they graze a cow or a few sheep.
W Whellan, *History, Topography and Directory of Durham*, 1894

The stone hamlet of **Cowshill** sits in a hollow under some bossy hills, seemingly offering little to the passing tourist motoring through on the A689. But there is more to discover here than a scattering of houses, a hotel and the quaint old church of St Thomas.

The two landscapes that fall either side of the main road through the hamlet offer something quite different to the walker. As you pick your way northeast of Cowshill along **Sedling Burn** (there's a large parking area just off the main road), the rough and pitted land bears all the hallmarks of quarrying and mining. Lead has been mined here since medieval times and **Burtree Pasture Mine**, about half a mile upstream, was considered one of the most productive in Weardale, producing in the region of a quarter of a million tonnes of lead by the time it closed in the late 19th century.

A prettier landscape of meadows, rushy pastures and the miner-farmer stone cottages and allotments of long ago trail along the foot of **Moss Moor** on the western side of Cowshill and the Killhope Burn. To access the network of footpaths traversing these beautiful grasslands, you'll need to locate Burtreeford Bridge: as you enter Cowshill on the A689 from the south, a secluded lane off to your left (by a prominent double-fronted house) descends past a cluster of houses to the bridge over Killhope Burn. You are now on the Weardale Way and can follow Killhope Burn upstream to the scenic **Whin Quarry**, which does an impressive job of mimicking a natural lake with towering dolerite walls.

For even more generous countryside views – and especially if you are a birdwatcher – you should follow the **Cowshill–Burnhope Reservoir road** southwest of Burtreeford Bridge for just under half a mile before striking off right below a farm and crossing the moorland fringe. The rougher, wilder allotment grasslands above on your left are the domain of curlew, snipe, golden plover and raptors like short-eared owls; sloping towards the burn are brighter meadows where there's more in the way of wildflowers. Incidentally, if you were to continue on the Burnhope Reservoir road, you'd enjoy some fabulous Pennine scenery (see page 214).

"The two landscapes that fall either side of the main road through the hamlet offer something quite different to the walker."

Lanehead's stone buildings climb a hillside a mile or so northwest of Cowshill and, if you didn't know about the places I'm about to describe, you may puff through this old hamlet without looking beyond the view of the dale, which is, it should be said, really very fine. If coming from Cowshill and travelling westwards, by the time you reach some dwellings you've missed one of the architectural highlights: **Heathery Cleugh Bridge**, a quintet of tall arches built in 1810 spanning the burn and giving the appearance of a miniature viaduct.

As you climb into the centre of Lanehead and round the sharp left bend, allow the little cottage on your right to catch your eye as well as the odd little box-shaped building with a door reached by steps. Built in the early 1800s, the cottage was a **police house**; the single storey building with a basement next door was the local lock-up. On departing the hamlet, a quaint chapel with a stone 'spirelet' appears by the roadside on your right. **Greenlaws Primitive Methodist Chapel** is now in private ownership but you may wish to pull over to have a quick look and take in the view of the meadows rising out of the valley.

¶¶ FOOD & DRINK

There are very few places to eat at the head of Weardale and even the **Cowshill Hotel** (DL13 1JQ ✆ 01388 537236 ⊙ noon–14.00 & 19.00–late daily) no longer serves food, though the somewhat shabby but authentic pub does serve pints and local chat, and has an open fire. For food, your closest options are Nenthead and the café at the Killhope Lead Mining Centre a few miles up the road.

14 KILLHOPE LEAD MINING MUSEUM

near Nenthead, DL13 1AR ✆ 01388 537505 ⊘ killhope.org.uk ⊙ Apr–Oct 10.00–16.30 daily (last admission 15.30); café on site; ♿

Embraced by moors bearing centuries-old scars from mining and quarrying, Britain's best-preserved lead mine is now one of the leading attractions in the North Pennines. There's a lot to see here – and do – this being an interactive museum where children (and adults) can have a go at splitting and 'washing' the rock for galena (lead ore) using machinery, a job once done by local lads. All the operational areas of the mine are laid out as they were, evoking the processes of extraction, transportation and separation. Infrastructure includes the wagon lines, washing floor (see below), mine shop (a cramped bunkhouse where workers lodged during the week) and the largest waterwheel in the North of England. You can also enter the onsite mine on tours (just remember to bring wellies).

The **washing floor** occupies the central area of the site. Raw rock extracted from underground was transported here using tubs on rails that emptied their contents into storage bays or **bouseteams** (stone partitions under the railway). From here, washer boys separated the lead ore – or galena – from waste material using water from the burn and a contraption that is essentially a large sieve. Children can have a go on these 'hotching tubs' and use the mallets – or 'buckers' – to break real rock.

Mining became increasingly mechanised in the 19th century with the assistance of the **Killhope Wheel** – a precious relic and one of only three waterwheels designed by the Victorian industrialist and hydroelectric engineer Lord Armstrong still in existence. Water from a purpose-built reservoir on the hilltop turned the wheel that powered machines in the adjacent 'jigger house' that crushed and washed the galena.

You'll need a hard hat and torch to go into the **mine tunnel**, all supplied by the museum as part of your entry fee. It's not one for the claustrophobic but most will find wading through the dark tunnel quite exciting, and you'll see where miners hacked into ore veins, and an underground waterwheel.

One of the most fascinating buildings is a two-storey house with a stables and **blacksmith's** occupying the ground floor, and the **lodging shop** – or dormitory – upstairs (next door to the mine offices). The authentically recreated rooms (the smithy houses the original forge) bring to life the dreadful conditions miners endured during the week, crammed into a small living area with poor ventilation, cooking and drying clothes over an open fire fuelled with peat. It's no wonder

VEINS & HUSHES

Evidence of lead mining in the North Pennines appears from medieval times, though it's very likely the Romans also mined here (land this rich in minerals so close to major Roman forts would surely not have gone unnoticed). Boom time came in the mid 18th century and lasted for over a hundred years, only to crash quite suddenly in the 1870s when cheaper markets for lead opened on the Continent. At its peak in the 1860s, the North Pennines produced a quarter of Britain's lead.

Lead ore (known as galena) forms **'veins'** – long ribbons, sometimes miles long, between the limestone that could be just a few inches wide or several feet thick. Finding these 290-million-year-old veins was key and much time and expertise was devoted to mapping the landscape and plotting its mineral veins, 400 of which were named in the North Pennines.

Early mining for lead involved digging shallow pits along the vein and extracting the dug rock using a simple bucket, rope and pulley. A hand roller known as a 'jack-roll' hauled the buckets to the surface – a system not dissimilar to raising a bucket of water from a well. Later, horses, turning a large wheel – or 'whimsey' – did the job.

By the 18th century, opencast mining dominated using a crude method called **'hushing'** involving building a dam at the top of a hill above a vein and, when sufficient water had collected, breaching it to allow the force of the water surging down the hill to strip away debris and loosen rock. Successive flushing in this way created gullies, which today look like natural gorges on the hillside but are very much artificial features. There's a good example above the Killhope Museum called Hazely Hush.

SCENIC DRIVE: COWSHILL TO NENTHEAD

The main road through Weardale rises steeply out of the hamlet of Cowshill to the famous lead mine at Killhope where only the odd farmstead, conifer plantation, chapel and cluster of cottages interrupts the expansive view of heavy moors pressing into each other and of the silver chain burn below. But, that's just a taste of what's to come. From Killhope to Nenthead, the A689 climbs to over 2,000ft at Killhope Cross, making this the highest classified road in England. Test your brakes before making the descent into Nenthead.

miners lived short lives, many of whom succumbed to lung disease – or 'the black spit' as they called it – before they reached half a century. A government inspector, quoted at the museum, wrote of their living quarters in 1842: 'I should think it no hardship to have to remain 24 hours in a mine, but I should be terrified of being ordered to be shut up a quarter of an hour in the bedroom of a lodging shop'.

The indoor **museum** and **Magnificent Minerals** display give a glimpse of the astonishing geology of the North Pennines. One of the most fascinating collections is the Victorian spar boxes – a folk art developed in mining communities that involved fashioning the purple, green and amber fluorite crystals, quartz and other rocks into miniature worlds: street scenes and grottos with little people. Displayed in wooden cabinets, spar boxes could be taken to exhibitions and country fairs.

A **reservoir** can be reached on a **walk** via wildlife hides in the adjacent forest where you may see red squirrels. And if you don't see them in the trees, you probably will in the museum car park where there are feeders.

BEYOND WEARDALE

Ⱥ **Carrshield Camping Barn** (page 311), **Mill Cottage Bunkhouse** (page 311)

From the head of Weardale, the North Pennine hills swell all around and the landscape as you head west into Cumbria or north into Northumberland offers more in the way of moorland and river scenery, with a scattering of remote farmsteads, villages and Methodist chapels. Two important places that continue the lead-mining story of the North Pennines are **Allenheads** at the head of the beautiful East Allen Valley, noted for its woodlands, grouse moors and winter skiing, and the stone village of **Nenthead**. The latter is reached by continuing west on the A689 from the head of Weardale, the road climbing to 2,044ft before making an exhilarating descent into this village at the top of the Nent Valley, a popular stopping point for Coast-to-Coast cyclists and where you can pick up a lovely lunch in the converted Methodist Chapel and visit the old lead mines.

15 ALLENHEADS

A sense of order pervades the buildings at Allenheads with its neat rows of miners' houses, workshops and office building, many of which were constructed under the instruction of Victorian engineer and mine agent, Thomas Sopwith, who was fixated with rules, punctuality and self-improvement – and presumably profit, this being the most important lead-mining area in Britain at one time.

Today, the village centre, which is reached off the B6295 by an easily overlooked slip road, is full of old-world character and seems to hide away in a wooded hollow inhabited by red squirrels. Allenheads' **Heritage Centre** (NE47 9HN ☉ daylight hours) is a good introduction to this Northumbrian village, its mining and farming heritage and community life in the 19th century. It includes a recreated blacksmith's and restored Victorian hydraulic engine once operational in the mine.

In addition to serving food and drink, the friendly **Hemmel Café** (page 222) also showcases the works of some talented local knitters and potters in its little gift shop. The **Allenheads Inn** stands prominently at the other end of the village, catching the eye with its vintage bicycles, road signs and mine 'tubs' (wagons) in the beer garden. Built in 1770,

SKIING IN THE NORTH PENNINES

Not opening today – snow disappearing
Ski-Allenheads' newsfeed, 2022

Don't expect Alpine runs and a fashionable après-ski scene, but fun is certainly guaranteed on **Ski-Allenheads**'s (⚡ ski-allenheads. co.uk), two 100yd beginner/intermediate slopes operated by rope tows above Allenheads. It's volunteer run and you'll need to be a member (easy to join online) to use the tows and hire equipment (a bargain at £5). Membership costs from £25 for the whole season. Do check the snow forecast before setting off; while the club reported 30 days of snow in recent years, the cover is unpredictable.

More experienced skiers and boarders should try the blue runs at **Yad Moss** (⚡ yadmoss.co.uk) in Alston or the **Weardale Ski Club** (⚡ skiweardale.com) near Daddry Shield with more challenging routes and longer ski runs.

it was the former home of the Beaumont family – one of the biggest mine owners, producing a quarter of all England's lead – but now opens its doors to weekend cyclists on the Coast-to-Coast and anyone on the hunt for a pint of real ale.

If you're interested to know more about lead mining, the old **mine yard** is on the other side of the road from the inn in the large car park where there is an excellent example of some bouseteems (page 208) and a few other historic buildings connected to the industry. Lead ore was extracted during a process of cleaning on the 'washing floor' before being sent to the smelting mill where it was melted into lead and silver.

Interpretation panels dotted around the village bring various aspects of Allenheads's industrial heritage to life, but there are a few buildings worth pointing out, including the long, single storey **mine offices** opposite the slip lane to the village centre, and the old **school** on the hillside. Built by Sopwith in 1849, he could spy on pupils from his office using a telescope; any pupil caught arriving just a few seconds late would be reprimanded. Note too, on the other side of the road from the offices, the cobbled **horse track** sloping into an old mine entrance.

Heading north from the rear of the Allendale Inn, in a couple of hundred yards, the lane passes a working **farm** dating to the early 1800s with a courtyard of quite some size. Cart sheds, byres, stables and haylofts face inwards to some slabs in the centre that mark where a central pool was once used for washing mine horses. You can see the courtyard from the road but there is no public access.

¶↑ FOOD & DRINK

The Allenheads Inn NE479HJ ✐ 01434 685200 ☉ 16.00–22.00 Mon–Fri, 14.00–22.00 Sat & Sun. An old-fashioned 300-year-old freehouse inn with a log fire, and outdoor tables that catch the evening sun. Local beers from Allendale and Great North Eastern Brewery Company draw in a local crowd on Friday evenings and jolly Coast-to-Coast cyclists at the weekend. Meals are now only served to guests in the simple B&B rooms upstairs.
Hemmel Café NE47 9HJ ✐ 01434 685568 ☉ summer 10.00–16.00 daily; winter 10.00–16.00 Thu–Sun. Popular café and gift shop in a converted cow barn attracting cyclists and day-trippers on fine days when tables in the sheltered courtyard get snapped up. When the weather turns, the log burner inside warms everyone up. The breakfast menu is fairly

1 A snowy view over Allenheads. 2 An abandoned mine near Allenheads.
3 Skiing in the North Pennines. ▶

extensive with the usual full English items and a hot veggie option, as well as pancakes and porridge. Lunches are mainly cold with a few hot plates (sausages and pies, bowl of chips, soup); cakes are delicious and made locally. Free wi-fi is helpful in this mobile-signal dead zone, and there's a little play area nearby.

16 NENTHEAD

There are no signs of poverty, but abundant signs of work; men and boys washing, sorting, and crushing ore, amid the splashing of water, the thumping of machinery, and clattering as of falling stones when the wagons from the mines drop their burden. From the heaps of ore at one end of the premises, to the slime-pits on the other, resolute industry prevails.

W White *Northumberland, and the Border,* 1859

A complete mining village (still with its mine) built by the Quaker-owned London Lead Company in the 18th century, Nenthead is hunkered beneath frowning hills with all the components that make the village so distinctively a North Pennine lead-mining settlement, built around a mine. Miners' terraces radiate from the centre, where there's a reading room ('Lead Company's Workmen's Reading Room'), fountain, school and chapel. Though the village sits just over the border in Cumbria, Nenthead continues the lead-mining story in such a visually striking way that it just had to be included in this guide.

The London Lead Company had a good deal of authority over residents and fostered an orderly community where houses were well kept and children obedient and educated. The afore-quoted author described this scene on his visit in 1859: 'What a clattering of clogs there was when the school broke up, and the children swarmed out upon the street! They are not remarkable for beauty, but they are remarkable for cleanliness, and appear to be robust alike in health and limb.'

"Exhibitions, music events and even theatre productions, all held in the chapel, have done much to enrich this lovely village."

Built in 1873, the Wesleyan chapel, now **The Hive at Nenthead** (page 226) is once again operating as a community space. Where worshippers used to sit on wooden pews in prayer, the congregation today is a mix of visitors and locals sipping coffees and admiring local artworks. The original organ is in situ and the decorative gallery, stained-glass windows and cast-iron columns have been carefully restored. Exhibitions, music events and

INSIDE A LEAD MINE

In the mid-19th century, the writer Walter White toured the North East, visiting a number of lead-mining villages in the North Pennines. On his travels, he made observations of the orderly lead-mining villages of Nenthead and Allenheads with their schoolhouses, chapels, reading rooms and mine offices as well as the mines and smelting mills and the miner-farmer countryside all around. He visited a school in Allenheads and asked the 40 or 50 children present who had seen the sea. Only three raised their hands. On one trip to Allenheads, he travelled underground through a mine where a wagon took him on a journey of a mile and a half, a candle lighting the way. He wrote the following description in *Northumberland, and the Border* (1859):

It was almost like going down a well, to descend the shaft, so copious is the drop from the sides... I saw how the vein of lead had been in places eight or nine feet thick, how it thinned off in places to an inch or two, in places to nothing... I saw veins of fluor-spare, intersected by threads of metal, and the various strata – limestone, shale, and clay, and in one of the veins a number of cavities full of beautiful crystals: wondrously beautiful they looked in the candle-light, like fairy grottoes. We crawled at times on hands and knees; we climbed and descended perpendicular ladders twenty fathoms or more, through openings so narrow, that with an inch or two additional breadth of shoulder you would stick. 'Tis grievesome wark,' said an old miner, who came panting up one of these chimney-like passages... And so we came to the 'forehead,' or one of the utmost extremities, where the men were working naked to the waist, and the heat and closeness were sickening... Then we returned to the wagon, and went up to shiver in the snow.

W White *Northumberland, and the Border*, 1859

even theatre productions, all held in the chapel, have done much to enrich this lovely village.

Cyclists on the Coast-to-Coast will find a handy repair shop in the village centre: **Nenthead Cycles** (✆ 01434 381324 ⊙ 08.00–18.00 daily), which has been open for years and the owner can sort out any wheeled problems.

Nenthead Mine and Smelt Mill is a short walk from the village centre (take the lane opposite the bicycle shop, with the playground on your right; the turn into the car park is on your left). Though no longer open to visitors as a museum, this fascinating site – which is one of the most intact in the North Pennines – has many stone buildings, shafts, dressing floors, dams, yards, workshops and structures dating to the early 1800s;

FOUR PENCE A DAY

Once a well-known folk ballad sang by miners and schoolchildren, this extract from *Four Pence A Day* recalls the work of the 'washer lad' whose job it was to pick out the shards of galena or lead ore from rock brought to the surface by miners. Keep these words in mind as you tour the mines at Killhope, Nenthead or Slitt Wood – still with their 'washing floors' (which retain their open character to this day) – and spare a thought for the local children who worked here, hands immersed in icy water, picking through rocks.

Ore's a-waiting in the tubs, snow's upon t'fell,
Canny folks they're sleeping yet but lead is reet to sell,
Come, me little washer lad, come, let's away,
We're bound down to slavery for fourpence a day.

It's early in the morning we rise at five o'clock,
Little slaves come to the foot to knock, knock, knock.
Come, me little washer lad, come, let's away,
It's very hard to work for fourpence a day.

Me father were a miner, he lived down in t' town,
'Twere hard work and poverty it always kept him down;
He aimed for me to go to school, but brass he couldn't pay,
So I had to go washing rake for fourpence a day...

it can be viewed from surrounding public rights of way including from a stony slope ascending the surrounding hill that passes several old mine shafts, some with their original rails trailing into arched mine entrances. As you wander up the slope, look for metallophyte plants (page 208) such as spring sandwort, mountain pansy, alpine pennycress and moonwort.

¶¶ FOOD & DRINK

The **Nenthead Community Shop & Post Office** (Vicarage Tce ☏ 01434 382359) services the village selling groceries and newspapers as well as cold snacks and hot drinks to take-away.

The Hive at Nenthead CA9 3PF ☏ 01434 408040 ⌖ hivenenthead.co.uk ⊙ 09.00–16.00 Wed–Mon ♿. This wonderful village hub and café in a restored Wesleyan chapel is testimony to the people of Nenthead, who clubbed together some years ago to bring back to life a community space that once stood at the heart of the village. The beautifully restored chapel operates as a café, serving mainly breakfasts and lunches but pizza nights and a licenced bar open at certain times through the year (check online for events). The lunch menu is mostly sandwiches and soups, but you'll also find a few hot meals (chickpea stew, curry, vegan burgers, pies) as well as a children's menu, cakes, tray bakes and scones etc. Also note Allendale's superb range of beers (Golden Plover is a firm favourite with many).

The Overwater Lodge Restaurant CA9 3NR ℘ 01434 381271 ⊙ 17.30–19.30 daily, plus occasionally for lunches but you'll need to phone ahead. Not a restaurant in the normal sense, this being an informal place to eat in the dining room of a private house in the village. Somewhat unusual, but look at the menu on the window: three courses (for £20) prepared with fresh ingredients, many grown by the cook including the salad leaves 'picked today', freshly baked bread and homegrown gooseberries (in the crumble). The two mains on offer when I last visited were organic pork fillet and peppers in a creamy sauce and free-range chicken with a pesto and tomato sauce (and on a previous visit: 'one of our own ducks roasted'). Call at least a few hours ahead to book. You'll find the restaurant 100yds from the bike shop (walk down the street with the playground on your right).

WOLSINGHAM SHOW

Weardale, County Durham

1st Weekend in September!

A *great* **WEEKEND** OF **FARMING LIFE** AND **COUNTRYSIDE** *entertainment!*

Our show grounds and the Show Barn are also available for hire throughout the year. Ideal for weddings, parties, outdoor events & much more. Please contact us for more information.

THE SHOW BARN

www.wolsinghamshow.co.uk
www.facebook.com/WolsinghamShow
email: info@wolsinghamshow.co.uk

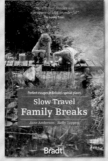

6
TEESDALE

Invigorated from its fall over Cauldron Snout, the River Tees flows eagerly through the remote, upper reaches of Teesdale entering a sweeping sun-filled mosaic of pastures, meadowlands and floodplains criss-crossed by drystone walls and dotted with old barns, farmhouses and remote Methodist chapels; this is a landscape reminiscent of Cumbria and the Yorkshire Dales, with the white-stone farms of the former and the hay meadows of the latter. The lasting memory is of lambs in fields of buttercups, farmers on quad bikes, powerful waterfalls, dolerite crags, hares sprinting along tracks and lapwings tumbling in enormous skies. You can see why many visitors call this Durham's prettiest dale.

Towards the head of the valley, **Widdybank** and **Cronkley fells** beckon walkers to their craggy slopes where Arctic-alpine plants – relics from the end of the last Ice Age – flower in spring. This is prime waterfall country too, home to some of England's biggest and most spectacular falls including **High Force**, which owes its height to geological events 295 million years ago.

Downriver from **Middleton-in-Teesdale**, one of the liveliest and most attractive towns in the dale, the landscape steps down a gear and the stone villages and farmsteads come every few miles: **Mickleton**, **Romaldkirk** and **Cotherstone**. Close by are two stunning smaller valleys: **Baldersdale** and **Lunedale**, both with their respective reservoirs and fine hay-meadow scenery.

Barnard Castle, at the eastern gateway to Teesdale, is a popular base for visitors exploring the lower reaches of the valley but many people come just to enjoy all that the market town has to offer: a plethora of antiques shops, the celebrated **Bowes Museum** art galleries, the town's

◀1 Barnard Castle. 2 The Bowes Museum has an internationally significant collection of European ceramics, including Sèvres porcelain and Italian Maiolica. 3 Approaching Barnard Castle.

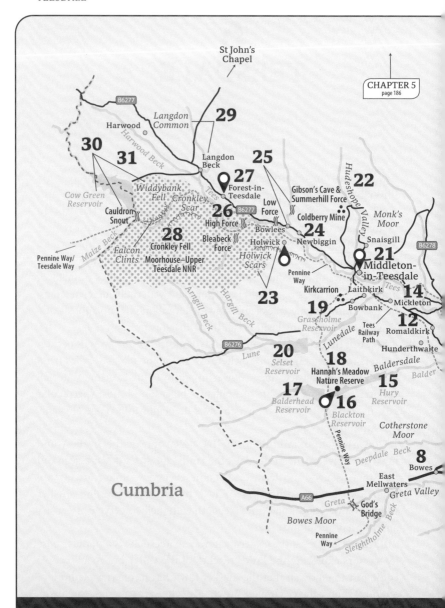

St John's
Chapel

CHAPTER 5
page 186

B6277

Langdon
Common

Harwood

29

Langdon
Beck

30

31

25

Harwood Beck

27
Forest-in-
Teesdale

Gibson's Cave &
Summerhill Force

22

Hudeshope Valley

Monk's
Moor

Cow Green
Reservoir

Widdybank
Fell

Cronkley
Scar

26
High Force

B6277

Low
Force

Coldberry Mine

Snaisgill

Cauldron
Snout

28
Cronkley Fell

Bleabeck
Force

Bowlees

24
Newbiggin

21

B6278

Maize Beck

Moorhouse–Upper
Teesdale NNR

Holwick

**Middleton-
in-Teesdale**

Falcon
Clints

Holwick
Scars

Pennine Way/
Teesdale Way

Pennine
Way

Kirkcarrion

Laithkirk

14

23

Arngill Beck

Hargill Beck

19

Bowbank

Mickleton

Tees

Grassholme
Reservoir

Tees
Railway
Path

12

Romaldkirk

B6276

Lune

20
Selset
Reservoir

Lunedale

18
Hannah's Meadow
Nature Reserve

Hunderthwaite

Balderdale

Balder

15
Hury
Reservoir

17
Balderhead
Reservoir

16

Blackton
Reservoir

Cotherstone
Moor

Pennine Way

Deepdale Beck

8
Bowes

Cumbria

East
Mellwaters

Greta Valley

A66

Greta

God's
Bridge

Bowes Moor

Pennine
Way

Sleightholme Beck

TEESDALE

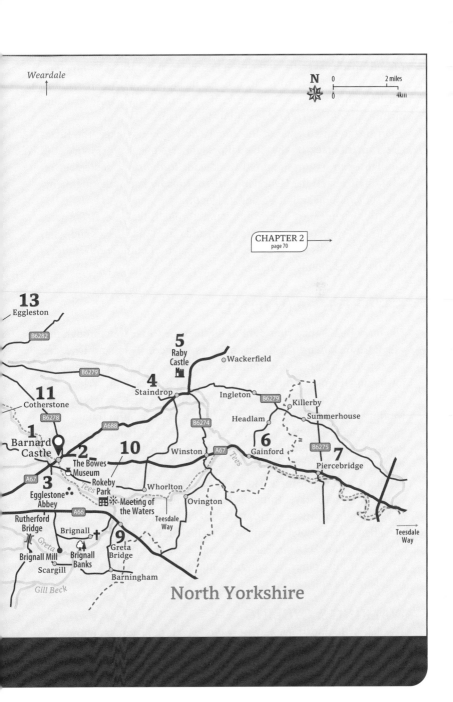

Weardale

N

0   2 miles

0   4km

CHAPTER 2
page 70

13
Eggleston

B6282

B6279

5
Raby
Castle

Wackerfield

4
Staindrop

Ingleton

B6279

Killerby

11
Cotherstone

Headlam

Summerhouse

B6278

A688

B6274

1
Barnard
Castle

2

10

Winston

A67

6
Gainford

B6275

7
Piercebridge

3
The Bowes
Museum

Rokeby
Park

Whorlton

Tees

A67

Egglestone
Abbey

Tees

Meeting of
the Waters

Ovington

Teesdale
Way

Teesdale
Way

Rutherford
Bridge

A66

Brignall

Greta

9
Greta
Bridge

Brignall Mill

Brignall
Banks

Barningham

Scargill

Gill Beck

North Yorkshire

ruinous medieval castle, and riverside trails to stone villages with good pubs and nearby historic attractions including **Egglestone Abbey**. Further downstream, on the outskirts of Darlington, is **Gainford** and picturesque old **Piercebridge** with its Roman fort.

On the southern edge of the county near **Bowes** village, the River Greta, a tributary of the Tees, flows under some hefty moors and through open pastures and old woodlands to the stone settlement of **Greta Bridge** and the Georgian estate of **Rokeby Park**, offering many miles of lonesome walking along its length.

In this chapter, we begin our jaunt through Teesdale at Barnard Castle, and work our way upstream, in and out of old villages and then deep into the hills of Upper Teesdale in search of outdoor adventures, waterfalls and mountain wildlife.

GETTING AROUND

The main B6277 road runs tight to the Tees the whole way through the valley from Barnard Castle upstream to Langdon Beck and over the Cumbrian border to Alston. It makes visiting many of Teesdale's villages, towns and hamlets efficient, but you wouldn't want to cycle many stretches of this road except for maybe the upper reaches, as it is narrow, winding and receives a fair amount of cars and heavy farm traffic.

Scarlet Band **bus** 96 (five daily Mon–Sat ⊘ scarletbandbuses.co.uk) between Barnard Castle and Middleton-in-Teesdale, via Cotherstone, Romaldkirk and Mickleton, follows the B6277; on Wednesdays it handily connects to three Hodgsons 73 services (⊘ hodgsonsbuses. com) for onward travel through the valley to Langdon Beck, stopping at Newbiggin, Bowlees (for the visitor centre and Gibson's Cave) and the High Force Hotel for the waterfall. For Eggleston, you'll need Scarlet Band bus 95 from Barnard Castle. East of Barnard Castle, there are several bus routes for onward connections to Darlington, Bishop Auckland and Durham.

WALKING & CYCLING

Teesdale is famous for its **river walks** which offer much contrasting scenery. The entire length of the Tees from its beginnings in Cumbria's Pennine hills to where it spills into the sea at Redcar near Middlesborough, is accessible along the 91-mile **Teesdale Way** which

---

ℹ TOURIST INFORMATION

In addition to the two places listed here, there are a few others in the valley where you could go for informal advice, including the community secondhand bookstore in Middleton, **The Village Bookshop** (Market Pl, Middleton-in-Teesdale DL12 0RJ ✆ 01833 641493 ⊙ Mon–Thu) which also sells local guides; and the **Teesdale Mercury** shop (24 Market Pl, Barnard Castle DL12 8NB ⊙ 08.30–16.00 Mon–Sat, 08.30–noon Sun) in Barnard Castle which stocks Ordnance Survey maps and local books.

Bowlees Visitor Centre Newbiggin DL12 0XF (signed off the B6277) ✆ 01833 622145 ⊙ March & Oct 10.00–16.00 daily; Apr–Sep 10.00–17.00 daily ♿. Run by the North Pennines AONB Partnership, Bowlees is a reliable source of information for Upper Teesdale, with a good range of maps and guides, and local staff with knowledge of the area.

The Witham 3 Horse Market, Barnard Castle DL12 8LY ✆ 01833 631107 ♂ thewitham.org. uk ⊙ 10.00–16.00 Tue–Sat, 11.00–15.00 Sun ♿. Community arts centre and café offering tourist information from a friendly team of staff and volunteers.

---

follows the route of the **Pennine Way** as far as Middleton-in-Teesdale before continuing eastbound past Barnard Castle, Gainford and Piercebridge as the primary river footpath. It probably goes without saying that the paths are long-established, clearly signed and easy to follow. Connecting rights of way in many places allow for circular walks along the Pennine and Teesdale ways. I've described some of my favourite river loops in this chapter on pages 244, 263 and 265 including descriptions of walks along the River Greta on the county's southern border.

In **Upper Teesdale**, the landscape is all meadows, stony riverbeds and powerful waterfalls under the gaze of some impressive fells with whinstone cliffs forming spectacular rock curtains in places. Widdybank Fell and Cronkley Fell are two recommended destinations for an extended hill walk (pages 306 and 302). They are also a joy for botanists with Arctic-alpine plants in spring, and views of flower-rich meadows, stone barns and remote farmsteads in the floodplains below.

In the **lower** and **middle** reaches of the dale (from Barnard Castle to Middleton-in-Teesdale), there's more in the way of wooded river walks and historic buildings and villages. **Baldersdale**, a minor valley and associated reservoirs west of the Tees, holds some wonderful flower grasslands accessible on foot (and also by bicycle along some remote country lanes; pages 270 and 278).

This being Durham, there's bound to be an old railway trackbed converted into a leisure path somewhere and indeed there is between Middleton-in-Teesdale and Cotherstone. A combination of the **Tees Railway Path** (pages 263 and 269) and Teesdale Way riverside path offers walkers the chance to make a circuit of the central Teesdale countryside via some old villages with excellent pubs (pages 263 and 265).

Cyclists can also enjoy the Tees Railway Path but will need off-road tyres for sections on grass. In the same vicinity, around Middleton-in-Teesdale, a few quieter roads here and there offer alternatives for cyclists (and motorists looking for a more scenic route), for instance, the fellside road above the B6277 between Middleton and Newbiggin is a beautiful length of tarmac offering outstanding landscape views. But these back roads will only take you so far and in the case of the Holwick road it comes to an abrupt end with no onward hard surface, but does provide close access to Low Force.

Teesdale's **reservoirs** are connected via some wonderfully quiet lanes, some with hardly any traffic at all, offering a few options for circuits of this remote 'lake district' region and its upland landscape. A recommended loop for cyclists from Mickleton begins along the southern shore of Grassholme Reservoir in the valley of Lundale before climbing over moorland to reach Blackton and Hury reservoirs where you can return to Mickleton via the northern or southern edge of these waters and the historic village of Romaldkirk.

TAXIS

Alan's Taxis Barnard Castle ✆ 01833 695860
Hodgsons Barnard Castle & Middleton-in-Teesdale ✆ 01833 630730. Covers the whole of the Teesdale area and further afield.

BARNARD CASTLE & SURROUNDS

A steady flow of farm vehicles and Land Rovers passes through the lively market town of Barnard Castle at the gateway to Teesdale, known affectionately throughout Durham as 'Barney' (a name derived from the 12th-century founder of the stone castle you see today, Bernard de Balliol). You could easily spend most of a day shopping for antiques

VIKING & SAXON PLACE NAMES

Take a look at the Ordnance Survey map of Teesdale (Explorer OL31) and you'll notice that many place names have a hint of Yorkshire about them, with plenty of riggs, laiths, thwaites, garths, holms and kirks indicating the Saxon and Viking influences of long ago – and that this whole area used to fall into Yorkshire before the county boundaries were reset in 1974. Note too that waterfalls here are known as 'fors', from the Old Norse meaning simply 'waterfall' (in Northumberland they are 'linn', an Anglo-Saxon word). Semantics aside, in many ways, the Teesdale landscape has more in common with the Dales of Yorkshire than the Durham valleys further north, with hay meadows criss-crossed by drystone walls, isolated farmsteads and barns built into walls.

and local crafts in the many independent boutiques, taking in several centuries of history at St Mary's Church and touring the medieval castle – but then you'd need another day to visit **Bowes Museum**, a must-see attraction on the edge of town famed for its lavish exterior, period rooms and superb 18th- and 19th-century art galleries, and to take a riverside walk along the Tees, perhaps to the ruins of **Egglestone Abbey** or **Rokeby Park**.

A few miles northeast of Barnard Castle is one of the leading attractions in the area: **Raby Castle** and the handsome village of **Staindrop**, which combined make for a recommended family day out. Due east of Barnard Castle, along the Tees towards Darlington, the river meanders past a scattering of picture-perfect old villages including **Whorlton**, **Gainford** and **Piercebridge** with its Roman heritage.

1 BARNARD CASTLE

Galgate's broad avenue of 18th- and 19th-century houses welcomes visitors entering Barnard Castle from the north. It's a fine introduction to this historic market town on the edge of Teesdale famous for its castle, independent shops and the celebrated Bowes Museum.

Horsemarket & Market Place

A good starting point is where Galgate meets **Horse Market** at a prominent elbow in the thoroughfare and by the town's imposing Methodist church. Before you get swept up in the busy street scene, there are a few places of interest set back from the Galgate/Horse Market corner. Flatts Road is a quiet street leading away from the Methodist church and old post office and connecting with Vere Road, site of a traditional **livestock market**. It's worth viewing if you're in town on a Tuesday morning or Wednesday afternoon when sheep and cattle are auctioned – a custom in Barnard Castle for over 130 years. Behind the Methodist church is an open area of parkland and the entrance to the castle (page 241).

From the top of Horse Market, take in a half-mile stretch of shops, galleries, cafés, restaurants and pubs lining the wide boulevard which slopes downhill to meet with the River Tees. Inching your way south, a number of independent boutiques, bookshops and antiques emporiums may catch your eye. A few to look out for include the superb **William Pete deli, bakery and butcher** (page 246), **Hayloft Emporium**, (an antiques shop tucked away at the back of a passageway between William Pete's two shops) and **Mouncey Fine Art** (ceramics and paintings).

The pavements are thronged with people on market days (first Saturday of the month) when **Market Place** hums with visitors musing over stalls laden with produce from around the North East and crafts produced by local artists. The stalls occupy the cobbled area outside a couple of independent bookshops where you can pick up local guides and maps, including the **Teesdale Mercury** shop (page 235). Providing education, welfare and entertainment for over 150 years, **The Witham** community arts centre (page 235), also on Market Place, is housed in the neoclassical former Music Hall and Mechanics' Institute. Today a lively programme of theatre, music, film, art and well-being classes feature throughout the year and especially during the **Summer Festival**, with free live-music concerts every Saturday and Sunday in July and August: ukulele, jazz, acoustic, indie and folk (go online to see the full programme). The rear garden is a peaceful spot away from the crowds in which to enjoy a light lunch from the café.

Buttermarket & The Bank

Buttermarket (also known as Market Cross), dating to 1747, is the conspicuous stone octagon building at the junction of Market Place and Newgate, marking the centre of Barnard Castle. It has served various civic functions over the centuries including a fire station, courtroom and dairy market. Test your eyesight here by searching for bullet holes in its weathervane – the result of an unofficial shooting contest between two men in 1804, using the vane as a target.

BARNARD CASTLE TOWN STROLL

A recommended short loop of Barnard Castle town centre and castle begins from the top of **Horse Market**. You can walk this route in either direction. Walk downhill towards Buttermarket (the stone octagon building), past all the shops, cafés and galleries lining Market Place. At **Buttermarket** you may want to turn left on to Newgate to visit **St Mary's Church** (on the corner) or the **Bowes Museum** (half a mile away); alternatively, continue straight down onto **The Bank**.

At the bottom of The Bank, do not cross into Thorngate but veer right onto **Bridgegate**. After 300yds or so you'll reach the medieval **County Bridge** (so called because it once formed the boundary between Durham and Yorkshire). Do not cross the river but take a pedestrian footpath off to your right that curls steeply up hill and round the base of the **castle** walls to emerge at the entrance to the ruined fortress, opposite parkland. Walk past the entrance to the castle and back to the top of Horse Market, by the Methodist church.

Opposite Buttermarket on the corner of **Newgate** is St Mary's Church (see below). The famous Bowes Museum (page 242) is a ten-minute walk along the same street. Continuing downhill from Buttermarket, however, is **The Bank**, Barnard Castle's well-known road of antiques shops (page 240). Halfway down The Bank, **Blagraves House** (an antiques shop was under construction at the time of writing) is a Tudor building with steps to its door and lays claim to being the town's oldest house – it was once visited by Oliver Cromwell, as the blue plaque above the doorway details – with a quartet of stone musicians playing above its windows.

Thorngate is a peaceful avenue connecting Barnard Castle's shopping streets with the Tees at the southern end of the town. A quiet stone avenue with 18th- and 19th-century houses, it offers direct access to the **riverside** over a footbridge by the side of a prominent old textile mill. On the south side of the water, turning left will lead you along the riverbank to the ruins of Egglestone Abbey (see walk description on page 244) and Rokeby Park (page 261).

Church of St Mary

Newgate, Barnard Castle DL12 8NQ (opposite Buttermarket) ✆ 01833 637018 ☉ daylight hours daily ♿

St Mary's is full of curiosities and history from the nine centuries since it was founded in 1130. At first sight, the church appears Victorian on account of its tower, which is indeed 19th century, but once you get

BARNARD CASTLE'S ANTIQUES SHOP TRAIL

Barnard Castle is well known for its antiques shops which are mostly concentrated on The Bank, a sloping street descending away from Buttermarket towards the River Tees. The **Collector Antiques** (25 The Bank, DL12 8PH ☉ by appointment ✆ 01833 637 783) specialises in fine-art restoration but also sells oils, watercolours and wooden furniture. **Mission Hall Antiques Centre** (51 The Bank, DL12 8PL ☉ 10.00–17.00 Mon–Sat, 13.30–17.00 Sun) is one of the largest emporiums in the town, with many items of furniture, paintings, china and glassware for sale. Next door is **Antiques Affair** (47 The Bank, DL12 8PL ☉ 10.00–17.00 Wed–Sat) with a select range of exclusive vintage finds. **Robsons Antiques** (36 The Bank, DL12 8PN ☉ 10.00–17.30 daily), on the other side of the road, mainly deals in glassware, silver plates and cutlery, and ceramics. **Blagraves House** (30 The Bank, DL12 8PN) is the latest antiques shop to open on The Bank (under renovation at the time of writing).

Elsewhere in Barnard Castle, look out for **Hayloft Emporium** (27 Horse Market, DL12 8LX ☉ 09.00–16.00 Mon–Sat) by the butcher's at the top end of the town, and **Inget Decorative Arts** (40 Horse Market, DL12 8NA ☉ 11.00–15.00 Mon–Fri, 10.30–16.00 Sat) specialising in Arts & Crafts furniture.

up close, you'll find so much of its present form dates to much earlier – to the Norman period and to the 15th century when the church was extensively remodelled and expanded.

Norman masonry survives in a few places including the south door (with much in the way of chevron detailing), the pillars in the **nave** supporting rounded arches (the octagonal pillars and pointed arches came later, in the 13th century), and the narrow windows on the north side of the chancel.

But, to understand many of the unusual features of St Mary's (blocked-up doorways, carved heads, piscinas too high to reach, boar carvings and so on), we need to look forward several hundred years to 1474 when **Richard III**, then the Duke of Gloucester, became Lord of Barnard Castle and spent a huge sum redeveloping the church from its simple Norman building with a nave and chancel into the wider and taller church that stands today. His plans included the construction of a religious college that was never realised owing to his death in battle. In recognition of his investment, you'll see his head carved in a few places, most conspicuously in the chancel arch: Richard III on the right; his brother, Edward IV, on the left. He was also responsible for the rood screen separating the holy chancel from the nave, which was then used for many secular public events. The screen no longer exists but the little doorway high up to the left of the chancel marks the entrance point to a balcony that once framed the top of the chancel.

The **font** in the north transept will catch your eye. It's Victorian but the significance of the unusual symbol repeated around the bowl is a mystery. More is known, however, of the stone effigy on the wall of two dancing boars carved either side of St Anthony, a favoured saint of Richard III's. Boar motifs – a nod to Richard III whose coat of arms features the animal – are seen elsewhere around the church, including by the side of a drain on the south transept. Incidentally, the boar is pictured on Barnard Castle's coat of arms to this day.

"The churchyard holds secrets too – of a cholera epidemic that caused the deaths of 145 residents of Barnard Castle in 1848."

The **churchyard** holds secrets too – of a cholera epidemic that caused the deaths of 145 residents of Barnard Castle in 1848, who were hastily buried in a mass grave at the bottom of the churchyard, marked by a memorial; a cheese press repurposed as a headstone (find the grave marker with a disc on its rear); and the tomb of a dapper George Hopper who is carved in stone on the side of his vault with the grim reaper appearing on the other side. Before you leave, cast your eye to the blocked-up north porch once housing the town's fire engine for over a hundred years.

Barnard Castle's castle

Corner of Galgate & Horsemarket, DL12 8PR ✆ 01833 638212 ☺ Apr–Oct 10.00–17.00 daily; Nov–Mar 10.00–16.00 Sat & Sun; English Heritage ♿ to some parts.

From the south, the ruined castle makes quite an impression commanding the top of a rocky bank above the Tees. From the centre of town, however, the castle is screened from view by a long run of houses; you will need to find your way (on foot) to its time-bitten walls by taking a path along the side of the Methodist church where Galgate meets Horse Market. The castle entrance is opposite parkland (a popular picnicking area) and a children's playground.

In the years following the Norman Conquest, a timber fort was raised on the naturally defensive site by landowner Guy de Balliol; this was rebuilt in stone by his nephew, Bernard de Balliol in the early to mid 12th century. Bernard, who also founded the town behind the castle (originally

'Bernard's Castle') is largely responsible for the fortress as it appears today, with its three main wards, keep and curtain wall, though many of the walls, including the thumping great Round Tower (which you can climb) were erected under his second son, Bernard II in the early 1200s. The castle exchanged hands many times within the same family and was briefly held by the Duke of Gloucester, later King Richard III, but it never fully recovered from a siege during the Rising of the North against Queen Elizabeth I in 1569, and by the early 17th century it had been abandoned.

Visitors enter through the North Gate into a wide grassy area, once the Town Ward, and can freely explore the site using the network of paths and walkways connecting the different zones and buildings. Though many of the stone structures exist only as low ruins or outlines today, long and remarkably intact lengths of the curtain wall, and towers standing to almost full height, remain.

2 THE BOWES MUSEUM

Barnard Castle, DL12 8NP ✆ 01833 690606 ⊘ thebowesmuseum.org.uk ⊙ 10.00–17.00 daily ♿

'Gloriously inappropriate' is how architectural writer, Nikolaus Pevsner, described The Bowes Museum, one of Durham's most distinguished art galleries, built in the style of a French château. The 19th-century mansion stands on the edge of Barnard Castle (a ten-minute walk from Buttermarket) above formal gardens and fountains and is astonishingly grand and ostentatious – fitting only for the treasures inside, not for the surrounding Durham countryside.

Just why such riches came to Teesdale is explained by the marriage in 1852 of its founders, John Bowes (a Durham man and illegitimate son of the 10th Earl of Strathmore who inherited his estate but not his title) and a French actress, Joséphine (also a fine landscape painter), who toured Europe many times amassing works for their picture gallery. Their love of the arts (and tremendous wealth) is much in evidence here, but neither lived to see the museum's opening in 1892. The gallery has continued to acquire works into the 21st century, which today includes one of the most important lace collections seen anywhere and vast collections of porcelain and European art including masterpieces by the likes of Canaletto, Gainsborough, Turner and van Dyck.

The purpose-built museum houses three floors of European paintings from the 15th to the 19th centuries, as well as ceramics, silverware and

THE CHARLES DICKENS TRAIL

If you should go near Barnard Castle, there is a good ale at the King's Head. Say you know me, and I am sure they will not charge you for it.
Newman Noggs in Charles Dickens's *Nicholas Nickleby* 1838

Dickens visited Barnard Castle while researching the notorious Yorkshire boarding school for *Nicholas Nickleby*, and stayed at the **King's Head** at 16 Market Place (opposite The Raby Arms and no longer an inn though the building itself is unchanged, still with its archway for horse-pulled carriages). He visited the **Bowes Academy** in nearby Bowes village (page 255) which provided inspiration for Dotheboys Hall in the novel and its cruel headmaster, Wackford Squeers.

Conditions at the real-life school (which still stands but is no longer a school) were by some accounts pretty horrific and the headmaster, William Shaw, was prosecuted when students went blind because of the unsanitary conditions, though the level of cruelty and poor conditions have probably been much embellished over the years. Shaw, and the inspiration for Smike – said to be George Ashton Taylor who died in 1822, aged 19 – are buried in the churchyard in Bowes.

costumes, displayed in galleries that sit next to rooms dressed with Second French Empire (the period between 1852 and 1870) furnishings from the Bowes's heady days in Paris entertaining artists and writers. In all, there are some 15,000 objects, including an extensive collection of Sèvres and 18th-century English porcelain, and the Fashion & Textile Gallery devoted to dress across several centuries: Victorian gowns to 20th-century haute couture.

In the upstairs **picture galleries**, famous works by Gainsborough, Turner, Canaletto, El Greco and Goya impress visitors (when the gallery opened in 1892, there were more Spanish paintings here than anywhere else in the country). Highlights include Canaletto's regatta scenes on Venice's Grand Canal, and Goya's intimate portrayal of his friend, Valdés, which rates as one of the museum's finest portraits.

Also don't miss Joséphine Bowes's sumptuous 'lit à la duchesse' (bed for a Duchess) with tumbling silk drapes cascading from a domed canopy, a purpose-built wooden botanical cabinet, Lady Ludlow's porcelain bird collection, and the **Blackborne Collection** of 17th-century lace.

The star attraction, however, is the 250-year-old life-size silver **automaton swan**, created in 1773 by the internationally known London jeweller and craftsman, James Cox, which catches a fish to the delight of all those gathered round to see the eccentric spectacle. It is displayed in a gallery devoted entirely to the performing bird and its creation. Since the Covid pandemic, the swan has not performed for fear her mechanism, which contains 2,000 moving parts, may have ceased up during the lengthy period of inaction; in 2023, following restoration, the swan will delight visitors once more in a new display area, to coincide with its 250th anniversary.

In the grounds of the museum is a children's play area and short woodland walk. A bright, upmarket **café** serves hot and cold dishes

Barnard Castle to Egglestone Abbey

❋ OS Explorer map OL31; start: southern end of Thorngate, Barnard Castle NZ049160; 3 miles; easy

This family-friendly riverside walk from Barnard Castle takes in the ruins of 13th-century Egglestone Abbey before returning to town along the wooded banks of the Tees and across gentle farmland, via the Teesdale Way.

1 At the southern end of **Thorngate** (350yds downhill from Buttermarket), cross the wrought-iron pedestrian bridge over the Tees, taking in the fine riverside views as you do so, and turn left when you reach the other side. A well-trodden woodland path skirts the back of some pretty cottages with gardens in full bloom during the summer and then some smallholdings before you reach a caravan park.

2 Pick your way through the friendly site (it's a little fiddly but you want to be heading uphill from close to the site entrance. There are plenty of people about during the summer who will point you in the direction of the abbey), ascending into open countryside along a lane with the caravan site now below you. Turn left off the lane through a gate by a hut painted with woodland animals, which takes you into a field. Continue across the next three fields, keeping the trees and the sound of rushing water to your left. At the end of the third and final field, squeeze your way between two stone pillars to reach **Abbey Lane** where you turn left, downhill.

3 After around 200yds you'll come to a road bridge (note the lovely humped packhorse bridge to your right). On the other side of the bridge, a fingerpost by a farm gate directs you into a field with the abbey ruins poking above a prominent hill. Enter this field, with the ruins on your left, and continue ahead (turn round to get a better look at the packhorse bridge) for around 100yds to a lone ash tree. Here, turn left up a steep bank to some stone cottages. **Egglestone Abbey** is ahead and accessed via a car park.

(page 246). The museum is a ten-minute walk from Buttermarket, in the centre of Barnard Castle; note that despite its name, it's not located in Bowes village.

🍴 FOOD & DRINK

Barnard Castle has no shortage of cafés, take-aways and pub restaurants and, despite the choice along the main road running through the centre of town, there are frequently queues at the weekend, such is the popularity of 'Barney'. On page 246 is a selection of some recommended places to eat, but also consider the two good Indian restaurants in town: the

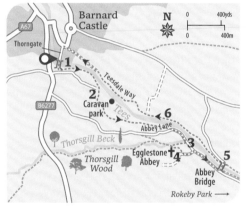

4 After exploring the ruins (this is a good spot for a picnic and the grounds are rarely busy), return to the car park and turn left on to the lane that curls downhill towards the river. At the handsome double-fronted cottage at the bottom, you meet another lane where you should turn right. At the traffic lights, turn left, crossing delightful **Abbey Bridge**, a tall arch of stone dating to 1773. Enjoy the plunging views of the Tees rushing through the wooded gorge below.

5 Now on the north side of the river, pick up a muddy footpath on your left which winds through oak, ash, holly and hazel trees to the riverbank. You are now on the **Teesdale Way**; Barnard Castle is 1½ miles ahead, as the signpost indicates. It's tempting to put your feet in the water here, but do take care as the river is fast flowing. After 300yds, exit the woodland by a kissing gate into a field.

6 Continue ahead across the next few fields. When you're opposite the caravan park, you'll need to cross over a (collapsed) fence into a field (where once stood a stile). Continue ahead through a gate and along a stony track to the outskirts of Barnard Castle. Cross the large green with a playground and re-enter the town along **Gray Lane**, which connects with the bottom of The Bank and top of Thorneygate. Turn right for Buttermarket and the centre of town.

Bengal Merchant (7 The Bank, DL12 8PH ✆ 01833 695857) and the extremely popular **Babul's** (9 Market Pl, DL12 8NF ✆ 01833 630575).

Café Bowes Bowes Museum, DL12 8NP ✆ 01833 690606 ⊙ 10.00–16.00 daily ♿. Within the sumptuous 19th-century surroundings of the Bowes Museum (page 242) is this surprisingly modern, bright and upmarket café featuring some local delicacies. Every appetite is catered for with light bites (scones, soups and sandwiches), afternoon tea, and more substantial dishes (try the Bowes rarebit made with Yorkshire cheese and Barnard Castle beer). There's also a children's and breakfast menu.

Clarendon's Café 29 Market Pl ✆ 01833 690110 ⊙ 09.30–15.30 Mon–Fri, 09.30–16.00 Sat ♿. A firm favourite with many locals in the centre of town and known further afield for its consistently good breakfasts (plenty of meat, veggie and vegan options), hot and cold lunches, afternoon teas (cakes and scones are some of the best in Teesdale and usually include lemon, carrot and chocolate and orange cakes plus a vegan brownie) and Sunday roasts. Meats from the butcher up the road, Teesdale cheese from Cotherstone and plenty of other locally sourced ingredients.

Fish & Chips 149 36 Galgate ✆ 01833 637332 ⊙ 11.30–late Mon–Sat, 11.30–19.00 Sun. What's the key to one of Barnard Castle's favourite fish and chip take-aways? Beef dripping. It's what makes the batter so crispy and, indeed, it was one of the lightest batters I've tasted on my travels in Durham. Expect to queue at lunchtime and especially during the evening. Dine inside or take-away.

William Peat Butchers Horsemarket, Barnard Castle ✆ 01833 638092 ⊙ 07.00–17.00 Mon–Fri, 07.00–16.00 Sat. Claiming the title of Teesdale's oldest butcher (and now also operating a deli and bakery), Peat's is legendary in Durham (and known as Castle Bank Butcher in a few other places). You'll find Peat's sausages on menus in the best restaurants and cafés in town, including Clarendon's and Café Bowes. All meats are sourced from local livestock markets, and most of the cheeses come from Durham and bordering counties including Cotherstone and Weardale cheeses. If you're self-catering, there's a huge choice including homemade black pudding and haggis.

The Witham 3 Horse Market, DL12 8LY ✆ 01833 631107 ⊙ 10.00–16.00 Tue–Sat, 11.00–15.00 Sun ♿. Bright, modern café with a sunny rear garden in a welcoming community and arts centre in the centre of town. Escape the busy streets and enjoy a light lunch of sandwiches, scones, soup or cake. Music concerts every weekend in July and August (page 238).

3 EGGLESTONE ABBEY

Abbey Ln, DL12 9TN ⊙ 10.00–18.00 daily; free entry but £2 parking fee ♿ limited but step-free access from the car park to the ruins which stand on bumpy grassland; English Heritage

The ruins of Egglestone Abbey appear quite wonderfully above the River Tees about a mile from Barnard Castle. Founded by Premonstratensian 'white canons' in the late 12th century, enough of its church, built 1250 on an even earlier building, remains standing to appreciate its nave, transepts and presbytery.

The **tomb** of Sir Ralph Bowes of Streatham (who died in 1482) went on a bit of journey before being returned to Egglestone in the 1920s; it now rests alone in the church crossing and is helpful for orientating yourself. With your back to the tomb and nave, look eastwards to the marvellously intact **eastern window** which is striking to this day. The sharp-eyed may notice the absence of a tracery; its four tall mullions dividing the window into five.

Turning left, continue your tour into the **north range**. The two-storey building was once the living quarters of monks before it was converted into an Elizabethan house in the years following the Dissolution of the Monasteries; it later housed farm workers. The vaulted **undercroft** is solid and largely unbroken. Little remains of the **cloisters**, but you gain a strong sense of its position by its stone outline.

The Teesdale Way traces the river from Barnard Castle, making a **walk** here a very pleasant option (page 244).

4 STAINDROP

It's hard to know where Staindrop's village green begins and ends, so long and sprawling is the settlement lining the A688 thoroughfare. But, don't let that description put you off from what is essentially a very attractive, well-kept old village, sandstone throughout, and with a few cafés and a striking church dubbed 'the cathedral of the Dales' on account of its considerable size.

"The finely carved rood screen separating the chancel from the nave is said to be one of the finest in the county."

While many features of **St Mary's Church** (Front St, DL2 3NH), at the eastern end of the village, point to the Norman period with its rounded arcades and chancel arch, it was originally a Saxon building (carved stones and even a sundial are incorporated into its walls) that was later significantly remodelled post-Conquest and again in the mid-13th century when the tower was raised. There's so much of interest inside: many effigies of the Neville family of Raby Castle (page 248), including one of a child as you enter the church on your left, the

13th-century sedilia (the triple arches built into the south wall) and pre-Reformation choir stalls and misericords. The finely carved rood screen separating the chancel from the nave is said to be one of the finest in the county.

¶¶ FOOD & DRINK

The Country Tea Shop 39 Front St, DL2 3NB ✆ 01833 660434 ⊘ 10.00–15.00 daily. Friendly traditional tea room, popular with elderly ladies tucking into scones and sandwiches. Besides sweet baked offerings, there are jacket potatoes and a couple of more substantial meals like scampi and lasagne and a roast on Sundays. Outside tables catch the morning sunshine – and all the comings and goings in the village.

5 RABY CASTLE

Staindrop DL2 3AH ✆ 01833 660202 ♟ raby.co.uk ⊘ castle: March–Oct 11.00–16.00 Wed–Sun (summer Tue also); deer park 10.00–16.00; Plotters' Forest: selected dates and times – check online; ♿ ground floor of the castle but the path to the castle is gravel; a level path runs throughout the deer park; the Plotters' Forest has an accessible boardwalk

Descending over the hills from the north, Raby Castle appears in the vale below, some seven miles from Barnard Castle, looking terrifically majestic with its stonking embattled towers connected by curtain walls and encircled by a moat and wider deer parkland. It's what children might call 'a proper castle', and rated by architectural historians as one of the finest medieval fortresses in England.

The castle's original name of 'Rabi' indicates its links with Denmark ('Ra' meaning 'boundary' and 'bi' 'settlement' in Old Norse) under the Viking ruler King Cnut in the 11th century. The oldest masonry (Bulmer's Tower) probably dates to around this period but the story of Raby Castle is really bound with one family and period: the Nevilles, who rebuilt almost the entire fortress in the 14th century. The Nevilles lived at Raby Castle until 1569 when 700 knights gathered at the castle under the part command of Charles Neville to stage a rebellion against Elizabeth I in support of Mary, Queen of Scots. The Rising of the North, as it became known, failed and Neville fled to the Netherlands never to return – except on canvas in the Barons' Hall. The Crown initially took possession of the castle before selling it to the Vanes, later the

1 Egglestone Abbey. 2 & 3 Raby Castle – including the Octagon Drawing Room.
4 St Mary's Church, Staindrop. 5 The Buttermarket in Barnard Castle. ▶

Lords Barnards who made a number of alterations in the 18th and 19th centuries as well as landscaping the parkland. Currently Raby is under the ownership of the 12th Lord Barnard who is a direct descendent of the Nevilles, and so the custodianship has come full circle.

Set in a 200-acre **parkland** where deer have roamed since Norman times, Raby's wider grounds and formal **Walled Garden** are worth allowing a few hours to explore. Most striking are the tremendously high yew trees that form an organic shaped wall (it takes two gardeners one month to cut it); unfortunately the gardens were under development at the time of writing and not open to the public.

Set back from the castle is the **Plotters' Forest**, an adventure playground in a young woodland where you will lose your children for a good hour or longer as they scamper off along walkways and climb wooden turrets. Depending on your style of parenting you may see this as an opportunity to enjoy a coffee and slice of cake at the on-site café at the top of the hill, though you have to be content with your offspring being heard but not seen. Those with very young children may find it taxing trying to keep an eye on them, despite all the fun.

Inside the castle

Entry into the rooms once you're within the curtain walls is via the formidable **Neville Gateway**. Notice how the courtyard (with the largest cobbles you may ever see) is not quite wide enough to turn a carriage, hence they travelled straight into the internal Entrance Hall and exited out the far door.

"French and German stained glass from the 12th and 16th centuries survives exceptionally well in the medieval chapel."

Inside, the rooms are impressive from the start – stately with huge chandeliers, drapes and paintings, but none comes closer in opulence and grandeur to the **Octagon Drawing Room**, intact from the 1840s when it was adorned with the jaw-dropping crimson and gold furnishings. My guide told me it took three years to build but five to restore. Also impressive is the medieval **Barons' Hall** where knights grouped for the uprising against the Crown. French and German stained glass from the 12th and 16th centuries survives exceptionally well in the medieval **Chapel** – an intimate space with an impressive rib vaulted roof and finely carved wooden pew ends depicting lions and hounds for courage and loyalty.

At the other end of the scale of lavishness is the servant's bedroom and butler's office, both furnished around 1900, but perhaps most historically fascinating is the **Old Kitchen** – a superb example of a surviving medieval kitchen, built around 1360 and little changed since then, except perhaps for the 1950s-era blue-gloss paintwork (the decorators even gave the grandfather clock a coating). Cooks will be in awe of the range, and the dazzling array of copper teapots, saucepans and jelly moulds. A passageway near the top of the ceiling runs around the kitchen and was used by servants entering the Barons' Hall and by soldiers on watch duty.

Raby Castle is stuffed with **curios**; a few to seek out are: an elaborate clock with two faces in the Small Drawing Room; ornamental Chinese pagodas in the library; a 19th-century diorama of a hot-air balloon ride over Raby; a Flemish painting within a painting in the Ante-library; a trinket tray of lockets, rings and miniatures in the Octagon Drawing Room; five outstanding Meissen porcelain animals in the Barons' Hall; wooden pew ends in the chapel; a stuffed fox curled up by the fire in the entrance hall; and over 300 copper jelly moulds in the medieval kitchen.

6 GAINFORD & SURROUNDS

⌂ **Headlam Hall** (page 311)

The rolling farmland between Barnard Castle and Darlington encloses some quaint old places that will catch the eye of passing travellers following the Tees or touring cross-country east of Staindrop (page 247). Country lanes connect the likes of **Wackerfield** with its charming run of white stone cottages and rural views; **Killerby** and **Summerhouse** – both lovely old villages with cottages facing their respective greens. Closer to the Tees

> *"Country lanes connect the likes of Wackerfield with its charming run of white stone cottages and rural views."*

is **Headlam**, dominated by a luxury spa hotel with perhaps the most elegant Georgian frontage of any country house you'll find in Durham. If you wander round the streets here you'll see a 17th-century dovecote within the grounds of the whitewashed Headlam Farm buildings. It's one of several **dovecotes** in the area, a distinctive feature of the Tees Valley.

Tracing the Tees east of Barnard Castle, a string of appealing villages come every few miles: **Whorlton**, a higgledy mix of stone cottages, a pub (see opposite) and a church about a generous green, reached by crossing a wonderful wrought iron chain suspension bridge (undergoing long-term restoration at the time of writing). Next downriver is **Ovington** with its lovely green and very tall maypole, followed by **Winston**, famous for its single-arched bridge dating to 1764 that was the longest in Europe at one time – so wide in fact that a spitfire was able to fly under the crossing (a film of the stunt is available to view on YouTube). As elsewhere, the riverside is accessible along the **Teesdale Way**, offering miles of walks.

One of the most historically interesting and attractive villages in the area, **Gainford** stands on the north banks of the Tees, eight miles east of Barnard Castle. The settlement's roots go back to Anglo-Saxon times when a monastic community with ties to Lindisfarne developed on the site where the parish church now stands. Occupying the southwest corner of the village green, **St Mary's** began life in the 9th century but what you see today is mainly Early English from the 13th century (look at all those fine pointed lancet windows) with medieval additions in the 15th century including the tower. There's much more to explore in the village including old farms, a fine terrace of Georgian houses (High Row) and a pub (the Cross Keys). Most of the historic streets lie on the south side of the A67. On the corner of High Row and Low Row is **Gainford Hall**, an imposing Jacobean manor (restored in Victorian times) and a nearby dovecote dating to roughly the same period.

Around half a mile west out of the village on the Teesdale Way leads to the enchanting **Whispering Waters** – a particularly picturesque stretch of the Tees – where stands **Gainford Spa**, a font-like basin dating to the 18th century spouting mineral water that overflows into the river. There's a pull-in area on the A67 from where you can walk to the spa through trees, guided by its sulphurous odour.

"Gainford Spa is a font-like basin dating to the 18th century spouting mineral water that overflows into the river."

On the south side of the Tees, public rights of way lead to the ruins of **St Lawrence Chapel** in the deserted medieval village of Barforth. A trio of lancet windows point to its 12th and 13th century beginnings before it was converted into a priest's home in the 16th century and later a farmhouse. There's another dovecote close by – a stout beehive creation and also late medieval.

¶¶ FOOD & DRINK

A few upmarket dining options, make the lower reaches of the Tees around Gainford an attractive place for holiday makers and couples looking for something more refined than most of the offerings in Barnard Castle and Darlington. Best known is the **Raby Hunt** in the village of Summerhouse (DL2 3UD ✆ 01325 374237), a two Michelin-star affair producing exquisite plates of food where you should expect to pay over £200 per person. Not on quite the same scale but above average dining nonetheless is the restaurant at the **Headlam Hall Hotel** (Headlam DL2 3HA ✆ 01325 374237) in the sumptuous surroundings of a Georgian country manor.

In addition to the two places listed here, other pub options to consider include: the **Black Horse** at Ingleton (DL2 3HS ✆ 01325 730374) for Italian dishes and Sunday roasts; **The Cross Keys** at Gainford (1 High Row, DL2 3DN ✆ 01325 730237) serving pies on a Friday night and roasts on Sundays; **The Four Alls** in Ovington (DL11 7BP ✆ 01833 627302) a friendly old pub opposite the village green (check out the very tall maypole) with a homely interior and beer garden and serving all the usual pub classics as well as regional ales.

The Bridge Inn Whorlton DL12 8XD ✆ 01833 316024 ⊙ 17.00–late Wed–Fri, noon–late Sat, noon–19.00 Sun. Friendly country inn to the east of Barnard Castle, serving burgers (including a vegan option), sausage and mash, cod and chips, scampi and so on. Enjoy the view across the tranquil village green from the outside tables. Reached via a four-mile walk along the riverside path from Barnard Castle, the Bridge Inn makes a very pleasant lunch stop on a loop of the Tees from Barnard Castle.

The Bridgewater Arms Winston DL2 3RN ✆ 01325 730302 ⊙ noon–14.00 & 17.30–21.00 Wed–Sat, noon–16.00 Sun; booking recommended ♿ ramp available but no disabled toilet. Housed in the village's Victorian schoolhouse, the Bridgewater oozes character with its fetching bell and snug interior with a fire, the scene of many a lesson. The school was converted into a pub soon after its closure in 1959; it's now an upmarket restaurant with an impressive wine list and a select number of lovingly prepared dishes: roast duck with orange and fennel, organic salmon, steaks, stone bass and shellfish linguine, beetroot and spinach curry, and Sunday roasts.

7 PIERCEBRIDGE

Old-worldly Piercebridge surrounds a leafy green on the north banks of the River Tees and is one of the most attractive and visited villages in the Barnard Castle area in part owing to its Roman heritage sites on the route of the Roman road, Dere Street.

If approaching from the south and before you reach the village, you may like to see the foundation stones of the **Roman bridge** that remain visible in a field south of the Tees (parking just off the B6275, a few hundred yards east of the George Hotel; cross a stile into a field where you'll find the stones), the river having changed its course since the early 3rd century when the crossing was constructed. Also on the south side of the river is the **George Hotel** whose tall antique clock inspired the nursery rhyme *Grandfather's Clock* (written in 1876 as a marching song by Henry Clay Work), and is the reason we call tall case-clocks by this name.

"On the south side of the river is the George Hotel whose tall antique clock inspired the nursery rhyme Grandfather's Clock."

Spanning the Tees today is a wonderfully elegant **medieval bridge** with three arches, the main entrance point from the south into the village. It's best viewed from a somewhat concealed riverside path on the north side of the crossing – the same trail leads to the ruins of a **Roman town** (east side of the village) with stones revealing the outlines of buildings. So often with places of great antiquity, all it takes is one seemingly unremarkable feature to bring the whole scene to life; in the case of the Piercebridge settlement – which may have gone by the Roman name of *Morbium* – it is a single drainage channel lining the side of a road. Suddenly, you can imagine people and traffic and the noise and sounds of soldiers, traders and civilians coming in and out of the buildings. The ruins are also accessible from the centre of Piercebridge, not far from the church, through a gate by the side of a residential house overlooking the green, the same open space that hides a large section of the fort under its grass.

After a stroll round the Roman ruins, church and green, which holds much rural charm, you could take lunch in The Fox Hole pub or visit the organic farm shop (see below).

¶¶ FOOD & DRINK

The Fox Hole DL2 3SJ ℘ 01325 374286 ◷ noon–19.00 Mon, noon–22.45 Tue–Sat, noon–19.00 Sun; kitchen closed Mon. Contemporary pub and restaurant with a stylish interior, wooden flooring and furnishings, and a straightforward menu (with pricey mains) of the usual pub dishes and a vegan option.

Piercebridge Organic Farm Shop & Butchery The Green, DL2 3SE ℘ 01325 374251 ◷ 09.00–15.30 Mon–Sat, 09.30–13.00 Sun. Three-hundred-acre livestock farm rearing cattle, pigs and sheep which are slaughtered on-site. We're not talking 'food miles' for the sausages, lamb, fillet steaks and burgers sold in the shop, but food *yards*. Also for sale are vegetables and a range of food cupboard items, eggs as well as coffees to take-away.

BOWES & THE GRETA VALLEY

🏠 **The Millbank Arms** (page 311) 🏠 **Mellwaters Barn Cottages** (page 311)

One of the lesser-known Durham valleys on the Durham border with Yorkshire and Cumbria, the Greta Valley is formed by its namesake river that rises on an extensive area of bleak moorland lying south of the A66. Most people's experience of the valley is from this fantastically high trans-Pennine route connecting Scotch Corner with Brough and the Lake District beyond. But for those who take time to explore the wooded gorge formed by the River Greta and the meadows and pastures rising out of the valley, you will be rewarded with some of the most untouched and secluded river scenery in Durham – and a picturesque ruin or three.

Bowes marks roughly the central point in the valley with open moorland to the west and more in the way of farmland and wooded river scenery east of the village. A beautiful stretch of waterway between Rutherford Bridge and Greta Bridge winds through **Brignall Banks** woods before entering the stone hamlet of **Greta Bridge** and the Georgian estate of **Rokeby** where the Greta joins with the Tees at a well-known beauty spot, the '**Meeting of the Waters**'.

8 BOWES

Bowes lies just south of the busy arterial route across the Pennines, the A66, on the site of an old Roman fort (now covered by the castle) and is an obvious stopping place on cross-Pennine journeys. While the village itself is attractive enough with its long thoroughfare of solid stone houses (and imposing Georgian Bowes Hall at the eastern gateway), it's the castle that most people come to see (those who make the mistake of visiting for the Bowes Museum will need to turn round and head to Barnard Castle, five miles away; page 242).

"A ruin maybe, but the bulk of the Keep remains, guarding what was once an important passage across the Pennines."

Bowes Castle (DL12 9HP ⊙ daily; English Heritage) is a brute of a keep – a 12th-century block with hugely thick walls sliced with arrow slits. A ruin maybe, but the bulk of the Keep remains, guarding what was from Roman times an important passage across the Pennines known as the Stainmore Pass. Set behind the main road through Bowes in a field with generous views all around, you can walk up to the Keep and enter the crumbling interior.

The castle looms over **St Giles Church,** the oldest parts of which (the nave and chancel) date to the time the fortress was raised in the 12th and 13th centuries, though – as with many old churches – it was extensively remodelled in medieval and Victorian times. One external feature worth finding is a heavily worn – though still clearly visible – stone relief of the Crucifixion in the south porch gable.

Dickens fans will find the former **Bowes Academy** (Dotheboys Hall in *Nicholas Nickleby*) and coach house on the main road at the western end of the village (look for a large sandstone building with seven bays on your left on leaving the village centre). Conditions inside the two-storey boarding school, now converted into flats, were said to be so cramped and unhygienic in the early 1800s that a number of the 200 students developed eye disease, for which the

"Dickens fans will find the former Bowes Academy (Dotheboys Hall in Nicholas Nickleby*) and coach house on the main road."*

infamous headmaster, William Shaw, was fined. Dickens met Shaw at Bowes in 1838, later immortalising the headmaster in his novel as the wicked Wackford Squeers.

While there are few reasons to warrant a longer stay in the village once you've had a wander and seen the castle, there are fine countryside **walks** direct from Bowes along the River Greta and up on to neighbouring moors, accessible via various routes including the Pennine Way. A seven-mile circuit connecting a variety of habitats starts on the eastern edge of Bowes, by the village hall, and heads downhill to meet the River Greta (don't cross Gilmonby Bridge but take the footpath off to your right). The Greta remains a close companion for almost four miles with the riverbank footpath guiding you upstream, initially through trees, to **Mill Force** – a wide stepped waterfall – and then along the Pennine Way across pastures on the south side of the Greta to **East Mellwaters**.

God's Bridge, another mile or so west (and three miles west of Bowes), marks a memorably scenic point on the Pennine Way where the limestone has been undercut by the river to form a natural bridge. From God's Bridge, follow the Pennine Way north, taking the tunnel under the A66 and then a farm track off to the right for a few miles

◀ **1** The 'Meeting of the Waters'. **2** Hannah's Meadow is a delight in early summer.

3 & **4** Oystercatcher and curlew are frequently seen in Baldersdale.

over blanket bog and grasslands to West Stoney Keld. The descent south off the hills crosses moorland managed for grouse and re-enters Bowes from the west.

Should you head south from God's Bridge, the Pennine Way climbs on to high ground tracing **Sleightholme Beck** upriver and over moorland to the highest pub in England, the **Tan Hill Inn** (see below), right on the Yorkshire border. I've seen adders in heather clearings up here so do take care with dogs.

¶¶ FOOD & DRINK

Cross Lanes Organic Farm DL12 9RT (use DL12 9SL for sat navs) ✆ 01833 630619 ⊙ 09.00–16.00 Mon & Wed–Sat, 10.00–16.00 Sun ♿. Ten miles east of Bowes is this superb farm shop and restaurant where almost 100% of food served in their café is organic: breakfasts, pizzas, burgers, falafel, sandwiches, lamb kebabs, Sunday roasts and salads. While the menu is not huge and the prices not small, the dishes are consistently very good (delicious cakes too) and the setting – with views of open farmland, outside tables, a children's playground and close proximity to a major road across the Pennines – makes this a winning combination for many travellers. Their well-stocked farm shop has everything you need for a cottage booking: a butcher's counter with grass-fed organic beef, some of the best rare-breed sausages you can find anywhere, kebabs, pies etc; a bakery; wide selection of pantry and household items; bottled beers from Barnard Castle's own brewery; and decent, frozen farm-made ready meals.

Tan Hill Inn Reeth, North Yorkshire DL11 6ED ✆ 01833 533007 ⊙ food noon–15.30 & 17.30–20.00; bar till after 23.00. Famous for being the highest pub in Britain, the Tan Hill sits amid moors and feels wonderfully remote. The freehouse is well known to Pennine hikers and periodically features in national news bulletins when snow drifts trap guests inside for days on end. Luckily the inn also offers B&B accommodation (and wild camping). It's not plush inside but the open fire and relaxed surroundings are a joyous sight to drenched walkers and the food, while pricey, is decent: burgers, fish and chips, pies, Sunday roasts and other pub favourites. One stand-out hearty plate is a coiled sausage inside a huge Yorkshire pudding, served with mash and veg.

9 GRETA BRIDGE & SURROUNDS

A mile upstream of the confluence of the rivers Greta and Tees, the old village of **Greta Bridge** (pronounced 'Greeta') clusters either side of its namesake 18th-century crossing, five miles southeast of Barnard Castle. A sandstone block known as The Square on the south side of the river is set around a courtyard and once housed a post office and inn. A trio of tall arched doorways recall its former use as a coaching inn when the

Scotch Corner to Brough road used to run through Greta Bridge. On the other side of the river is the Morritt Hotel, which makes much of Greta's Dickens connection (the author was said to have stayed in the village while researching *Nicholas Nickleby*).

The nearby Georgian mansion, Rokeby Park (page 261), and tranquil wooded riverside attracted 19th-century artists and poets including J M W Turner, John Sell Cotman and Sir Walter Scott whose favourite spots are accessible to visitors today, including where Cotman painted the elegant bridge over the Greta. His 1805 watercolour remains an accurate representation to this day.

Greta sounds enticing, I know, but I must be honest and mention that the appeal of the place is diluted somewhat by the continuous background rumble from the A66. Away from this busy trans-Pennine road, however – and especially if you follow the riverside trail to Brignall Mill – the traffic roar is soon replaced by the sound of water and birdsong.

Footpaths line both sides of the beautiful **River Greta**, opening up long lengths of the wooded waterway and wider valley to those on foot, with the northern banks offering the clearest paths – but even they are somewhat perilous and overgrown in places with steep drops through the gorge. The five-mile stretch of river between Greta Bridge and **Rutherford Bridge** is particularly scenic – densely wooded for the most part – with

"The nearby Georgian mansion, Rokeby Park, and tranquil wooded riverside attracted 19th-century artists and poets."

an abundance of early-flowering plants colouring the understorey of **Brignall Banks**, where warblers and all the common woodland birds sing all through spring. 'O Brignall Banks are wild and fair, And Greta woods are green, And you may gather garlands there, Would grace a summer queen' wrote Sir Walter Scott.

If you didn't want to walk the whole way to Rutherford Bridge, there's a straightforward there-and-back **walk** along the northern banks of the Greta to the deserted medieval village of **old Brignall** and its churchyard, one mile west of Greta Bridge. Take the 'Greta Walk' footpath signed for Brignall Mill from the north side of the old bridge (the same side as the Morritt Hotel), entering grassland by way of stone steps on the side of the bridge wall. The raised grassy embankment to your right is an old **Roman fort**, the 2,000 year-old perimeter wall clearly visible. Follow the edge of the woodland with the River Greta below to your left and ignoring the turning for Brignall Village near a ruin. You will soon reach the abandoned church and walled burial ground in a wide, open pasture. The lichen-covered tombs and headstones – some of them three hundred years old – enclosed in **St Mary's churchyard** are a poignant reminder that a village centred around this site for over half a century before stones from the church were moved uphill in the 1830s to what is now known as Brignall. All that remains of the roofless church are the crumbling walls of the chancel and arched window in the east gable – the only obviously ecclesiastical feature besides a piscina. On your return to Greta Bridge, you may like to make a detour to the river which is reached by turning off the main path into woodland. Slippery in damp weather, the muddy trail descends steeply to the Greta and the locally-famous **Scotchman's Stone** – a huge boulder lying half in the river and the subject of one of Cotman's paintings in the early 1800s.

To extend this walk to **Brignall Mill**, a circuit of around nine miles from Greta Bridge, rejoin the footpath just beyond St Mary's old churchyard, entering woodland over a stile and down steps, then tracing the river upstream in the deep gorge for a further 2½ miles. This is a rewarding route – devoid of people – through beautiful Brignall Banks woods and crossing open pastures but remaining in close company with the Greta for lengthy stretches. The mill now provides holiday accommodation but retains many historic features visible externally from the right of way, including the old water channels. Return to Greta Bridge on the south side of the gorge, first by crossing the Greta at Brignall Mill and turning left. You can make a detour to **Scargill Castle** (a medieval three-storey gatehouse) in half a mile and return to the River Greta along Gill Beck and the fetchingly named Hardy Wife Wood. The final leg to Greta Bridge is across open countryside with good views and plenty of upland birdlife, via Crook's House and Wilson House.

¶¶ FOOD & DRINK

Coghlaus Barningham DL11 7DW ✆ 01833 625295 ⊙ 10.30–16.30 Tue–Sat. Barningham village bears down on the Greta Valley from the south, a two-mile uphill climb from Greta Bridge. Housed in an old coach house, Coghlaus specialises in afternoon teas but also serves quiche, soup, ploughman's sandwiches and a few hot plates. There's also an on-site deli shop and bakery.

The Morritt Hotel Greta Bridge DL12 9SE ✆ 01833 627232. Making much of its literary link with Charles Dickens, who was said to have stayed in the village while working on

Nicholas Nickleby, this upmarket hotel with a spa has a few dining areas catering for non-guests: a relaxed but smart bar area (decorated with murals depicting Dickens' novel) and an attractive garden backing on to meadows. If the distant rumble of traffic is too intrusive, you can also dine in the wood-panelled interior of the restaurant, which is aimed at couples. Fish and chips, steak, pies, sausage and mash, fishcakes, all priced around £13 a plate.

10 ROKEBY PARK

DL12 9RZ ✆ 01833 631342 ⬦ rokebypark.com ⊙ Jun–Aug 14.00–17.00 Mon & Tue; call or check online for up-to-date visiting times ♿ ground floor only

> I have been all morning pulling about my pictures and hanging them in new positions to make more room for my fine picture of Venus's backside by Velasquez which I have at length exalted over my chimney piece in the library. It is an admirable light for the painting, and shows it in perfection, whilst by raising the said backside to a considerable height the ladies may avert their downcast eyes without difficulty, and connoisseurs steal a glance without drawing in the said posterior as a part of the company.
>
> J B S Morritt of Rokeby writing to his friend, Sir Walter Scott in September 1820

Set back from the Tees, the wondrous neo-Palladian villa, Rokeby (once known as 'Rookby' because of the large number of corvids in the trees), stands in parkland laid out in the 18th century, a few miles from Barnard Castle and bound by the Tees and Greta on two sides. This still being a family home, the mansion is only open at certain times of the year but is worth visiting for those interested in stately homes from the Georgian era with plenty of antiques, paintings and intricate plasterwork to catch your eye, a wonderful 18th-century Print Room and two rooms particularly unchanged since the 1700s. Velazquez's *The Toilet of Venus*, better known as *The Rokeby Venus*, was sold to London's National Gallery in 1906 but a copy still hangs here for visitors to 'steal a glance', alongside many other works and porcelain collected on Grand Tours.

"The Rokeby Venus, *was sold to London's National Gallery in 1906 but a copy still hangs here for visitors to 'steal a glance'.*"

Anne Morritt, resident here in the mid-1700s and described as 'a most ingenious lady', produced a large number of intricate needlework 'pictures' copied from the paintings of famous artists of the day. The 40 works of hers on display are some of the most treasured possessions in the house.

A **walk** in the grounds to the River Greta is highly recommended. Where the river joins with the Tees at a beautiful place, the '**Meeting** of the Waters', captured by Turner and where Sir Walter Scott penned the ballad 'Rokeby'. You can reach the very site by following the Teesdale Way or a well-signed footpath from nearby Greta Bridge.

LOWER TEESDALE: COTHERSTONE TO MICKLETON

Upriver from Barnard Castle, road and footpath dip in and out of a string of attractive stone villages along the Tees. They each have their individual charms and historical buildings of note and all are set within some of Durham's finest countryside, where a riverside ramble followed by lunch in an old pub are the order of the day.

11 COTHERSTONE

> I descended from heather to pastureland, and then my way carried me further downhill amongst meadows and woodlands, until ahead I could see the slender spire of a church peeping from the trees. And so I entered Cotherstone.
>
> Alfred Wainwright, *A Pennine Journey*, 1939

All that remains from the Norman period, when Cotherstone was 'Codrestone' in the Doomsday Book of 1086, are the earthworks of a castle that once capped a prominence above the confluence of the rivers Balder and Tees. As you enter the smart, well-kept village today, which is topped and tailed with two greens, East Green and West Green, most of what you see is 19th century with some earlier buildings dotted about. The village expanded in the years following the development of railway transport in 1868, and a few terraces have a distinctly railway village feel to them. Wainwright's 1939 observation that 'its houses are large and of good appearance, its roads neat and its hedges well-trimmed, and there is a church handsome enough to grace the finest avenue of a city' holds firm to this day.

"Walks on to Cotherstone Moor, which rises to the west, could be combined with a search for the Butter Stone."

A stream trickles through **East Green**, adding to Cotherstone's rural charm but it is **West Green** where visitors tend to gravitate to for its pubs and proximity to the riverside paths.

THE BUTTER STONE

In the hills above Cotherstone, by the side of a lonely road to Bowes, stands a peculiar large boulder with a little 'well'. If you didn't know its history, you'd probably overlook the Butter Stone, a curious relic from around the time a plague ripped through Teesdale in 1663. In order to safely trade produce during this period, farmers would deposit goods by the stone and then watch from a safe distance while customers collected their purchases, leaving their coins in the little well which was filled with (disinfecting) vinegar.

The stone, which is Grade II listed, is marked on Ordnance Survey maps at ♥ NY999183 and conveniently stands close to the road between Cotherstone and Bowes (not far from the most northerly of two fingerposts by the side of the road).

Another way of accessing the stone, and enjoying a scenic **walk** across Cotherstone Moor at the same time, is to take the paved track from Briscoe Farm (a few miles west of Cotherstone), parking in a little pull-in area at the end of the track by a farm gate and following the bridleway in a southeasterly direction towards the aforementioned road. The stone appears in the grassland to your left on reaching the road. There are beautiful views up here, with Teesdale laid before you.

If you were to take an evening stroll along the back lanes that curl behind the Fox & Hounds pub, you'd be walking in the footsteps of medieval villagers. Look over the walls of **Leadpipe Lane** and you'll see some fine examples of medieval 'strip' fields; in fact the village is surrounded by them, as a glance at an Ordnance Survey map reveals.

Picnickers will find plenty of spots to take lunch by the **River Tees**, reached by taking a footpath signed just before the bridge at the northern end of Cotherstone; goosanders, dippers and wagtails are a familiar sight here. A popular **walk** follows the Teesdale Way trail north through woods for two miles to Romaldkirk (page 265). After a very good lunch in the Rose & Crown pub (page 265), return across countryside along the Tees Railway Path – a flat-ish route with expansive views of the hills and rolling pastures, and an impressive viaduct. Another favourite river and woodland ramble is to Barnard Castle following the Teesdale Way downstream and returning along the river's northern bank, a circuit of around seven miles.

Walks on to **Cotherstone Moor**, which rises to the west, could be combined with a search for the Butter Stone (see above) or the prehistoric decorated stones at Goldsborough Rigg (page 272). These 'cup and ring' marked stones are thought to have religious or sacred significance and

COTHERSTONE CHEESE

Cotherstone's well-known creamy cheese has been produced in Teesdale for hundreds of years; now just one farm continues the tradition, run by an elderly lady. You'll find the cheese stocked in most good delis, butchers and local shops in Teesdale including McFarlane Family Butchers in Barnard Castle and Samuel James's coffee shop in Middleton. Supplies are limited, however, this being a two-person production, so if you see it for sale, you may want to make your purchase there and then.

are scattered below a rocky outcrop, itself a stunning spot overlooking Baldersdale and its reservoirs.

¶ FOOD & DRINK

The Fox & Hounds DL12 9PF ✆ 01833 650241 ⊙ food: 18.00–20.30 Mon–Wed, noon–14.00 & 18.00–20.30 Thu, noon–14.00 & 17.00–20.30 Fri & Sat, noon–16.00 Sun (note times change seasonally); bar open later ♿. Traditional 300-year-old inn busy with locals, farmers, visitors and walkers and serving decent pub dishes and Sunday lunches. I recommend the fish and chips, which you can also order to take away for very reasonable prices. Cheese from the village dairy features heavily on the menu including in a chicken dish, topped on a ratatouille gratin and in their 'fox lair salad'.

The Red Lion DL12 9QE ✆ 07871865118 ⊙ 18.00–22.30 Mon, Wed, Fri & Sat, 15.00–21.00 Sun. This cracking old pub of cottage proportions has been serving beers to a local crowd since 1738 and has all the appeal of a rural community drinking hole whose landlord is passionate about his beers, some brewed locally, and where the background soundtrack is of people chatting rather than music. The Red Lion boasts two dominoes teams, doesn't serve food and there's an open fire. That's all you need to know.

12 ROMALDKIRK

🏠 **The Rose & Crown** (page 311)

> A threatening sky next morning could not rob Romaldkirk of its charm. It had been too dark last evening to appreciate its quiet beauty, but now I found that I had unknowingly spent the night in an arbour of great loveliness. I found no other place in Teesdale quite so pleasant as Romaldkirk.
>
> Alfred Wainwright, *A Pennine Journey*, 1939

Romaldkirk is a perfect English village. It appears out of the surrounding meadows and is instantly alluring with its neat 18th-century stone houses around a wide village centre, renowned pub/restaurant (see below), old church and lanes filled with the chatter of sparrows and songs of thrushes. People amble along in the middle of the road and stop to chat. It's that kind of a place.

A sweet square of cottages conceals a side entrance into the church ground. Some masonry in **St Romald's** goes back to Anglo-Saxon times and a good deal remaining dates to the Norman period, particularly the nave arcade and aisles. An effigy of a medieval nobleman (in chain mail) who died in battle against the Scots in 1305 lies in the north transept, unusually with his legs uncrossed. Another medieval curiosity to note is The Devil's Door, a conspicuously blocked-up opening seen on the facing wall as you enter the church. It was sealed in medieval times and supposedly keeps the devil at bay. Also on display is an ampulla that would have once belonged to a pilgrim and contained holy water.

At the north end of the village, a fetching old railway signal by the side of the road indicates where the **Tees Railway** once passed Romaldkirk. Today it's a mixed-used leisure path (page 263) but has been diverted at this point and walkers will need to pick up the route where indicated by signs.

If you look at an Ordnance Survey map of the area (OL31) there's an obvious **walk** to neighbouring Cotherstone that makes use of the Tees Railway Path (page 269) and Teesdale Way to form a popular circular route of four miles. The path passes close to the stone hamlet of Hunderthwaite.

¶¶ FOOD & DRINK

The Rose & Crown DL12 9EB ✆ 01833 650213 ☉ noon–14.30 (bar area and outside; restaurant on Sun) & 18.00–20.30 (restaurant only) daily. 'The Rose and Crown was out of the question for me; it looking much too fine and expensive and would have scrutinised me from head to foot, I knew.' So thought Alfred Wainwright when he visited in the 1930s. His words ring true today, at least the bit about it being fine and expensive, but not the welcome, which is altogether warmer, even for this 21st-century weary hiker. Nonetheless, I avoided the tables in the main wood-panelled, carpeted dining room set for couples, with candles lit, and instead headed into the snug, rather more informal bar room where a fire was crackling.

The owners of the Georgian inn have kept the décor smart and discreet while embracing the building's 300-year-old charms. Prices are surprisingly reasonable for expertly put together dishes such as fillet of cod with potatoes, mushroom and leeks; venison bourguignon pie, 'hog roast' sausages (famously produced by Peat's butchers in Barnard

Castle. While the menu is small, the plates are beautiful, using seasonal produce, a good deal of which is sourced from Durham or neighbouring counties. Clearly, this is one of the best pub restaurants in the dale. With that in mind, make sure you book ahead, particularly because tables get reserved in advance by guests staying in the hotel.

13 EGGLESTON

⚑ Hill Top Huts (page 311)

Eggleston lies on the north side of the Tees beneath heather moors. It's an attractive, oddly shaped village trailing down a steep hillside and best known for **Eggleston Hall Gardens** (DL12 0AG ✆ 01833 650230 ☉ 10.00–17.00 daily ♿ but uneven paths) and its café, where plants and fruit trees have been cultivated for over 400 years. Set in the grounds of Eggleston Hall (not open to the public), which was built in the early 19th century off the back of lead-mining money, the gardens, nursery, beehives and restored greenhouses are enclosed by Victorian walls and will entice even those who don't intend to buy any plants. If you are here to shop, you are in for a treat as the variety and quality is said to be excellent. There's also an artist's workshop (☉ 11.00–14.30 Thu & Fri, 11.00–16.30 Sat & Sun) housed in the gardener's cottage within the walled garden. Victoria Bellas Carter works with coloured tissue paper to create lively, detailed scenes of gardens and meadows that are so intricate you can hardly believe the collages have not been painted. 'The key is to stop the dyes in the tissue paper from bleeding too much,' she says of her affordable works.

A roofless **chapel** dating to the 17th-century is reached at the end of a very short garden path in an overgrown corner of the gardens behind a gate signed for 'the old churchyard'. It is like stepping into the pages of *The Secret Garden*. The ruin stands (just about) looking picturesque through the bushes and must have been dilapidated for some years for such a thick-waisted tree to sprout through its centre and rare snake's-head fritillaries to establish inside the building.

Eggleston and its gardens can be reached on foot from the **Teesdale Way** that winds through a delightful stretch of woodland by the river before diverting uphill by a handsome medieval bridge (rebuilt in the 17th century).

◀ **1** Kirkcarrion Bronze Age burial site. **2** Picturesque Cotherstone. **3** St Romald's at Romaldkirk. **4** Hayberries Nature Reserve is a great place to look for lapwings.

¶¶ FOOD & DRINK

Eggleston Gardens Coach House Café Eggleston DL12 0AG tel: 01833 650553 ♿.
Adjacent to Eggleston's walled garden is this modern, reasonably-priced café and gift shop
in a restored coach house with a sunny patio area. I recommend the quiches and £10 platters
(their Winter Warmer includes a shot of soup, a sticky sausage, bacon and cheese fries,
smoked-cheese rarebit and salad). They also serve afternoon teas, cakes, sandwiches and a
few more substantial dishes such as lasagne and steak burgers.

14 MICKLETON

A few miles upriver from Romaldkirk and a similar distance downriver
from Middleton-in-Teesdale lies the village of Mickleton with its old
sandstone cottages, school, farms and surrounding meadows. An
evening stroll through the village pondering the former life of converted
stone buildings and stopping at the Blacksmith's to catch sundown in
the beer garden is a very enjoyable way to spend a few hours if staying
in the area.

Low Side is the lane set back from the main road through the village
where there's a pretty old church and many flower-filled cottages,
converted byres and a dovecote. Round the corner on Mill Lane, a
fetching old farm set around a yard with a long barn on one side may
catch your eye.

Railway path walkers (see opposite) will find the countryside above
Mickleton hugely enjoyable with its meadows sloping gently to the
Tees, lapwing-filled skies, farmers doing their rounds, and a few places
to picnic and take in all these sights. **Hayberries Nature Reserve**
(♥ NZ991229) is one such place, reached from the B6281 between
Eggleston and Mickleton (and signed from the road). The wide grassy
vale (once an old quarry) edged with birch, oak and sycamore trees and
with valley views lends itself well to a rug and sandwiches. Apart from
the wildflowers, and a lake inhabited by amphibians, the star attraction
is a colony of sand martins in a fenced-off area concealing the quarry
face, the perfect nesting place for the birds. You'll see them in flight from
March and all through summer; they can be distinguished from their
similar-looking cousins, the house martin and swallow, by their duller
plumage: brown with a pale underside and distinctive dark neck band.

On your way out of Mickleton heading west towards Middleton-
in-Teesdale, the hamlet of **Laithkirk** with its church born out of
a 15th-century tithe barn is worth a few moments of your day, as is

TEES RAILWAY PATH

Gentle countryside walks in Durham rarely get better than the Tees Railway Path: a well-marked route between **Middleton-in-Teesdale** (there's a car park between Middleton-in-Teesdale and Mickleton on the B6277 that marks the northern end of the path at ♀ NY951245; postcode DL12 0PL will take you close to the car park) and **Cotherstone** (♀ NZ011192; close to postcode DL12 9PH, reached from the Bowes to Low Lathbury road). It's flat and easy most of the way and suitable for all age groups, with pretty rural views of stone farms, rolling grasslands, drystone walls and hedgerows, and old villages with excellent pubs and within easy reach of the trail.

Trains ran between Barnard Castle and Alston along this line for just over 100 years until it closed in 1964, later reopening as a six-mile mixed-use trail between Cotherstone and Lonton (close to Middleton-in-Teesdale) suitable for walkers, cyclists (mountain bikers only owing to the grassy tracks and muddy patches) and horseriders. A diversion at **Romaldkirk** (page 265) takes you away from the original line but does pick its way through the delightful village where you can pause for food and drinks.

The line roughly follows the River Tees along its southern side and never really rises high enough for the countryside to feel remote or challenging; and for the most part you will remain on the green slopes rising out of the valley on bare or grassy ground.

While it is a linear route, you may want to make use of the Teesdale Way riverside path to vary the return from Middleton or Cotherstone. A popular circular route including both these paths is between Cotherstone and Romaldkirk where there are good pubs. On the outskirts of Cotherstone, the path crosses the nine-arched **Balder Viaduct**.

Kirkcarrion Bronze Age burial site, a landmark and popular walking destination, identified by its copse of trees on top of a hill (see page 278 for information on both these places).

🍴 FOOD & DRINK

The Blacksmith Arms DL12 0JY 🖉 01833 640605 ⊙ 15.00–late Tue–Fri, noon–late Sat & Sun; food until 20.30 Tue–Fri. I heard about the Blacksmith's from the owner of a local campsite who told me they make excellent sourdough pizzas. The menu is pretty straightforward with just a handful of options but what they serve up (washed down with a local beer) is very good. Seats on the opposite side of the road in a peaceful beer garden filled with the song of thrushes make this a favourite spot for an easy early evening meal in the summer (hot in the midsummer sunshine at 21.00 as I write this). Incidentally, if you're walking the Tees Railway Path, the Blacksmith's is a short walk down Bail Hill Road from the Mickleton Station Picnic Area and car park.

BALDERSDALE

🏠 **East Briscoe Farm Cottages** (page 311)

Trapped by a trio of reservoirs (Balderhead, Blackton and Hury), the River Balder escapes at the lower end of the chain, flowing under 18th-century Hury Mill Bridge on its way to the Tees at Cotherstone. Despite the part played by Victorian and then 1960s engineers in creating these lakes, the old farms and drystone walls trailing across pastures and meadows to reach the reservoirs belong to the Dales of yesteryear when the river rushed freely from surrounding moors. On the facing fells, the distinctive stepped profile of the land reveals where the alternating layers of limestone, shale and sandstone have worn away at different speeds over millennia.

My lasting memory from a visit to Baldersdale one evening in early spring is of curlews baubling above rushy pastures, oystercatchers and redshanks guarding stone walls, farmers tending to lambs, and the waters below like giant steel disks. Two months later, and my eyes would be cast to the grasslands in full bloom along the southern side of the valley.

Some of the most stunning flower-filled **meadows** lie below **Hury** reservoir and its southern shores and can be viewed from an exceptionally quiet paved lane, perfect for cyclists, running up the valley from Briscoe Farm to Willoughby Hall. Buttercups and clovers flower in abundance along with wood crane's-bill, yellow rattle, meadowsweet, devil-bit scabious and knapweed, and are best viewed in May, June and July. A public footpath along the higher slopes of these fields varies the return for those on foot, completing a circular **walk** of around three

TROUT FISHING IN DURHAM'S RESERVOIRS

Durham's reservoirs are well known for their trout fishing. Derwent and Grassholme are replenished weekly with trout from fisheries and are therefore the most popular fishing waters owing to the larger size of catches. At Balderhead, Blackton, Selset and Cow Green, the waters teem with wild native brown trout; Hury is fly-fishing only. Purchase permits online at 🖥 watersideparksuk.com or at the fishing shop in Grassholme. According to Northumbrian Water, who run the reservoirs and fisheries, the trout are descendants of native upland 'brownies' which lived in the rivers before they were dammed. They are 'lightning quick and very hard fighting'.

miles. Another route for walkers that begins from Briscoe Farm climbs over Cotherstone Moor to the Butter Stone (page 263).

From Willoughby Hall, if you continue westwards from Hury to Blackton Reservoir, the lane rises through rougher ground into the territory of the curlew, snipe, and lapwing; the views become more expansive and sheep wander freely; there's no one here but you.

15 HURY RESERVOIR

A few miles west of Hunderthwaite & five miles west of Cotherstone; two car parks: the northern car park (♥ NY967197) is close to Hury and Strathmore Arms farms and has a toilet ♿; the southern car park (♥ NY967192) is reached from Briscoe Farm on the Cotherstone–Baldersdale road.

Constructed in the late 19th century, Hury is divided in two and is the smallest in the chain of Baldersdale's reservoirs and surrounded by some beautiful meadows (see my description opposite of a wildflower grasslands trail) and patches of woodland offering something to the walker, cyclist and those less mobile (the quiet paved lane on the south side is suitable for wheelchairs as there is rarely any traffic). Two car parks with picnic tables at either end of the dam offer easy access to both shores and their respective permissive paths. A three-mile loop of the water takes in the lake scenery, the crenelated walls of the reservoir and wildflower meadows in the southeast corner, and can be combined with a longer walk to neighbouring Blackton Reservoir and Hannah's Meadow nature reserve.

16 BLACKTON RESERVOIR

Access on foot via the Pennine Way; parking for the northern side of the reservoir is provided in a car park above Balderhead Reservoir, just west of the entrance to Hannah's Meadow nature reserve at ♥ NY928187; parking for the southern shore is at the dam between Blackton and Hury reservoirs at ♥ NY950186.

Varied scenery and habitats around the middle of Baldersdale's three reservoirs awaits walkers on the three-mile reservoir circuit that can be combined with a jaunt on to Cotherstone Moor or to Hannah's Meadow nature reserve (page 273).

Tussocky islands and damp grasslands at the head of the water provide a mosaic wetland habitat supporting a range of wildfowl and wading birds and you are likely to see oystercatchers, lapwings and curlews hereabouts, particularly from March until July. On the open water and in the shallows, geese and ducks are common and easily viewed from a **bird hide** on the shores below Low Birk Hatt Farm. A permissive path from the hide traces the northern banks of the water in a clockwise direction, eventually meeting with the dam between Blackton and Huɪy and the reservoir's overflow funnel – a kind of giant plughole.

Back at the head of the reservoir, **Blackton Bridge** marks the midpoint of the Pennine Way. Following the long-distance path north, you'll pass through Hannah's Meadow nature reserve (see opposite); south will take you to the southern shores of the reservoir and the moorland beyond.

A network of trails traverse the pastures and fields rising above the reservoir to the south, offering views for miles across Baldersdale. If you look up to Cotherstone Moor, you'll see a prominent rocky outcrop accessible on foot following Alfred Wainwright's *A Pennine Journey* trail to **Goldsborough Rigg** (signed from the quiet lane above the south shore) from where there are sweeping views of the dale. A scattering of rocks below this landmark are covered in **Neolithic cup and ring** depressions (around ♀ NY956177).

17 BALDERHEAD RESERVOIR & THE HEAD OF BALDERSDALE

Car parking at either end of the dam (east end of the reservoir). The northern car park (♀ NY928187) is reached from a track off the road (signed for the reservoir) from Hunderthwaite and Romaldkirk, a few hundred yards up the valley from the Hannah's Meadow turn off and the Pennine Way. Crossing the dam takes you directly to the southern car park at ♀ NY926178

Flooding the western end of the valley is the largest of Baldersdale's three reservoirs with a perimeter of around five miles. The River Balder was dammed here in the mid-1960s creating a new reservoir to service developing industries on Teesside. While the water itself holds little interest beyond its inherent scenic qualities, the surrounding farmland, meadows and grassy moorland offer many miles of uninterrupted hiking across access land where you are unlikely to see anyone at all (unless you visit during the grouse-shooting season from 12 August until 10 December).

Two car parks at each side of the dam facilitate access into the hills above the reservoir. The best-known **walk** is to the top of **Shacklesborough** (♀ NY909170) – a flat-topped hill at 1,490ft above sea level, encircled at the top by some crags. It's reached in 1½ miles

HAY TIME

A North Pennine hay meadow in summer is a sight to behold: swathes of yellow rattle, pignut, meadowsweet, great burnet, clovers, lady's mantle, buttercups and wood crane's-bill. You won't see all these plants in flower at the same time, and the grasslands change colour throughout the season: the yellows of late spring, and rusty reds and purples when great burnet and melancholy thistle flower in July are particularly striking.

High-altitude meadows like those found on the southern edge of **Ilury Reservoir** in Upper Teesdale, above **Ireshopburn** in Weardale (north side of the Wear), **Hannah's Meadow** in Baldersdale, and around **Widdybank Farm** and **Holwick** in Upper Teesdale are exceedingly rare in England. Of the estimated 2,500 acres of traditional upland hay meadow left in the UK, 40% is in the North Pennines.

from the southern car park by following a track to Water Knott outdoor education centre and then quad bike tracks across Galloway Rigg to the summit of Shacklesborough. The final ascent to the cairn and trig point is a rocky scramble, best approached from the north. But wait for the view: the North Pennines unfolding before you to the north, the rolling landscape of the Yorkshire Dales to the south.

A **walk** round the reservoir is possible from the north by following the wonderfully peaceful lane running west of Hannah's Meadow (see below) and the reservoir car park entrance. At the end of the road (incidentally, there's a parking area here), the track continues in a rougher form as a bridleway trailing round the slope of **Hunderthwaite Moor** past some nice old sheepfolds to reach the head of the **River Balder** at the confluence of Balder Beck and Black Beck. Footbridges carry you over the streams to a track that traces **Great Ay Gill** upwards on to the grouse moors and the summit of Shacklesborough. The return is via Galloway Rigg and Water Knott (see above), and then across the dam. Hannah's Meadow can be visited at this point before returning to the northern car park.

18 HANNAH'S MEADOW NATURE RESERVE

Hunderthwaite DL12 9UX; signed off the unclassified road five miles west of Romaldkirk via Hunderthwaite ♀ NY934187

Trapped in an ecological time warp, two glorious hay meadows above the northern shores of Blackton Reservoir provide a glimpse of the traditional grasslands that used to flower across the Dales before modern farming methods changed in the post-war era.

Hannah's Meadow

❄ OS Explorer map OL31; start: at the top of Hannah's Meadow where the Pennine Way crosses the road ♥ NY934190 (park by the side of the road or at Balderhead Reservoir northern car park ♥ NY928187); 1¼ miles; easy.

E njoy wildflowers in abundance (May to early July) on this easy walk suitable for all ages through grasslands, with a short stretch along Blackton Reservoir to its bird hide. It's still a rewarding walk for birdwatchers outside of the flowering season.

1 Access to the reserve is via a farm gate at the side of the road (♥ NY934190). You'll see a Pennine Way fingerpost signed for Clove Lodge, pointing downhill to High Birk Hatt Farm. Go through the gate and down the paved track. At a prominent fork, take the left-hand track, ignoring the one to the farm, which you will pass on the return leg of this walk.

2 A short way ahead, a boardwalk crosses the top of the famous **Hannah Hauxwell hay meadow**, leading to an old barn, some 200 years old, with a stone-flagged roof. Today it acts as an information point and is a good starting place for learning about the wildlife on the site. If you're looking for a place to eat sandwiches, there's a delightfully placed bench outside the barn from which to watch the house martins and maybe a kestrel hovering overhead. Return to the paved track and continue downhill over a couple of cattle grids (note the stone stile in the wall) and through a copse.

3 Low Birk Hatt Cottage on your left is where Hannah lived. There's no public access but you can stroll down to the water's edge ahead by first following the Pennine Way fingerpost. **Blackton Reservoir** is seen through an old iron gate; a footpath here leads to the north

Before the Durham Wildlife Trust took over the running of the site in 1988, these upland meadows – now one of the rarest habitats in the UK – were managed by an extraordinary farmer, Hannah Hauxwell, who lived alone at Low Birk Hatt Farm without electricity or running water, working the 80 acres of land for over half a century in the traditional way: cutting the sward after the flowers have seeded and without adding anything to the soil.

Hannah achieved national fame as an elderly farmer in the years following a newspaper article titled 'How to be happy on £170 a year' and later a TV documentary, *Too Long a Winter*, filmed in 1973, which followed her tending to her cows in the snow and candidly reflecting on hardship, loneliness and getting by in the dale. 'I existed during the shore of the reservoir, as a sign on the farm gate indicates. It's a very short diversion along a permissive path that stays close to the water and is a tranquil spot to watch the ducks and take in the reflections of the trees from the bird hide.

Return to the iron gate and continue on your walk with the reservoir on your left (ignore the 'circular walk' markers pointing right).

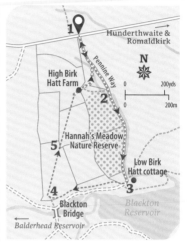

4 Don't cross Blackton Bridge but instead go through a metal gate and follow a stony track. After 30yds, look for wooden steps on your right rising steeply uphill to the stone wall at the top. Head up and go over the stone stile in the wall. Strike diagonally across the field aiming for two prominent old trees in the corner. High Birk Hatt Farm is now back in view.

5 When you reach the sycamore and ash trees, go through the farm gate to the left of the trees and cross the next field, aiming for a farm gate. Walk towards **High Birk Hatt Farm**, following the public footpath that winds round the front of some early 19th-century byres, a barn and the farmhouse, which are wonderfully unchanged, still with their stone flagged roofs. Ahead, the track merges back with the Pennine Way for the return to the top road.

winter and truly lived during the summer,' she said of her life on the isolated farm.

Hannah eventually retired from farming and lived her final years in the nearby village of Cotherstone where she died in 2018, but the farm she spoke of as if it were part of her very being remains as it was, untouched by modern methods of farming and silage production, with many native grasses and plants including adder's tongue fern, yellow rattle, buttercups, pignut, ragged robin, wood crane's-bill and great burnet flowering at different times from May to early July before the meadows are cut in the time-honoured, low-impact ways of yesteryear.

Low Birk Hatt is now in private ownership and there is no public access to the buildings on the shores of the reservoir (though you can

TOM CURTIS/S

JOE DUNCKLEY/S

RADOMIR REZNY/S

see the farm entrance on the walk described on page 274), but you can enjoy Hannah's fields at any time. And it's not just the wildflowers that are rather special here; when I walked through the reserve one summer, I saw a barn owl exiting a derelict barn at the head of the reserve.

LUNEDALE

⋀ High Side Farm Camping (page 311)

The River Lune drains the southern and eastern slopes of Mickle Fell and Little Fell into **Selset** and **Grassholme reservoirs**, a few miles west of Middleton-in-Teesdale, before spilling into the River Tees. Sloping gently to the water's edge are the meadows and sheep-grazed pastures divided by the drystone walls so familiar in these parts and that make this dale – and neighbouring Baldersdale – so scenic. Even if you don't intend to explore the upper reaches of the valley and the foreboding moorlands beyond, you may want to motor through the dale, taking in the views from the B6276 Brough road or, for a less hurried jaunt with views of the reservoirs, the unclassified West Pasture Road from Mickleton – also a great route for cyclists.

19 GRASSHOLME RESERVOIR & THE SOUTHERN REACHES OF LUNEDALE

Most visitors to Lunedale venture only as far as the south shores of **Grassholme Reservoir** (1½ miles from Mickleton; DL12 0PW takes you to just past the turn off; ♥ NY948225; ✆ 0345 1550236) where there's an observatory, fishing shop, picnic areas, toilets ♿, sailing club and a three-mile permissive path round the lake (partially closed at the time of research owing to works on the dam). The popularity of Grassholme has increased in recent years with the opening of the new **Grassholme Observatory** (West Pasture Rd, DL12 0PW ✆ 0345 1550236 ⬙ grassholmeobservatory.com ♿) above the fishing shop. It's run by the former director of the observatory at Kielder Reservoir in Northumberland and the talks are engaging and offer something for everyone: from family astronomy evenings and astrophotography to 'Aurora Nights' and late-night sessions that run into the early hours of

◀ **1** Middleton-in-Teesdale. **2** Grassholme Reservoir. **3** The Lune Railway Viaduct. **4** The Lune Valley.

A BICYCLE TOUR OF LUNEDALE & BALDERSDALE

A stunning eight-mile loop of Lunedale and Baldersdale starts one mile west of Mickleton-in-Teesdale by the junction with a paved track connecting the two valleys (second lane on your left, if you're coming from Mickleton, and close to the southeastern corner of Grassholme Reservoir). The road climbs a hundred feet through increasingly rough pastures until you are on the heather tops looking across the two dales (a blaze of pink greets travellers in August; courting wading birds in early spring). The descent south reveals **Hury Reservoir** and more in the way of homesteads, farms and hedgerows as you tootle through picturesque **Hunderthwaite** to **Romaldkirk** where a well-deserved drink at the pub awaits. The final leg back to **Mickleton** (good food and drink here too) is all off road along the Tees Railway Path (page 269).

the morning. According to staff: 'on these evenings, the Observatory will turn its eyes to the skies and hunt out some of the treasures of our Milky Way galaxy, such as nebulae – glowing clouds of gas and star clusters, which dazzle like diamonds strewn on the velvet sky.'

West towards Selset Reservoir, the **Pennine Way** crosses Grassholme by a multi-arched stone bridge before continuing south into Baldersdale. There's a quiet parking area here (♥ NY929216) and it makes for an alternative destination to the busier area around the sailing club and observatory. You can pick up the lakeshore trail here or follow paths on to Mickleton and Hunderthwaite moors.

20 THE NORTHERN REACHES OF LUNEDALE & SELSET RESERVOIR

The **Lune Railway Viaduct** hits you head on as you cross the River Lune half a mile north of Mickleton. From under its arches the road begins its climb through the hamlet of **Laithkirk** on the B6276. The strikingly long **Laithkirk Church** greets you at the top of a steep bank. It began life as a 15th-century tithe barn and was later converted into a place of worship in 1826 with no division between its nave and chancel. Its sundial bares the inscription: 'watch and pray 1865'. Twenty yards down the road is an old byre house dating to the early 19th century, which once housed livestock downstairs and people upstairs.

Half a mile west of Laithkirk is **Bowbank**, a hamlet with a scattering of old cottages and farms and nearby Bronze Age burial mound,

Kirkcarrion (♥ NY940238), a prominent tumulus crowned by a copse of pine trees. Known locally as Caryn's Castle, the archaeological site is visible for miles around. Discovered by a farm worker in the early 1800s, it was probably the burial site of a chieftain and once contained a funerary urn. Access is via a right of way off the B6276 (about a quarter-mile west of Bowbank).

The road continues on its gentle incline passing old farms, barns and cottages with the reservoirs twinkling in and out of view every so often, but by the time Hargill Beck is behind you the landscape becomes increasingly featureless, with snow posts standing by the roadsides.

Remote and under visited, **Selset Reservoir** appears somewhat bleak around the dam side of the lake, but the scenery becomes increasingly picturesque the further west you venture, with conifer and broadleaved trees softening the water's edges and heather moors muscling in on the scene. Selset's shores are accessible from a few places on foot, or from the car park in the northeast corner of the water (♥ NY916216), where you can **walk** across the dam wall or take the shoreline path. A popular route runs south across the dam and then along the south side of Grassholme Reservoir. Like other reservoirs in the region, Selset offers excellent wild brown trout fishing (page 270).

Above Selset's water, the valley rises into the surrounding hills providing some challenging **hiking** up on to grouse moors pitted by mining activities from several centuries ago and to the crags below the summits of several hills. Clear grouse shooters' tracks provide swift access from the Brough road up on to the moors at a few points including from **Hargill Bridge** for a hike to **Bink Moss** (a desolate place with a summit of just over 2,000ft) or up the side of **Arnhill Beck** for a killer ascent to **Standards** (of a similar height to Bink Moss and with equally expansive views of the North Pennines). Continuing through the valley on foot leads to one of Teesdale's most remote waterfalls, **Arngill Force** (♥ NY847234).

"Above Selset's water, the valley rises into the surrounding hills providing some challenging hiking up on to grouse moors."

If you're exploring the reservoir from the B6276 road to Brough, about a mile west of where the road crosses the head of the River Lune, look out for the **Lunehead Stone Circle** (♥ NY851204) by the south side of the road. The prehistoric arc of six stones combines with a further two outlying boulders to make an oval shape of around 33ft in diameter.

MIDDLETON

21 MIDDLETON-IN-TEESDALE & AROUND

🏠 **Brunswick House** (page 311), **The Hill B&B** (page 311)

Lively Middleton stands at the gateway to the upper reaches of Teesdale and is your last reliable place to pick up supplies before heading into the hills, but it is also a very pleasant town to visit for a few hours with its small number of independent craft and antiques shops and inviting places to eat.

A main thoroughfare runs through the **town centre**, flanked by a wide, linear green on one side and smart stone houses on the other and mixed with shops and cafés. There's a convivial atmosphere with locals chatting outside shops, waving at acquaintances passing in cars and its streets busy with visitors, walkers and cyclists saddling up after lunch.

The Kings Walk & Hudeshope Valley

✳ OS Explorer map 31; start: St Mary's Church on Town Head lane (west end of Middleton)
📍 NY947260; 1¼ miles; fairly easy with some moderate climbs and descents

This is a very enjoyable short woodland walk suitable for families, with a stretch along the Hudeshope Beck where there are some little falls and places to picnic. Note that Beck Road (the yellow track on OS maps) is paved and suitable for pushchairs and wheelchairs. For a longer walk, at the half-way point climb steeply into open countryside to Aukside and return to the start of this walk via hay meadows. Alternatively, you could continue tracing the beck three miles due north to reach the head of the Hudeshope Valley in an area littered with archaeological monuments from the lead mines of long ago (page 284). Note that even on the route set out below it's easy to become confused by the becks, so do take a map and gain a general sense of how the paths connect to each other before you set off.

1 From **St Mary's Church**, walk up **Town Head** on the pavement for a quarter of a mile until you reach a prominent fork in the lane (there's a parking area here, incidentally).

2 Turn left on to **Beck Road**, entering woodland. The scent of wild garlic will hit you immediately if walking this route in early spring.

3 After 100yds, a dirt path rises through pine trees to your right with a Raby Estates notice pinned to a tree marked for the **Kings Walk**: follow this well-trodden permissive path through the woods. A meadow soon appears on your right.

On Chapel Row (the cobbled lane with a Co-op) a lovely little boutique sells traditional hand-made children's cardigans, blankets and toys; further up is a run of buildings with old frontages and awnings including **J. Raine & Son** (DL12 0QA ✆ 01833 640406), a hardware store selling outdoor clothing and equipment. A helpful community-run secondhand bookshop located in the old Town Hall opposite the Teesdale Hotel, **The Village Bookshop** (Market Pl, DL12 0RJ ✆ 01833 641493 ○ 10.00–17.00 Mon–Thu), sells local guides, trail leaflets and Ordnance Survey maps.

Middleton's medieval origins are revealed in a few places, strikingly in the churchyard of **St Mary's** where rests a window tracery belonging to an earlier church that previously stood here from the late 13th century. The current church is pretty solidly Victorian but take a look at the stone building reached by steps nearby: the detached belfry, a rarity, dates to the mid 16th-century.

4 After a few hundred yards, where the path swings sharply uphill to the right, take the path to the left descending through trees to meet with **Snaisgill Beck**. Cross the little footbridge over the water and turn left, continuing through trees until you reach a lane by **Hudeshope Beck**.

5 Turn left on to Beck Road; there are lovely picnic and paddling spots hereabouts and a pleasing spout waterfall ahead. Look out for dippers on exposed rocks in the riverbed.

Stroll down the lane, keeping left of the river until you come to a track off to your right (continuing ahead is the straightforward route back to the start).

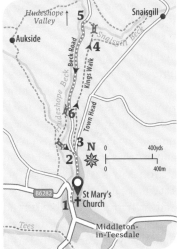

6 Take this spur and cross the green metal bridge. The beck is now on your left and you should follow it downstream, crossing it again when you reach a wooden bridge. Climb through beech trees to meet with the lane, and retrace your steps to the church.

The period most referenced around town, however, is the 1800s when Middleton was an important lead-mining centre and the northern headquarters of the Quaker-owned London Lead Company. You may notice some rather more grand houses among the Victorian terraces including those on **Masterman Place**, built for the most valued lead-mining employees, and **Middleton House** on Hude (a short walk northwest of the centre on an elevated road above the valley). Once the chief mine agent's house and office, this Georgian mansion was designed by architect Ignatius Bonomi in the early 19th century and has housed a fair number of politicians and royalty over the centuries since it changed hands into private ownership and became at various times a lodge for grouse shooters.

For a hundred years, the London Lead Company played a central role in the development of Middleton and so workers' houses, a school, chapels and various other buildings connected to the mine company, all dating to the heyday of the industrial boom in the early 19th century, feature prominently in the town. Look out for the wonderfully unchanged old fire station on Masterman Place and piped water taps built into stone walls – a luxury at one time (a curved wall on the junction of Masterman Place and Newton houses a good example). One of the most telling relics from this period is the **Bainbridge Fountain** (opposite Samuel James's coffee shop on Horsemarket), an ornate cast-iron memorial erected in 1877 with a canopy covering the figure of a child. Funded by employees of the mine company, the fountain is dedicated to the mine agent at the time, and matches an almost identical one in Nenthead (page 224).

"Look out for the wonderfully unchanged old fire station and piped water taps built into stone walls."

Prosperity was amplified by the opening of the Tees Valley Railway in 1868 that connected Middleton with Barnard Castle for both passengers and the transportation of lead and stone, though by then the market for lead was in decline and the town reverted to farming as its principal industry by the early 1900s. Farming continues to thrive on the verdant pastures that surround, with cattle and sheep traded a few times a month at the **Auction Mart** on the south side of Middleton Bridge on the B6277. As for the railway line, which remained open until the 1960s, it now operates as a leisure path perfectly placed to facilitate walks and cycle rides between a number of villages in lower Teesdale (page 269).

Around Middleton

You can access the surrounding countryside directly from the town centre on foot by following a few walking trails, described here and in leaflets available in the secondhand bookshop opposite The Teesdale Hotel. For a stroll along the **riverside**, pick your way along Masterman Place and Newtown to the Tees.

Away from the valley bottom, there are lengthy **walks** up on to the moors behind the town, or south following the Pennine Way over Crossthwaite Common and into Lunedale. The Hudeshope Valley is a fascinating place to explore with much in the way of abandoned mining architecture and fellside scenery (page 284). On the western edge of the town and trailing north from the Hude is a delightful footpath linking several flower-filled hay meadows with **Aukside** (you can return via Hudeshope Beck and the Kings Walk; page 280).

Lanes above the main arterial road to Barnard Castle are similarly rich in meadow scenery, and I strongly recommend the quiet road connecting Middleton with Newbiggin to **cyclists** (and motorists taking a leisurely pace through the valley), for the grasslands and the far-reaching views across the valley – with Kirkcarrion prehistoric burial site (page 279) always in view above Grassholme Reservoir.

¶¶ FOOD & DRINK

A cluster of coffee shops and cafés offering breakfast and lunch face the town centre on the streets around Horsemarket, including Samuel James (see below) and **The Tees'pot** (Bridge St, DL12 0QB ✐ 01833 640717 ◷ 09.00–16.00 (sometimes later) Thu–Tue), a friendly café serving good breakfasts. The choice is more limited for an evening meal but there is a decent **fish and chip shop** on Market Place (DL12 0RJ ✐ 01833 640404 ◷ 11.30–14.00 & 16.00–19.30 Tue, Fri & Sat, 16.00–19.30 Wed & Thu) at the western end of town. Opposite is **The Teesdale Hotel** (Market Pl, DL12 0QG ✐ 01833 640264), an 18th-century coaching inn serving a feast of meat dishes (burgers, pies, steak, Teesdale lamb and a few fish plates) and a small number of vegetarian/vegan meals.

Samuel James Deli Café 4 Horsemarket, DL12 0SH ✐ 01833 641235 ◷ 08.00–18.00 daily. Everything is spot on here: the strong coffee served alongside a chilled glass bottle of water, the tempting deli counter filled with cheeses from the Durham Dales and surrounding counties, the generous bowls of homemade soup, the knobbly scones filled with fruit, large squares of flapjack, and the tables in the sun outside where you can watch all the comings and goings about town.

22 HUDESHOPE VALLEY

🏠 **The Quirky Quarry** (page 311)

At the western end of Middleton, a road signed for Stanhope leads steeply uphill for three miles into one of the most prosperous lead-mining areas of the 19th century. Today it's one of the most peaceful valleys in the Dales. A circuit of Hudeshope, starting from St Mary's Church in Middleton, can be completed by either walking upstream following Hudeshope Beck (page 280) through woodland and past some delightful little falls, or on wheels along a lonesome paved road via Snaisgill, which I highly recommend both for the built heritage, the wonderfully bleak fellsides and eerie serenity of the place. But cyclists be warned, it's a hell of a climb out of Middleton.

As you travel upstream beyond Snaisgill, **Skears limestone quarry** and **limekiln** (♀ NY948271) come into view. Ahead, the open land is cut by a number of artificial gullies called 'hushes' (page 219), excavated centuries ago by the release of a deluge of water to reveal the lead vein, known as the **Skears Hushes**; further up the valley is **Marl Beck Mine**

"The views through the valley are spectacular: all meadows and pastures divided by walls trickling down the slopes of the valley."

(♀ NY94962872), still with its old mineshop house where miners would lodge overnight and a number of grassed over spoil heaps, mine shafts and scree slopes. It doesn't sound beautiful but the natural landscape features dominate and the views through the valley are spectacular: all meadows and pastures divided by walls trickling down the slopes of the valley, and extensive heather moorland on the fell tops. Besides livestock, the only other life I saw up here one evening in August were some wheatears, a kestrel hovering above a scree slope and a Royal Mail van delivering post to some isolated farms.

As you round the head of the valley, **Coldberry Mine** (♀ NY941289) comes into view with its tumble-down mine buildings. A couple of tracks lead to the mine lodgings, stable and smithy, now inhabited by sheep sheltering from the wind, but still standing almost two hundred punishing winters after they were built. There's something quite haunting about the place and with a little imagination you can picture all the activity, noise and commotion associated with a productive 19th-century mine. Above the buildings, and seen for miles around, is a deep chasm in the hillside known as the **Coldberry Gutter**. This gash in the hill – over 1½ miles long – is generally considered to be a hush caused by mining activities but recent studies suggest it may have been created by glacial meltwaters at the end of the last Ice Age and is suitably rounded and tunnel-like.

UPPER TEESDALE

On a sunny June day, the five miles to High Force are a joy to the naturalist, the geologist and the botanist... this is a place to linger, to rest awhile in sylvan sweetness, and dream.
Alfred Wainwright, *Pennine Way Companion*, 1939

Outstanding meadow and moorland scenery span the wide aperture of Upper Teesdale between Middleton-in-Teesdale and Langdon Beck, an area with less in the way of villages and amenities but more natural

BIRDWATCHING IN UPPER TEESDALE

Exceptional numbers of breeding **wading birds** inhabit the meadows and pastures rising out of Teesdale's valley basin – probably in greater densities than anywhere else in England. Curlews, lapwings, redshanks, snipe and oystercatchers are particularly conspicuous but also look out for yellow wagtails and black grouse (in a few specific locations, page 304). A couple of superb areas for spring and early summer birdwatching are Widdybank Fell and around Langdon Beck YHA, Harwood Beck, Holwick and, a little further south, Baldersdale, though there are many others.

On the **moorland** plateau, keep watch for golden plovers, merlins and short-eared owls. Red grouse and meadow pipits are everywhere of course. There's plenty of heather habitat for breeding hen harriers, but nests are extremely rare and only really occur on the RSPB's Geltsdale reserve over the border in Cumbria, and away from the shooting estates where they are sometimes persecuted.

The **whinstone cliffs**, such as at Holwick Scars, are worth scanning for ravens and peregrine falcons and you may even hear a ring ouzel singing in a wooded gully or from shrubs sprouting from the rocks.

River-dwelling birds including dippers, grey wagtails and goosanders inhabit many burns and rivers in the valley.

The above sightings apply mostly to spring and summer; come autumn, the waders feast at the coast, but from over the North Sea come migrant geese and ducks to sit out the following few months on this windswept barren landscape (it's mild here in comparison to Scandinavia). With them comes an influx of thrushes to the valleys: redwings and fieldfares gorge on thorn-bush berries and in the **juniper woods** north of High Force.

delights: nationally renowned waterfalls, **High Force** and **Cauldron Snout**, and superb wildlife watching and hiking opportunities. Birders in spring and early summer won't want to be without their binoculars, but who needs them when a flock of 60 lapwings tumbles through the valley?

Moorhouse – Upper Teesdale National Nature Reserve encompasses a broad sweep of this landscape, famous for its bird and plant life and variety of rare upland habitats: juniper woods (page 298), blanket bog, upland hay meadows (page 273) and limestone grasslands. There are plants up here that have hung on since the Ice Age and they are of national significance, particularly the eye-catching blue spring gentian and Teesdale violet. Birders and botanists should make **Cow Green Reservoir**, **Widdybank Fell** and the **Harwood Beck** valley top of their list of places to visit. The Pennine Way and an old packhorse route, the Green Trod, over **Cronkley Fell** will also guide you to some of the best spots (pages 300 and 302).

23 HOLWICK & HOLWICK SCARS

🏠 **Low Way Farm** (page 311)

Crouched below a columnar wall of igneous whinstone three miles from Middleton-in-Teesdale and cut off to the east by the River Tees, **Holwick** has remained in relative isolation for hundreds of years. 'Hol' is Old English for 'hollow' incidentally ('wic' is commonly found in many Anglo-Saxon place names and means 'dairy farm'). The village's heyday was in medieval times and much of the layout of Holwick – along a single lane and surrounded by ridge and furrow cultivation – points to this period, though its origins probably date to the Bronze Age. Prehistoric funerary cairns, Iron Age roundhouse settlements and ancient tools from different times certainly indicate farming communities have inhabited this area continuously for millennia.

It's a fascinating place to explore and you'll find a number of things of architectural, historical and geological interest here and in the wider area around the River Tees. A walk along the main lane running through the village reveals the stone farmhouses, cottages, byres and walls built at different times over the last 300 years. Under the cliffs, some interesting

1 Low Force. **2** Bowlees Visitor Centre, a former Methodist Chapel. **3** Look out for waders, including snipe. **4** Dippers can be spotted along the rivers in this area. **5** Summerhill Force.

Holwick to Bowlees

✳ OS Explorer map 31; start: Holwick village ♥ NY906270; 3 miles; easy.

Avoid the crowds and enjoy the flower grasslands sloping away from the Tees and the impressive cliffs of Holwick Scars on this circular meadow and riverside amble through some of Teesdale's finest countryside with diversions to a couple of waterfalls.

1 Approaching Holwick from the east, you'll pass the old village pub – now permanently closed – and, half a mile later, a run of cottages on your left and a lone cottage a little ahead on your right. By the fingerpost just past this house, climb over the stile into a meadow and make your way down to the Tees (aim for the line of trees at the bottom), crossing a few long fields and enjoying the profusion of buttercups, clovers, bluebells and pignut in nearby meadows. The distinctly rounded stones in some walls are known as 'clearance stones', gathered from surrounding grasslands where they were deposited by ice sheets many thousands of years ago, their edges smoothed from being ground together.

2 Climb over a stile on meeting the Tees to join the **Pennine Way**, turning right and then left down a bank a short way ahead to reach **Scoberry Bridge**, which you should cross. The river runs fast here but there are a few bathing and paddling areas on the north side by the flat, grey slabs of rocks – an outcrop of 'cockleshell limestone' containing fossilised shells and the remains of creatures that swam in the then-tropical waters of this area some 350 million years ago. Even if you don't get your feet wet, this is a beautiful picnicking spot.

3 Take the footpath leading away from the river and across the buttercup meadow ahead to a farm gate. Once through the gate, veer right and continue across the next meadow to a footbridge over a beck in the corner of the field.

4 Cross the water and continue up the bank with woodland on your left (don't go through an opening in the wall on your right). Head through a gap in the wall at the top and follow the track through meadowland stuffed with wildflowers in summer, veering right ahead.

5 At a farm gate, turn right on to the road and then first left (signed for Newbiggin Chapel). Continue up this pretty lane into the timeless village of **Newbiggin**. A little beck is reached at the top of the lane, which is hidden by trees but you'll be guided by the sound of its falls. Opposite the beck there's a delightfully placed bench by Brooklea cottage.

6 Back on the lane, follow the road up and out of the village, with Brooklea below on your right. At the top of the hill, an outstanding view awaits of Holwick Scars cliffs and fells to the northwest.

7 Just before the road rounds a bend to the right, strike off left into a field signed with a finger post. Head for a gate in the middle of the field and then a barn in the next. Skirt the barn to its left and head for a gap marked with yellow tape on a fencepost. Stone steps in the wall take you into the next bumpy pasture with houses to your left. Stay close to the wall. Cross the next two fields, heading for woodland.

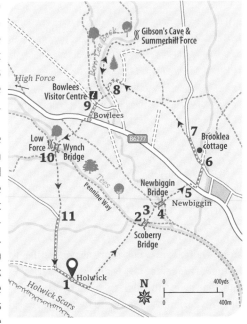

8 You are now at the top of the Bowlees visitor car park and on the trail for **Gibson's Cave and Summerhill Force**, which are reached by first turning left then right past a black car-park gate signed for toilets. Continue on the well-trodden footpath keeping the beck on your left all the way to the **waterfall**. Retrace your steps to the car park and then to the **Bowlees Visitor Centre** (pages 235 and 295) and former chapel (for hot and cold drinks and light lunches).

9 With your back to the front entrance of the chapel, head down the lane to meet the main road by a quaint letterbox. Turn right then, after 20yds, left into a meadow (clearly signed for Low Force). In summer, enjoy the wildflowers, before entering a beech woodland by a gap in the wall.

10 Ahead is **Wynch Bridge**, famous for its views of **Low Force** and for being the earliest suspension bridge in Europe when it was built in 1741. The present bridge is the third reincarnation and still uses iron chains and handrails. On crossing the Tees you have three options. The first is to go up the stone steps following the Pennine Way north to gain a closer look at Low Force (if walking this route in summer, note the orchids in the meadow on your left) otherwise you could turn immediately left and follow the Pennine Way downriver, eventually meeting with Scoberry Bridge where you can retrace your route to Holwick (this mile between Low Force and Scoberry Bridge was described by Alfred Wainwright as 'the most ▶

Holwick to Bowlees (continued)

◀ beautiful of all' for its assemblage of river rocks and abundance of wildflowers, and I too found the damper grasslands hereabouts utterly enchanting with orchids and cuckoo flowers amid all the buttercups, forget-me-nots, clovers and pignut). The third option from Wynch Bridge, described here and shown on my map, goes through the kissing gate and returns to Holwick via a slightly different route, first crossing a meadow with more orchids to the sweetest of packhorse bridges. Beyond the bridge, the path curls round a little bank where mountain pansies grow from May to August. Be careful not to trample the plants nor disturb the nesting lapwings in summer. Go through a prominent gap in the stone wall and into a meadow with a barn. Cross the meadow, keeping the barn on your left. There's a break in the wall halfway along, marked with a post. Cross the next meadow to meet a paved lane.

11 Turn left and follow the lane uphill back to the village, its grey-brown houses almost camouflaged by the backdrop of the cliff walls of the same colour. The rolling fields south of Holwick tell of Ice Age glacial movement and are filled with lapwings, oystercatchers and curlews in spring and summer.

stone walls form a corridor perpendicular to the village. Note too the funnel arrangement of walls where stock were driven from the moors and channelled through the wider end and into the passageway to reach the drove routes. Looking eastwards across countryside to the Tees, the meadows gently bow horizontally in unison, revealing the movement of ice sheets during the Ice Age.

The **Holwick Scars** form a formidable wall and backdrop to the village, appearing rather spectacularly from a distance to those travelling along main routes through Teesdale. The columns were formed 295 million years ago from cracks resulting from the molten rock cooling and contracting. Its grey walls of whinstone prove too irresistible to climbers (stringent rules apply because of the sensitive nature of the site to wildlife) and hikers who can reach the top of the cliffs by following the lane north out of the village and then on to a track used by grouse shooters. Most walkers, however, will be content to view the crags from afar, perhaps on a circular **walk** to Bowlees across the meadows below Holwick (page 288).

*"The **Holwick Scars** form a formidable wall and backdrop to the village, appearing rather spectacularly from a distance."*

¶ FOOD & DRINK

Farmhouse Kitchen Low Way Farm, DL12 0NJ ☺ Easter–end Oct 10.30–17.00 Sat & Sun. I can't think of a more perfectly placed spot for lunch or a pick-me-up cup of tea after a walk to see the nearby cliffs or waterfalls. As I write this from a picnic table in the sun-filled cobbled courtyard, my view is of lambs in meadows, the rock-strewn fells of Holwick Scars and a redstart in bushes by the beck. I can hear the wind in the trees, the incessant chatter of chaffinches and thrushes, and the occasional 'peewit' of lapwings flying overhead. My lunch is a substantial cheese salad sandwich and pot of tea, but I could have opted for a meat filling, a toastie or all-day breakfast. Karen runs the café and is friendly and helpful. Two bunkhouses here cater well for Pennine walkers and are open all year round.

24 NEWBIGGIN

> We rode through rain and wind to Newbiggin-in-Teesdale. Being but a poor horseman, and having a rough horse, I had just strength for my journey and none to spare; but, after resting awhile I preached without any weariness.
>
> John Wesley, founder of Methodism, writing in his journal, dated 16 June 1784

Newbiggin's **Wesleyan Chapel** provides a focal point in this otherwise delightfully unstructured village and is one of the earliest of all Methodist churches (now privately owned), first welcoming worshipers in 1760. John Wesley's journal shows he visited Newbiggin several times and preached from the pulpit inside.

Methodism aside, the small village on the hillside is not famed for anything other than simply being one of the most picture-perfect places in the whole of the dale – a snapshot of Teesdale in miniature with its merry beck running through the village green, over a couple of little falls and past whitewashed stone houses, farmsteads and outbuildings below moors dividing Teesdale from Weardale. Views of the lush wider landscape seep through narrow lanes and breaks in the linear arrangement of houses drawing the eye to the meadowscape beyond the village – all stone barns and boundary wall; wildflowers and old-man trees. Woodland shrouds the Tees in the valley bottom but it's the striking cliffs of Holwick Scars that are most demanding of your attention.

Records of Newbiggin date to the medieval period but almost every building you see today is 18th and 19th century from when the village expanded with the prospering lead-mining industry. Little has changed architecturally since, and while the public buildings along the B6277 no longer service the community, they remain intact including, from east to

WHIN SILL & WATERFALLS

An imposing igneous dolerite rock, the Great Whin Sill – or 'whinstone' as it is often known – appears in a number of spectacular locations in Teesdale and around the North East. Being extremely hard and resistant to erosion means the dolerite stands firm while surrounding softer rocks erode away over thousands of years, leaving these impressive vertical intrusions. The North East is famous for it, particularly where the Emperor Hadrian built his wall and medieval kings raised their castles (Dunstanburgh and Bamburgh in Northumberland for example). Here in Teesdale, **Holwick** and **Cronkley scars** are striking examples forming columnar curtains but, perhaps most memorable, is where the Tees rushes over whin ledges – or 'sills' – to form impressive waterfalls like **High Force**.

In places where the once-molten dolerite has intruded through limestone, the hot rock caused the limestone to 'bake' forming a white grainy marble known as sugar limestone. It's special, not just geologically, but because of the rare plants it supports (page 300). One of the best places to see both the whin sill and sugar limestone is at **Cow Green Reservoir** (page 304). Patches of the crumbly white marble are visible in a number of places in the grasslands and close to the paved track from the car park to the top of **Cauldron Snout**, itself one of the finest waterfalls in Durham and which splashes over a steep staircase of whinstone.

Not all of Teesdale's waterfalls owe their height to the erosion-resistant whinstone however, **Summerhill Force** near Bowlees gushes over limestone and the resulting cave formed behind the waterfall is a result of softer sandstone and shale erosion below. It's strikingly different to the likes of High Force with its columnar walls and has more in common with Hardraw Force further south in the Yorkshire Dales.

west, a former inn (the white cottage with four windows set back from the north side of the road and formally the mine agent's home), reading room (above the old hearse house, identified by its arched carriage doorway) and post office opposite. The quaint single-storey village school (now Brooklea cottage by the bridge over Newbiggin Beck) closed in the 1950s but its position by a jingly stream is particularly fetching. A well-placed bench makes this a nice spot to open a flask of tea.

A glance at an Ordnance Survey map will reveal a good number of short **walks** direct from the village: a couple of footpaths link the north and south ends of the village completing a short circuit of Newbiggin in around a mile, or you could walk to **Gibson's Cave and waterfall** (see opposite and page 288). A longer hike from Newbiggin could take you on to Hardberry Hill above the village, or over the fell to the Hudeshope

Valley to see the old mines. But a leisurely stroll through the village (the top lane, not the main B6277) will reward in equal measure with its views and summer wildflowers and potential to picnic by the burbling beck in a wonderfully tranquil spot.

25 BOWLEES, GIBSON'S CAVE & SUMMERHILL FORCE

Visitor Centre, Bowlees, DL12 0XF ✆ 01833 622145 ⊙ Apr–Sep 10.00–17.00 daily; Mar & Oct 10.00–16.00 daily ♿

The old Methodist chapel in the quaint hamlet of **Bowlees** is now a popular **visitor centre** and **café** (in an area with limited information sites and places to eat) operated by the North Pennines AONB Partnership and is the access point for visits to the nearby waterfall. On sale in the little shop are maps and an excellent range of local trail guides and leaflets detailing the area's geological and natural history wonders, as well as some local crafts and artworks. A simple display cabinet showcases minerals found in this UNESCO Global Geopark (page 12) including: a block of the special 'sugar limestone' you may have already seen in its natural setting on nearby fells; galena, the rock extracted all over the Dales by 18th- and 19th-century miners; and most of the 'ites': witherite, siderite, baryte, limonite and fluorite to name a few.

The infrastructure in the woods around the visitor centre (plenty of parking spaces, toilets, picnic benches and so on) facilitates visits to nearby **Gibson's Cave** which forms an amphitheatre around a secluded waterfall, **Summerhill Force**. Unsurprisingly, the footfall is pretty high and on sunny weekends in summer the place is thronged with day trippers and you may have trouble finding a spot to park. As for the walk to the waterfall, there's usually a steady trail of families working their way through the woods along the lovely beck.

"Gibson's Cave forms an amphitheatre around a secluded waterfall, Summerhill Force. Unsurprisingly, the footfall is pretty high."

But don't let this put you off; Summerhill Force is a beauty – just try and visit at the extremes of the day or outside of the café opening hours to enjoy the merry little beck, wildflower grasslands and cascade in relative peace.

To **walk** to Gibson's Cave and Summerhill Force (unsuitable for pushchairs and wheelchairs because of steps), take the muddy path

following the shallow beck upstream. It's not particularly well signed and you may wonder whether to cross the stream by the footbridge after the toilet block (you can, but you'll need to recross the stream by making your own stepping-stones route further up). Alternatively, keep the beck on your left the whole way to the waterfall. The first point of interest, beyond the black metal gate, is an old **limestone quarry** and grassland oasis. Wildflowers are abundant on the flat ground and cliff walls and include some wonderful rarities like the greater butterfly orchid. Cuckoo flowers, water avens, buttercups and wild strawberries are easy to spot in the warmer months. One late summer, I saw a profusion of peacock butterflies here enjoying the scabious flowers.

Knapweed, devil's-bit scabious, harebells and clovers flower the path sides as you continue upstream following the peat-stained beck and the sound of rushing water all the way to **Gibson's Cave** and **Summerhill Force** (plenty of stone-throwing opportunities on your way, kids). 'Gibson' was a local outlaw, incidentally, who hid in the secluded cave. Water has eroded the sandstone and shale walls of the cave faster than the band of limestone at the top of the cliff, undercutting the harder rock and resulting in the concave walls. This fascinating geological process allows the daring to walk behind the jet of water spilling from the limestone precipice above. Watch you don't slip, prepare to leave with damp clothes, and keep in mind that the waterfall is retreating upstream as the erosion causes the limestone overhang to periodically fall away. I applaud any parent who manages to leave here with dry-footed children. But isn't this just the most delightful of waterfalls? A long plume, gushing from around 50ft high into an amber pool.

¶¶ FOOD & DRINK

The café in the Bowlees Visitor Centre is the obvious choice but also consider the short walk from Low Force to Holwick where the Farmhouse Kitchen (page 291) offers a good range of lunch items and a wonderfully scenic setting.

The Falls Café Bowlees Visitor Centre, DL12 0XE ✐ 01833 622145 ⊘ 10.00–16.00 daily ♿. A tray of cheese scones had just come out of the oven when I last visited this welcoming café by the side of the main road through Teesdale, housed in an old Methodist chapel. They were some of best I've tried on my travels in Durham and I've subsequently learned the

◀ **1** High Force waterfall. **2** Black grouse, Langdon Common. **3** Newbiggin.

café is well-known locally for them. Other items on the small menu include ploughman's sandwiches, soups, sausage rolls, toasties and cakes. Location wise, the Visitor Centre is very well-placed for Pennine Way walkers and anyone travelling through the dale, and I have found it a useful halfway point for a number of walks in the area, as well as being one of the best places for consistently good coffee in Teesdale.

26 HIGH FORCE WATERFALL

🏠 **High Force Hotel** (page 311) parking (small fee) at High Force Hotel, Alston Rd (the B6277), DL12 0XH 📞 01833 622336 ♿

> **The thunderous crash of its waters can be heard from afar: they fall without grace, in a furious rage. It is a spectacle all should see.**
> Alfred Wainwright, *Pennine Way Companion*, 1939

Geological events 295 million years ago triggered what would create the biggest waterfall in England. Molten rock forced upwards through the earth spread through softer rocks before solidifying to create a flat, erosion-resistant sheet or 'sill'. The softer sandstones, shale and limestone at High Force have worn away over millennia, undercutting the harder whin sill, which outcrops spectacularly in the Tees here forcing the entire river to plunge some 70ft over its grey cliff edge into a boiling cauldron of white water. It's one of the greatest natural attractions in the North, both for its power and height, and the theatre of crags, woods and moors in which its performance is staged. The spectacle caught the eye of J M W Turner, who painted the fall depicting a secondary spout that occasionally gushes over an adjacent precipice after storms, but that was in the early 1800s before the Tees was dammed upriver creating Cow Green Reservoir.

"A well-marked trail through birch, beech and conifer trees involves crossing a beck by a little footbridge."

The **rock strata** – whinstone at the top, limestone at the bottom and sandstone and shale in between – are easily distinguished as you take in the gushing torrent in its full glory from the viewing platform, reached on a 20-minute **walk** from the High Force Hotel (where you can park for a small charge). The walkway to the fall is on the other side of the road to the hotel; here you must pay Lord Barnard of Raby Castle a couple of pounds (use the honesty box in low season – there's a staffed ticket hut from Easter–Oct).

The wide, gravel path is just about suitable for wheelchairs and rugged buggies, and though it may be a bit of a bumpy ride, it does offer a splendid view of the River Tees in the deep gorge below. Once you've had your photo taken by the waterfall, those on foot can climb a steep flight of steps and return to the hotel via mixed woodland. It's a pleasant, well-marked trail through birch, beech and conifer trees and involves crossing a beck by a little footbridge. I saw a red squirrel at the top of the bank on my last visit.

So that's the more accessible (and touristy) way to reach the waterfall, but what about the tempting footpath you can see on the far side of the gorge? That'll be the **Pennine Way**, accessible in a few miles from Bowlees or Forest-in-Teesdale and permitting a view of High Force from the south side of the gorge (and avoiding the admission charge in doing so). The walk from Bowlees is the most popular because it also takes in Low Force (High Force's little sister downriver) but I've described both routes in the walk box on page 298.

It's possible to reach the High Force Hotel via a Wednesday-only **bus** service (page 234) from Middleton.

¶¶ FOOD & DRINK

High Force Hotel High Force, Forest-in-Teesdale DL12 0XH ✆ 01833 622336 ◷ 08.00–11.00 & noon–21.00 (20.00 in winter) Mon–Sat, 08.00–11.00 & noon–18.00 (last bookings 15.00) Sun. Smart old inn with a good reputation for its food and beautifully decorated hotel rooms. Wooden furnishings and oil paintings on walls in keeping with the building's heritage. Expect to pay above average prices for Teesdale lamb and veg, steak, fish and chips, burgers and the like.

27 FOREST-IN-TEESDALE

There is no forest at Forest-in-Teesdale. This may not surprise you if you know that some 'forests' refer to post-Conquest hunting grounds, and so it's likely that the hamlet you see today would have always had a similar open character with heath, grassland and some trees supporting deer.

Forest-in-Teesdale is a tiny place with a few farms, a lonely Wesleyan Methodist Chapel by the side of the road (no longer in public use) and, remarkably, a primary school with a handful of children, and is well positioned

"Forest-in-Teesdale is a tiny place with a few farms, and a lonely Wesleyan Methodist Chapel by the side of the road."

as a starting point for **walks** along the River Tees or to Cronkley Fell – the craggy hill on the far side of the valley. The Hanging Shaws parking area

Four waterfalls walk

✳ OS Explorer map OL31; start: Hanging Shaws car park, Forest-in-Teesdale ♀ NY867299; 5½ miles; easy route, muddy in places and some steps.

This linear walk takes in four impressive falls – **Bleabeck Force**, **High Force**, **Low Force** and **Summerhill Force** – along a fairly easy-to-navigate path that largely follows the Pennine Way, tracing the Tees through some beautiful scenery. If you do the walk on a Wednesday, it's possible to bus back from Bowlees (page 234), providing you time your walk well, but otherwise it's a two-car job (or walking back the way you came).

For the ultimate waterfall walk, you could park further up the valley at Cow Green Reservoir and take in **Cauldron Snout**. To do this (which stretches the walk to 11 miles), follow a paved track for 1½ miles to the top of the cascade from the car park and work your way down the side of Cauldron Snout to Maize Beck (easier than it sounds), then follow the Pennine Way under Widdybank Fell and along the banks of the Tees to Forest-in-Teesdale where you pick up the route described below.

1 From **Hanging Shaws car park** at Forest-in-Teesdale, turn right on to the B6277 and walk for 100yds to where a track leads off on the left into fields by a cattle grid (signed for Birk Rigg). Cross the cattle grid and go down the track, through a farmstead (a bit fiddly but basically cross a few fields to meet with the river at the bottom of the grassy slope by a green metal footbridge).

2 Cross the River Tees and turn left, joining the **Pennine Way** for the steady climb past a farm and up a hillside thickly covered with juniper bushes. This is the largest **juniper woodland** in England, a rare habitat vulnerable to a die-back disease, and whose dense branches support black grouse and overwintering thrushes. Ahead is **Bleabeck Force**, a delightful cascade rushing over blocks of dolerite; a mile or so downriver is **High Force**, which you will hear roaring long before you peer over the head of the precipice to see the furious deluge.

3 Continue eastbound on the Pennine Way for a really impressive view of High Force, and onwards to **Low Force**, which is quite some waterfall in its own right, not as high, but a thrilling broad cascade nonetheless. In spring and early summer look out for yellow globeflower, mountain pansies, bird's-eye primrose and water avens, and orchids in the surrounding damp meadows. A sculpture of two sheep stands by the side of the path just beyond Low Force – a popular photo-taking spot with families.

just off the B6277 is more or less opposite a right of way running through pastures and round a farm to meet with the Tees by a footbridge. You can pick up the Pennine Way here for a walk to High Force and the other

4 If you are still yearning for more waterspouts, it's an easy walk from the **Bowlees Visitor Centre** to **Summerhill Force**, a beauty of a waterfall in a shale cave. To reach Bowlees, cross **Wynch Bridge**, a thrilling suspension footbridge of some local fame, affording views of Low Force, and pick your way through the bluebell woods on the north side of the Tees. Exit the woodland by a gap in the wall and cross the flower meadows ahead to the main road (the B6277). Turn right, then left after 20yds by a Georgian letterbox. Bowlees Visitor Centre (housed in the old chapel) is straight ahead at the top of the lane.

5 For Gibson's Cave and Summerhill Force, skirt round the visitor centre and work your way through the car park, past the toilet block and picking up the footpath from a black metal gate spanning the track. Don't cross the beck but keep it on your left as you follow the well-trodden footpath upstream the whole way to the waterfall, passing an old quarry on your right (botanists will find much of interest here). A quarter of a mile ahead, guided by the sound of splashing water, is Summerhill Force. Return to the visitor centre the same way.

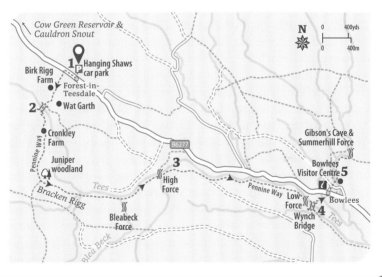

falls in the area (see above), or continue across the flood plains to access Cronkley Fell (page 302). Note the well placed Langdon Beck youth hostel up the road that has been welcoming hikers for years.

PLANTS ON THE EDGE

Upper Teesdale supports a rare assemblage of plants that are thought to have survived since the last glaciation, including two species found here and almost nowhere else in mainland Britain: the spring gentian (bright blue and unlikely to be confused with any other plant), and the Teesdale violet. Both plants flower from May to June. Also look out for alpine cinquefoil and hoary rockrose in early spring, bird's-eye primrose (May–June), and spring sandwort, alpine bistort and hoary whitlowgrass throughout summer.

The most productive spots for Arctic-alpine plants are where you see exposed sugar limestone – a crumbly marble with sugar-like texture, which was formed by the heat from the molten whin sill rock 'baking' the carboniferous limestone millions of years ago. Swathes of this rare habitat were destroyed when Cow Green was flooded in the 1970s to make the reservoir but you'll find good outcrops on Cronkley Fell and Widdybank Fell.

The Teesdale Special Flora Trust runs events for those interested in the valley's wildflowers. See ⟁ teesdalespecialflora.uk.

28 CRONKLEY FELL

Forest-in-Teesdale ♥ NY842285 (summit)

The humps, bumps and rock stacks at the top of this flat hill form an unusual summit and a delightful picnicking area that is sheltered in many places from the wind but exposed enough to be simultaneously bathed in sunshine. Take your time to enjoy all the major hills of the North Pennines undulating across the panorama, including Cumbria's Cross Fell, Great Dun Fell and Little Dun Fell (all nudging 3,000ft). Around you, in fenced off enclosures affording protection from rabbits and sheep, are **rare plants** with a lineage dating to the last Ice Age. Nowhere else in England apart from here and a handful of other spots in the valley can you see the startling blue trumpets of the spring gentian (they usually flower between the second week in May and the third week in June). Other Arctic-alpine species that together with a large number of other rarities are known as the 'Teesdale Assemblage' (see above), include Scottish asphodel, mountain avens, hoary rock-rose, moonwort, bird's eye primrose and Alpine meadow rue. Their existence is reliant on climate and the special geology of the site; their endurance thanks to the conservation efforts of government

1 Hiking at Cronkley Scar. **2** Langdon Beck. **3** Cronkley Scar is home to rare plant species, including Scotch asphodel. **4** Red grouse at Widdy Bank Farm. ▶

DAVID FORSTER/A

GEMMA HALL

DAVEMHUNTPHOTOGRAPHY/S

JOJOO64/S

Forest-in-Teesdale to Cronkley Fell

✤ OS Explorer map OL31; start: Hanging Shaws car park, Forest-in-Teesdale ♥ NY867298; 7 miles; moderate

Well-known for its rare plants, Cronkley Fell attracts botanists from afar in spring and early summer to see species such as the spring gentian in bloom around exposed sections of sugar limestone. Plants and rocks aside, this is a spectacular route both for the far-reaching views of Pennine summits, the birdlife in spring, and delightful river and meadow scenery on the return leg along Maize Beck.

I've outlined the route here but it is a little fiddly to explain in full with all the manoeuvres through the farms, and you're better off using your sense of direction and a map rather than a description of every turn and farm gate.

1 From **Hanging Shaws car park** in Forest-in-Teesdale, turn right on to the B6277, then left after 100yds (signed for 'Birk Rigg') by a fingerpost. Go over the cattle grid and continue down to the farm, keeping right round the black barn with the fence-line on your right. Goldfinches feast on thistle seeds hereabouts; and free-range hens, belted Galloway cattle, flybys of swallows and repeated calls of 'that'll do' from the farmer to his dog complete the rural scene. Go through a gate in the wall and continue downhill, passing an old building on your right. Forty yards later, turn right into a field and to a metal farm gate. Go through this gate and turn left keeping close to the fence-line and walking downhill to a green metal footbridge over the river.

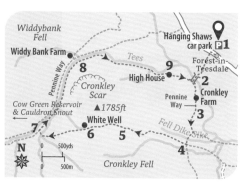

2 Cross the River Tees and pick up the **Pennine Way**, following it to **Cronkley Farm**. Don't go through the farm but instead take a diverted route as signed. Head for the craggy hillside reached

agencies and local botanists. Geology is critical and you'll notice the fenced off areas encircle outcrops of the perfectly named sugar limestone (page 300). The best time to view the plants is from May to July.

via a few gates and turns in the path. Notice the marsh marigolds and globe flowers in the damp grasslands. Work your way upwards through the juniper thicket of **High Crag** and its many ferns and foxgloves.

3 Round the back of the crags, follow the Pennine Way through a gap in the wall, turning left along a slab path with the drystone wall on your left. Continue along the slab path with patches of upland meadow flora to the top of a hill by two prominent marker stones. Part company with the Pennine Way here, veering a little right.

Ahead, cross the wall by the kissing gate and over Fell Dike Sike stream. The path veers slightly left before hitting a T-junction with another wide, grassy path, the **Green Trod**.

4 Turn right and view your destination ahead, watching where the clear grassy track curls round the summit of **Cronkley Fell** with a drystone wall to the right. Someway up there's a well-positioned boulder with a 'seat' for out of breath hikers. The path continues round the side of the hill and then begins ascending steeply again with a deep chasm to your left.

5 At the top you'll see the first of the fenced enclosures protecting the wildflowers. Continue across the summit, through two rock stacks 150yds apart and then across a broad plateau with another much larger plant enclosure on your right, enjoying wide views of the flat-topped moors.

6 Cross **White Well** (a limestone outcrop over a spring) and continue downhill to a prominent grassy bowl, guided by piles of stones. Begin the steep descent off the fell, making for the corner of a fence-line, then, at the bottom of the hill, strike off across a damp meadow to reach the **River Tees**.

7 Turn right and follow the wide, rocky river for a couple of miles downstream, keeping close to the water's edge and avoiding the temptation to climb upwards through heather – it only gets thicker and more impassable. After crossing a fence-line by a gate, you'll eventually pick up an intermittent boardwalk.

8 Opposite Widdy Bank Farm, go through a gate and continue ahead across the rushy pasture and past grazing cattle.

9 At **High House**, make your way through a couple of gates before crossing into a meadow and following the well-trodden path to the footbridge. Retrace your path to Forest-in-Teesdale.

Reaching the plateau of Cronkley Fell is straightforward from Forest-in-Teesdale following the Pennine Way and then the old drovers' route, the Green Trod, for the final ascent. I recommend the circuit over the western slopes of the fell and along Maize Beck (page 298).

5AM AT THE BLACK GROUSE LEK

lek ⇥ a small gathering of birds performing a courtship ritual; from the Swedish *leka*, meaning 'to play'

It's just gone 5am. I'm sitting in my car on Langdon Common by the side of an unclassified road linking Langdon Beck with St John's Chapel, staring into a lead-grey sky. This is the third time I've come to see black grouse perform their early morning courtship ritual, staged here every day in early spring in the exact same spot in the exact same field, year on year.

As the morning light brightens the graphite tones, I can just make out the facing fellside and I begin scanning the field in front. The wind hisses through the course grasses; snipe drum, hares run; and then comes the first bird call: a curlew. His cry, a wave of sorrow – a soundtrack perfectly suited to this desolate upland terrain of blanket bog, heather and rough pastures, and yet so inappropriate for the time of year. But, as if to lift the mood, a pair of lapwing take to the sky, their dolphin-like repertoire of clicks and squeaks rather silly and incongruous.

And then I see them: coal black with bushy white tail feathers. They're bigger than their ubiquitous cousins, the red grouse, and bolder in colour. I count 21 individual males – up from 12 and 18 on previous visits. They strut in the grassy arena like athletes about to take up their starting positions; somewhere

29 LANGDON BECK & LANGDON COMMON

🛏 **Langdon Beck YHA** (page 311)

The Langdon Beck Hotel, surely one of the most remote inns in England, stands at the head of Upper Teesdale at an important junction where your onward journey will either take you up across Widdybank Fell to Cow Green Reservoir; through the Harwood Valley and into Cumbria on the Alston road; or across Langdon Common into Weardale. The Langdon Beck–St John's Chapel road (page 307) is one of the highest and truly great mountain roads in England: all open moorland, peat bogs, snow posts and huge skies. The curlew is a perfect companion up here. The hotel at Langdon Beck serves drinks and food but it's a funny old place, mainly the haunt of farmers and the odd cyclist.

30 COW GREEN RESERVOIR, WIDDYBANK FELL & CAULDRON SNOUT

Cow Green Reservoir is a bleak metallic sheet of water surrounded by green slopes with stupendous views of the highest Pennine hills and one of the best upland birdwatching and wildflower sites in the UK on its in the long sward the hens – grey-brown and smaller – settle into their ring-side seats to watch potential mates display their dominance and prowess.

The battle begins: the cocks face each other in pairs about a yard apart, tail feathers fanned, wings dropped and with a look of intent; they lower and lengthen their necks then charge, jousting their opponent, locking together, jumping and tussling. When the combat is over, one bird turns and sees another challenger through the tussocks: he advances and goes in again for another round. All the while, the strangest low burbling sound comes in waves on the breeze. After half an hour or so, the cocks are out of fight and they begin to drift away, absorbed into the long grass; s. another day.

VIEWING THE BLACK GROUSE L

The best place to view the black grous is on the unclassified road branching the B6277, about a quarter of a mile we of the Langdon Beck Hotel. Go over two cattlegrids and 500yds later you'll see a pull-in gravel area on your right by a fence-line. The grouse perform in a flattish area of grass your side of the river about 400yds to the southeast. You must arrive before dawn and always stay in your car with the engine turned off. Do not get out of your car or walk across the fields as this will certainly disturb these rare birds.

doorstep in the form of Widdybank Fell. Cow Green's leading attraction for most visitors is **Cauldron Snout**, a powerful cascade that storms through a rocky chasm of dolerite below the reservoir, before flowing as the River Tees under the rock-strewn whin sill cliffs, known as **Falcon Clints** – and later, Cronkley Scar.

The waterfall is reached by following a clear paved **path** (suitable for wheelchairs and bicycles; no need for a map) for 1½ miles from the Cow Green Reservoir car park (♀ NY811309) to the dam, where you can pick up the Pennine Way (don't cross the dam). It's a bit of slog down the lane from the car park but if you're excited by the special plant life in these parts, there's plenty to distract from the otherwise rather tedious walk. Limestone grasslands are all around but you'll also see some fenced off patches containing sugar limestone (page 300). Spring gentians and the Teesdale violet are two star species among other rarities including Alpine meadow-rue, the peculiar-looking fern, moonwort, and Scottish asphodel (Teesdale is pretty much the only place in England where the species grows). Outside of the flowering season (roughly May–July), there's not much to see, however. One of the rarest sites for this special

'estroyed when the reservoir was dammed
'able water supply for Teesside and its

aimble-footed will be able to descend
airway down the side of the waterfall to
tom and view Cauldron Snout in its entirety,
o step. Look out for dippers as you make your

e bottom of the fall, heading east on the Pennine Way
Maize Beck as your companion, I recommend returning to
Green via a well-trodden loop of **Widdybank Fell** via Widdy
ank Farm. The entire circuit is around seven miles. As the footpath picks its way under the **Falcon Clints**, those interested in ferns will find one of the country's most exciting sites for bryophytes. Northern buckler fern, lemon-scented fern, mountain male fern, beech fern and green spleenwort are some of the species growing among shrubs here, including bearberry which also sprouts from the crags. Cronkley Fell's cliffs on the other side of the river add to the volcanic drama of the valley.

At **Widdy Bank Farm** – a wonderfully remote working farm with some beautiful hay meadows stuffed with wildflowers – you leave the Pennine Way, heading north on a track that eventually connects with the Langdon Beck–Cow Green road where you turn left and head uphill back to the car park at the reservoir. As the grasslands give way to pastures and then moors, red grouse are easily startled during the final leg on the tarmacked lane. It was around here one summer's evening that I watched a number of hares and grouse and even saw, very fleetingly, a merlin. As soon as the light dipped, the wildlife seemed to emerge at the same time from the heather and grasslands to reclaim the lane. On a different occasion, very early in the morning in March, I saw more wading birds around here than I think I have ever seen. Using your car as a bird hide is a good way to see the wildlife on this exposed hillside and minimise disturbance.

31 HARWOOD BECK

If visiting Cow Green Reservoir or staying in the Langdon Beck area, I thoroughly recommend a walk or cycle ride (though by car works too) through the lovely little valley formed by Harwood Beck, which is reached by continuing northwest from Langdon Beck along the assemblage of plants was destroyed when the reservoir was dammed in the 1960s to provide a stable water supply for Teesside and its burgeoning industries.

At the end of the track, only the nimble-footed will be able to descend the huge rocks that form a stairway down the side of the waterfall to look back up from the bottom and view Cauldron Snout in its entirety, splashing from step to step. Look out for dippers as you make your way down.

Once at the bottom of the fall, heading east on the Pennine Way with the Maize Beck as your companion, I recommend returning to Cow Green via a well-trodden loop of **Widdybank Fell** via Widdy Bank Farm. The entire circuit is around seven miles. As the footpath picks its way under the **Falcon Clints**, those interested in ferns will find one of the country's most exciting sites for bryophytes. Northern buckler fern, lemon-scented fern, mountain male fern, beech fern and green spleenwort are some of the species growing among shrubs here, including bearberry which also sprouts from the crags. Cronkley Fell's cliffs on the other side of the river add to the volcanic drama of the valley.

At **Widdy Bank Farm** – a wonderfully remote working farm with some beautiful hay meadows stuffed with wildflowers – you leave the Pennine Way, heading north on a track that eventually connects with the Langdon Beck–Cow Green road where you turn left and head uphill back to the car park at the reservoir. As the grasslands give way to pastures and then moors, red grouse are easily startled during the final leg on the tarmacked lane. It was around here one summer's evening that I watched a number of hares and grouse and even saw, very fleetingly, a merlin. As soon as the light dipped, the wildlife seemed to emerge at the same time from the heather and grasslands to reclaim the lane. On a different occasion, very early in the morning in March, I saw more wading birds around here than I think I have ever seen. Using your car as a bird hide is a good way to see the wildlife on this exposed hillside and minimise disturbance.

31 HARWOOD BECK

If visiting Cow Green Reservoir or staying in the Langdon Beck area, I thoroughly recommend a walk or cycle ride (though by car works too) through the lovely little valley formed by Harwood Beck, which is reached by continuing northwest from Langdon Beck along the in the long sward the hens – grey-brown and smaller – settle into their ring-side seats to watch potential mates display their dominance and prowess.

The battle begins: the cocks face each other in pairs about a yard apart, tail feathers fanned, wings dropped and with a look of intent; they lower and lengthen their necks then charge, jousting their opponent, locking together, jumping and tussling. When the combat is over, one bird turns and sees another challenger through the tussocks: he advances and goes in again for another round. All the while, the strangest low burbling sound comes in waves on the breeze. After half an hour or so, the cocks are out of fight and they begin to drift away, absorbed into the long grass; show over for another day.

VIEWING THE BLACK GROUSE LEK

The best place to view the black grouse lek is on the unclassified road branching off the B6277, about a quarter of a mile west of the Langdon Beck Hotel. Go over two cattlegrids and 500yds later you'll see a pull-in gravel area on your right by a fence-line. The grouse perform in a flattish area of grass your side of the river about 400yds to the southeast. You must arrive before dawn and always stay in your car with the engine turned off. Do not get out of your car or walk across the fields as this will certainly disturb these rare birds.

doorstep in the form of Widdybank Fell. Cow Green's leading attraction for most visitors is **Cauldron Snout**, a powerful cascade that storms through a rocky chasm of dolerite below the reservoir, before flowing as the River Tees under the rock-strewn whin sill cliffs, known as **Falcon Clints** – and later, Cronkley Scar.

The waterfall is reached by following a clear paved **path** (suitable for wheelchairs and bicycles; no need for a map) for 1½ miles from the Cow Green Reservoir car park (♥ NY811309) to the dam, where you can pick up the Pennine Way (don't cross the dam). It's a bit of slog down the lane from the car park but if you're excited by the special plant life in these parts, there's plenty to distract from the otherwise rather tedious walk. Limestone grasslands are all around but you'll also see some fenced off patches containing sugar limestone (page 300). Spring gentians and the Teesdale violet are two star species among other rarities including Alpine meadow-rue, the peculiar-looking fern, moonwort, and Scottish asphodel (Teesdale is pretty much the only place in England where the species grows). Outside of the flowering season (roughly May–July), there's not much to see, however. One of the rarest sites for this special

SCENIC ROUTE:
LANGDON BECK TO ST JOHN'S CHAPEL

A spectacular journey on a quiet unclassified road, first into the folds of gently sloping hills clothed in white grasses and grazed by sheep and then steadily ascending **Langdon Common**, following the snow markers up and up on to a peaty plateau with the scars of mining here and there and exposed rock and shale. Eventually you reach the highest point on the broad moor between the two valleys at 2,057ft. Weardale is before you: a valley peppered with hamlets and farms and a few lines of forest and meadows divided by drystone walls rising from the river and up the far side of the facing hills. Now for the thrilling descent between **Harthope Moor** and **Chapel Fell**: a 17% gradient as the road sign warns. The coarse grasslands of the fells soften with decreasing altitude, becoming greener hay meadows as the road winds past stone barns, cottages and the wooded Harthope Burn for the final run into the quaint village of St John's Chapel.

B6277. A quieter and more picturesque introduction to the valley is experienced by taking a paved lane off the Langdon Beck–Cow Green Reservoir road.

Descending towards the river and the farm at **Lingy Hill**, all the scenic features that make Upper Teesdale so alluring come together: isolated two- and three-hundred year old farm buildings; free-range lambs on the road; a collage of flower meadows and pastures lining the valley sides; farmers tending to livestock; a lone Methodist chapel; the shallow, stony beck; barns built into drystone walls; and the skies thronged with lapwing, curlew, drumming snipe, redshank and oystercatcher. I even encountered black grouse by chance in one of the meadows below Binks House.

As you progress westwards through the valley along the northern fell slopes, the tell-tale signs of lead mining pockmark the landscape: all ripples, bumps, mounds and crumbling stone walls.

ACCOMMODATION

The following is a hand-picked selection of some recommended places to stay in Durham, with a mix of hotels, B&Bs, self-catering cottages, hostels, bunkhouses and campsites to suit a range of budgets. When researching, I favoured independent accommodation that caught my eye – perhaps because the owners celebrated local food, the building was historically interesting or the views outstanding – but what they all offered were well-kept rooms, a friendly welcome and great service.

The hotels, B&Bs and inns featured in this section are indicated by a ♠ under the relevant heading nearest their location within chapters; self-catering cottages, hostels and bunkhouses by 🏠 and camping by ⅄.

Where you see the ⅃ symbol, you can expect step-free accommodation (most with accessible bathrooms too) but facilities do vary so it's best to check before booking. Also note that where you see the symbol next to holiday cottage companies, not all properties in their portfolio will be wheelchair accessible.

Go to ⊘ bradtguides.com/durhamsleeps for full reviews of each place listed.

1 DURHAM CITY

Hotel

Hotel Indigo 9 Old Elvet ⊘ durham. hotelindigo.com ⅃. Imposing red-brick 1892 mansion, skilfully converted into an upmarket, modern hotel with a Marco Pierre White restaurant. Sumptuous original tile work and stained glass.

B&Bs & inns

Castle View Guest House 4 Crossgate ⊘ castle-view.co.uk. Eighteenth-century terraced house with cathedral views and walking distance to the riverside and historic centre. Spacious, modern rooms.

Durham Castle Palace Green ⊘ durham. ac.uk. Simple university rooms in the Norman Keep (many en suite; two opulent state rooms). University holidays only (Dec, Easter, Jul, Aug & Sep). Breakfast served in the medieval Great Hall.

Forty Winks Guesthouse 40 South St ⊘ 40winksdurham.co.uk. Nine opulent suites facing the peninsula on one of Durham's finest historic terraces. Versailles styling here and there, plush fabrics, chandeliers and fancy toiletries.

Hatfield College North Bailey ⊘ durham. ac.uk ⅃. Basic student rooms (Jul, Aug & Sep only) for those on a budget in one of the oldest university colleges, situated along a side lane from the cathedral.

The Victoria 86 Hallgarth St ⌂ victoriainn-durhamcity.co.uk. Famous pub known for its beers, with refurbished, unpretentious mid-range rooms. No breakfast. Five min walk to the historic centre.

Self-catering
52 Old Elvet ⌂ 52oldelvet.com. Georgian townhouse remodelled into 12 luxury apartments, a few hundred yards from historic Elvet Bridge.

Durham Riverside Apartments New Elvet ⌂ durhamriversideapartments.uk ♿. Apartments with kitchens and river views, a short stroll from the peninsula.

Woodland Barn Holiday Cottage South Durham ⌂ https://woodlandbarn.rentals. Luxury two-bedroomed self-contained barn conversion close to the River Wear, a five-minute drive south of Durham University. Good base for exploring the city and countryside.

2 VALE OF DURHAM
Hotels
Blackwell Grange Hotel Darlington ⌂ blackwellgrangehotel.com ♿. Impressive 17th-century mansion in parkland on the outskirts of Darlington, with a pool. Essentially a modern, boutique hotel though rooms vary in size and opulence.

Lumley Castle Chester-le-Street ⌂ lumleycastle.com. Impressive fortress on a hillside above Chester-le-Street. High prices for atmospheric rooms with much theatre and medieval styling.

Park Head Bishop Auckland ⌂ aucklandproject.org ♿. Large new contemporary hotel well-situated in the town for visits to the galleries and historic buildings.

Rockliffe Hall Darlington ⌂ rockliffehall.com ♿. Red-brick, Victorian mansion, now a five-star hotel with a spa, golf course and Orangery restaurant. Also self-catering houses and apartments.

Thomas Wright House Byers Green ⌂ thomaswrighthouse.com ♿. Small boutique hotel with restaurant in an unassuming village between Durham and Bishop Auckland. Luxury touches and two suites with hot tubs.

B&Bs & inns
Burnhopeside Hall Lanchester ⌂ burnhopeside-hall.co.uk. Elegant Georgian country house set in acres of gardens and woodlands by the River Browney. Large en-suite bedrooms and local food for breakfast (some home-grown and reared!).

Dowfold House Crook ⌂ dowfoldhouse.com. Detached Victorian house in farmland on the outskirts of Crook. Three mid-range, comfy rooms. Eco-conscious owners full of enthusiasm for their local food suppliers and home-produced ingredients.

The Old Post Office Lanchester ⌂ theoldpostofficelanchester.com. Friendly, mid-range B&B in a central village location, boasting breakfasts made with regional produce.

The Pickled Parson Sedgefield ⌂ thepickledparson.co.uk. Neutrally decorated, compact rooms, plus a good restaurant, in the centre of Sedgefield.

The Saxon Inn Escomb ⌂ saxon-inn.com. Opposite Escomb Church and a short stroll to the Wear. Traditional old inn serving food with simply furnished, inexpensive rooms.

Self-catering
Teesdale Cheesemakers Butterknowle ⌂ teesdalecheesemakers.co.uk. Two glamping huts with verandas and kitchenettes set in peaceful sub-Pennine farmland. Run by a cheese-making couple who also operate a café specialising in farm-produced food.

3 DURHAM HERITAGE COAST
Hotels
No.16 Seaham ⌂ no16seaham.co.uk. Clean, modern rooms (no breakfast), a few hundred yards from the seafront in the centre of Seaham.

Seaham Hall Seaham ⬧ seaham-hall. co.uk ♿. Georgian mansion by the sea on the outskirts of town. Luxurious (and expensive) but not stuffy. Good restaurant, and the hotel spa is one of the very best in the North East.

Camping

The Barn at Easington Easington Colliery ⬧ thebarnateasington.co.uk. A beautiful site on farmland near Hawthorn Dene (a 15-min walk to the beach) with distant sea views. Basic facilities and very quiet. Also camping pods, caravans and a wood cabin to hire.

4 DERWENT VALLEY

Hotels

Derwent Manor Boutique Hotel Allensford, nr Shotley Bridge ⬧ derwentmanorhotel. com. Large hotel (and four cottages) with pool and spa in countryside setting. Plush décor, good-value rooms.

Lord Crewe Arms Blanchland ⬧ lordcrewearmsblanchland.co.uk ♿. Beautiful, pricey rooms (thick heritage fabrics and luxury touches) in a historic medieval inn. One of the best restaurants in the region.

Inn

Derwent Arms Edmundbyers ⬧ derwent-arms. co.uk. Compact rooms in a popular inn with a good reputation for its food, close to Derwent Reservoir. Also one self-catering apartment.

Hostels & camping

Low House YHA & campsite Edmundbyers ⬧ lowhousehaven.co.uk. Friendly hostel in a low-rise run of three 18th-century cottages, with its own quirky pub and campsite.

Starlight Camping & Caravanning Castleside ⬧ 07513 151669. Basic campsite with a flat, green pitch and views across the Derwent Valley; two-person shepherd's hut for hire.

West Wood Yurts Gibside ⬧ gibsideyurts. co.uk. Yurt 'village' and luxury camping pods

(hot tubs included) on National Trust-owned farmland. Access to the Gibside estate outside of opening hours.

Hidden Retreat Glamping Shotley Bridge ⬧ hiddenretreatglamping.co.uk. Two large luxury pods (each sleeping four) with hot tubs in a peaceful setting on the edge of Shotley Bridge, by the banks of the Derwent.

5 WEARDALE

B&Bs

Bonners Lodge Waskerley ⬧ bonnerslodge. co.uk. Family-friendly, inexpensive B&B and touring caravan site with donkeys, alpacas and goats. In open countryside on the edge of the Dales.

Westgate Manor Westgate ⬧ westgatemanor. co.uk. Old-fashioned opulence pervades this Victorian country manor on the edge of Westgate and close to Slitt Wood. A good base for walkers.

Self-catering

Bowlees Cottages Wolsingham ⬧ bowleescottages.com. Collection of four mid-range large holiday cottages on a farm with a pool. Good for families and large parties.

Low Cornriggs Holiday Cottages Cowshill ⬧ cornriggsfarm.co.uk ♿. Two inexpensive small holiday cottages in the upper reaches of Weardale, designed with disabled people in mind.

Stanhope Castle Stanhope ⬧ stanhopecastle. co.uk. In the centre of town, the medieval castle keep and associated buildings now form eight pricey self-catering cottages. Expect a lot of bling and faux medieval styling for your money.

Woodcroft Farm Frosterley ⬧ woodcroftfarm. co.uk. Two homely, inexpensive cottages set in farmland near the south banks of the Wear. Also glamping pod cabins.

Bunkhouses & camping

Barrington Bunkhouse Rookhope ⬧ barrington-bunkhouse-rookhope.com.

Somewhat eccentric independent hostel, once a Victorian school. Popular with Coast-to-Coast cyclists. Campers welcome.

Bonners Lodge Caravan Park (see opposite)

Carrshield Camping Barn West Allen Valley ⬦ carrshieldcampingbarn.co.uk. Wonderfully restored 19th-century mine shop in beautiful rural surroundings not far from Allenheads. No-frills modern camping barn (no mattresses, sleep on raised wooden 'benches').

Mill Cottage Bunkhouse Nenthead ⬦ millcottagebunkhouse.com. Nestled by the side of an old lead mine, now a heritage site, this welcoming independent bunkhouse sleeps six.

6 TEESDALE

Hotels

Headlam Hall Headlam, nr Gainford ⬦ headlamhall.co.uk ♿. Seventeenth-century spa hotel in clipped-to-perfection landscaped grounds on the edge of the Dales. Country elegance at its finest.

High Force Hotel nr Bowlees ⬦ raby.co.uk/high-force/hotel. Sophisticated upmarket country hotel opposite the gateway to England's biggest waterfall.

B&Bs & inns

Brunswick House Middleton-in-Teesdale ⬦ brunswickhouse.net. Stone-built Georgian guesthouse with five en-suite rooms. Clean and modern; excellent breakfast.

The Hill B&B Middleton-in-Teesdale ⬦ thehillbandb.co.uk. Simple, comfortable rooms in a Victorian town house. Good location for exploring Teesdale.

The Millbank Arms Barningham, Greta Valley ⬦ themilbankarms.com. Characterful pub and restaurant dating to 1690. Stylish country rooms with plenty of nods to the past. Superior accommodation for mid-range prices. Also three holiday cottages for similar rates.

The Quirky Quarry Snaisgill, Middleton-in-Teesdale ⬦ thequirkyquarry.co.uk. Off the beaten track, nestled in the wooded Hudeshope Valley. Small mid-range B&B with three fresh, modern rooms and a shepherd's hut. Spectacular views.

The Rose & Crown Romaldkirk ⬦ rose-and-crown.co.uk. Best known for its superb restaurant, this peaceful old village pub has seven rooms upstairs and five 'courtyard' suites to the rear (with limited wheelchair access). Luxury touches, above average prices.

Self-catering

East Briscoe Farm Cottages Cotherstone ⬦ eastbriscoe.co.uk ♿. Five inexpensive cottages (with use of an on-site pool and games room) enclosed by beautiful Baldersdale countryside.

Hill Top Huts Eggleston ⬦ hilltophuts.co.uk. Twelve huts in a field above Eggleston village; simple facilities and furnishings.

Low Way Farm Holwick ⬦ lowwayfarm.co.uk. Wonderfully peaceful spot surrounded by meadows and within walking distance of Teesdale's famous waterfalls. Two modestly furnished, inexpensive cottages and two camping barns.

Mellwaters Barn Cottages Bowes ⬦ mellwatersbarn.co.uk ♿. Four humble cottages designed with disabled people in mind. Picturesque farmland setting in the Greta Valley, close to the Pennine Way.

Hostels & camping

High Side Farm Camping Bowbank, Lundale ⬦ highsidefarmcampingglamping.co.uk. Small, adults-only tent and touring caravan site with beautiful sloping views across Lundale. Warm welcome and very well kept.

Langdon Beck YHA Upper Teesdale ⬦ yha.org.uk/hostel/yha-langdon-beck. Perfectly situated for walkers and cyclists exploring the wilder parts of Teesdale. Simple, clean, rarely very busy. Wake up to a cacophony of bird calls in spring.

Low Way Farm camping barns Holwick ⬦ lowwayfarm.co.uk. One large and one smaller camping barn with basic facilities.

INDEX

Entries in **bold** refer to major entries; those in *italics* refer to maps.

INDEX OF ADVERTISERS

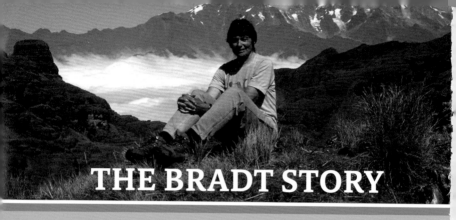

THE BRADT STORY

In the beginning

It all began in 1974 on an Amazon river barge. During an 18-month trip through South America, two adventurous young backpackers – Hilary Bradt and her then husband, George – decided to write about the hiking trails they had discovered through the Andes. *Backpacking Along Ancient Ways in Peru and Bolivia* included the very first descriptions of the Inca Trail. It was the start of a colourful journey to becoming one of the best-loved travel publishers in the world; you can read the full story on our website (bradtguides.com/ourstory).

Getting there first

Hilary quickly gained a reputation for being a true travel pioneer, and in the 1980s she started to focus on guides to places overlooked by other publishers. The Bradt Guides list became a roll call of guidebook 'firsts'. We published the first guide to Madagascar, followed by Mauritius, Czechoslovakia and Vietnam. The 1990s saw the beginning of our extensive coverage of Africa: Tanzania, Uganda, South Africa, and Eritrea. Later, post-conflict guides became a feature: Rwanda, Mozambique, Angola, and Sierra Leone, as well as the first standalone guides to the Baltic States following the fall of the Iron Curtain, and the first post-war guides to Bosnia, Kosovo and Albania.

Comprehensive – and with a conscience

Today, we are the world's largest independently owned travel publisher, with more than 200 titles. However, our ethos remains unchanged. Hilary is still keenly involved, and **we still get there first**: two-thirds of Bradt guides have no direct competition.

But we don't just get there first. Our guides are also known for being **more comprehensive** than any other series. We avoid templates and tick-lists. Each guide is a one-of-a-kind expression of an expert author's interests, knowledge and enthusiasm for telling it how it really is.

And a commitment to wildlife, conservation and respect for local communities has always been at the heart of our books. Bradt Guides was **championing sustainable travel** before any other guidebook publisher. We even have a series dedicated to Slow Travel in the UK, award-winning books that explore the country with a passion and depth you'll find nowhere else.

Thank you!

We can only do what we do because of the support of readers like you – people who value less-obvious experiences, less-visited places and a more thoughtful approach to travel. Those who, like us, take travel seriously.

Bradt GUIDES

TRAVEL TAKEN SERIOUSLY